THE
ENGLISH
TRIP
OF 1910

TORONTO, SIR HENRY PELLATT,
THE QUEEN'S OWN RIFLES
AND THE PRESS GANG

MIMA BROWN KAPCHES

 FriesenPress

One Printers Way
Altona, MB R0G 0B0
Canada

www.friesenpress.com

Cover Image: The QOR marching over the Holborn Viaduct to the Guildhall in London. Toronto Public Library, Special Collections, Baldwin Room. Canada Army, Queen's Own Rifles, 1910, S79. 5.1.3.

ISBN
978-1-03-831058-3 (Hardcover)
978-1-03-831057-6 (Paperback)
978-1-03-831059-0 (eBook)

1. HISTORY, MILITARY, CANADA

Distributed to the trade by The Ingram Book Company

TABLE OF CONTENTS

FOREWORD

In the annals of history, there are moments that stand as testament to the unwavering spirit and courage of those who serve their nation. The year 1910 witnessed such a remarkable chapter in the saga of The Queen's Own Rifles of Canada, a journey that would become an indelible mark in the rich tapestry of Canadian military heritage.

This book, chronicling The Queen's Own Rifles of Canada's extraordinary expedition to England in 1910, is a tribute to the brave souls who ventured across the vast expanse of the Atlantic Ocean. They carried with them not only the pride of their regiment but the aspirations of a young nation. Within these pages, readers will embark on a captivating odyssey that transcends borders and generations, a story that encapsulates the essence of camaraderie, valour, and the unyielding determination of those who don the uniform in service to their country. In particular, it highlights the important role that embedded newspaper reporters played in documenting this story for the Canadian public.

Through meticulous research, firsthand accounts, and scouring historical documents, Ms. Brown Kapches unveils the intricacies of the Riflemen's journey, from the shores of Canada to the heart of England. It explores the challenges they faced, the friendships forged, and the cultural exchanges that took place during their time abroad. The narrative captures the spirit of the age, painting a vivid picture of a bygone era when the world was on the brink of war, and nations were forging alliances that would shape the course of history.

May this book continue to inspire and resonate with all who cherish the spirit of honour, duty, and patriotism.

C. Boileau, CD
Lieutenant-Colonel
Commanding Officer
The Queen's Own Rifles of Canada

PREFACE

In the summer of 1910, the City of Toronto was enthralled with the celebration of the fiftieth anniversary of the formation of the Queen's Own Rifles of Canada. The QOR, based in Toronto at the University Avenue Armouries, was a proud Toronto volunteer regiment that had come to the City's and Canada's defence during that half-century.[1] The commanding officer of the QOR that year was the wealthy Canadian financier Sir Henry Mill Pellatt. Pellatt was a staunch supporter of the QOR; he was a man who had risen in the ranks from a rifleman to CO in his thirty-four years of membership.

Pellatt was a controversial figure; some thought him shameless in his pursuit of British honours, resulting in his being awarded with a knighthood in 1905.[2] His financial endeavours had made him incredibly wealthy though his business fiascos eventually resulted in his penury, but in 1910 he was at the height of his financial and military prowess. He had yet to commence construction of the monument that is most associated with his vainglory—his home on the hill, Casa Loma. But Sir Henry, as he was affectionately called by his regiment, had dreams, and he only dreamed over the top. His plans for the 1910 semi-centennial of the QOR were no exception.

Sir Henry planned events in Toronto to honour past and current members of the QOR with garden parties, parades, historical pageants, and a gala ball! His generosity was extravagant, and he committed to covering all expenses. For several weeks in April, May, and June the city and members of the QOR focused on rehearsals and plans for the celebrations for seven days, from June 18 to 24, when Toronto citizenry was fascinated with the QOR and their military history. Thousands cheered at parades and attended the historical pageant extravaganzas staged at Exhibition Park. Once the Toronto celebrations were completed, attention turned to the next significant event marking the semi-centennial, the "English Trip."

Pellatt and the QOR, with the support of the Canadian and British governments, arranged for a regiment of QOR men to travel to England to train with the British Regulars during their summer manoeuvres at Aldershot in August and then take part in the full army manoeuvres on the Salisbury Plain in September. To that end, over 600 Toronto men— tall, young men—enlisted in the QOR as members of this regiment, a provisional one formed for the sole purpose of going to England. These riflemen, officers, buglers, and bandsmen went to England on this, the trip of a lifetime. For young Toronto men this trip was a skylark, for in his planning Sir Henry gave them an incredible gift. The trip was, as the press said repeatedly at the time, "at his own expense!" Pellatt covered all the major costs: transportation, salaries, and other outlays, and while the Canadian and the British governments covered some expenses, he met most of them.

For the soldiers, the most important feature of the trip was that they would receive salaries for the seven weeks they were away from their employers, their jobs were guaranteed when they returned, and they were to be paid by Pellatt for their military service. The trip included a week in Lévis, Québec, east and west transatlantic crossings, training in Aldershot, manoeuvres, and best of all, a week of free time in London.

Although most of the young men who signed on for the trip were students, bank clerks, or shopmen from stores like Eaton's, there were six men who went on the trip as reporters. These men earned their salaries while they were overseas. Five of the newsmen joined the QOR, and one accompanied the trip but did not enlist. The young reporters wrote for Toronto daily papers, and their stories were often front-page news where they were given their first experience of a byline! The men in the regiment, who tented together, were nicknamed the "Press Gang" by the QOR. Once in England, the military training for the men was a challenge, but the evenings were free to explore London, and their articles relate adventures of the trip from their points of view. Over time there were some near-miss disasters and humorous tales indeed. [3]

The events of 1910 will be the focus of this history, and the stories of these youthful pressmen form the thread of continuity, beginning with their involvement in the rowdy elections of the Toronto Press Club in January of 1910, following them through the summer pageants and the English trip, and then after the return home, their lives until their passings. The lives of a few others of the QOR provisional battalion will also be charted, and the life of Pellatt will be followed until his death.

Ultimately, little is known about most of the men who went on Pellatt's journey, so what we learn from the reporters is a representation of what it was like to be a young Canadian man in 1910, and what it was like to live in Toronto over 110 years ago. In retrospect, it was a naïve and innocent time. Even though there were rumbling of political discord in Europe, and it was thought that war would occur, for those on the English trip, war was the furthest thing from their young minds. When war was declared in 1914, men in Toronto quickly enlisted, and some thought that the journey they were about to embark on was a lark, but why would they think that? Is it possible that the lark of 1910, which was followed with great interest by Torontonians, gave them the false impression that going overseas with military was exactly that?

How is it that this history of over 600 young Torontonians of 1910 has finally come to light? It began with the discovery of an article written in the *Toronto World* by J.N.M. Brown from 1910. The story was filed from the Queen's Own Rifles while in England, and his byline listed him as a correspondent soldier in the unit. I am related to Brown, but he was not my grandfather, as you might expect; he was my father. I am his youngest child (a daughter) of his second marriage. I have few memories of him and apart from knowing that he was a journalist, I knew little else. Over the years, I have searched for his articles with little success, since he mostly wrote without a byline. After finding the *World* article, I realized that no one had written in detail about the QOR trip to England, or the QOR jubilee celebrations in Toronto, or the role Sir Henry Pellatt had in planning and financing this eventful year. This book will address that void, and additionally, this will give me the chance to meet my father.

This is a complicated and interesting story about Toronto. The English trip was Sir Henry Pellatt's gift to over 600 young Toronto men, and as Nineteen Ten(ers), they never forgot his generosity and their memories of their wonderful adventures of 1910.

CHAPTER

1

The Press Gang

The providers have even gone to the length of putting up and furnishing a press tent for members of the regiment and others representing the Toronto papers.[4]

At the beginning of the second decade of the twentieth century, industrialization led to Toronto becoming the urban centre driving the economy of Ontario and some might say Canada.[5] The excitement of the growth and development of the city led to optimism that Toronto in 1910 was the best city in Canada and that Canada was the best country apart from England, the "mother-country," in the British Empire. This attitude of somewhat cocky self-assurance was echoed in the press of the day. In 1910 it is possible to focus on six young men, journalists, who all started their careers at approximately the same time, and as a group of like-minded men with not too dissimilar backgrounds they existed as a cohort. Although their lives would eventually take different directions, in 1910 they were colleagues, friends, and perhaps rivals—after all they were competing for the same scoops for their papers. This is not a new or unexpected story, as all newspapers hire inexperienced cubs; however, the events of 1910 make their stories unique not only for their own lives but for the history of the city of Toronto.

As reporters, membership in the Toronto Press Club was expected, although not mandatory. In Toronto, in 1909–1910, the club was a unique environment. "There are few clubs more democratic and more exclusive than the Toronto Press Club. Practically every man connected with the editorial, reportorial, and art departments of Toronto's newspapers and magazines is a member. . . . No matter how steeped in gall the pens which address one another on rival pages, within the warming circle of the Press Club all is geniality and good-fellowship. Light and airy persiflage is the order of the day, and shafts of humour wing their way unbarbed."[6] In other words, when at club meetings it was no holds barred, probably fueled by a lot of alcohol.

The one event that captured all the members' attention was the campaign and election of club officers over January and February of each year. "So it happens that to be an officer of the Press Club is a token of one's personal popularity among the members of the craft, and the annual elections are fought on strictly personal lines. All of one's past, present and future is raked up and exposed for view. Every trick known to politicians, save the 'roorbach,' is practised. The roorbach is not used because the worst has already been said."[7] A "roorbach" was a mid-nineteenth century term for a forgery published for political purposes.[8]

The nominations for positions were announced January 14, and then two weeks later the elections were held. In the fortnight leading to the elections, it's safe to say all hell broke loose on the campaigns, and 1910 was a banner year for shenanigans.[9] The campaigning began in earnest and the *Globe* coverage of it was delightfully verbose. A meeting was held to grill the candidates and otherwise cause mayhem:

> The most amusing and exciting meeting at which Mayor
> Geary has yet presided was held in the assembly room
> of City Hall yesterday afternoon, when a mass meeting

of the members of the Toronto Press Club was held. During the occasional intervals of quietness, the various candidates for office at the approaching elections were permitted to address the meeting. Cheers and counter cheers, campaign literature, and all the tricks of election-eering were made use of with a splendid brutality. The "hecklers" were out in full force, and jokes on candidates were conspicuous by their plentifulness. A continuous string of alleged cablegrams from eminent politicians and Canadian newspapermen in England showed the widespread interest aroused in the elections. Two empty beer bottles, some flags, and a policeman were present, but the policeman was not used.[10]

Of the meeting, it was reported that "Each candidate was subjected to a severe heckling from which he emerged more or less alive. But the audience was responsive. When one candidate urged the electors to elect him as 'a watchdog on the treasury' the audience barked a conglomerate bark like a dog show and howled the candidate down."[11] One important feature of the campaign was the posters: "Reams of campaign literature were written and distributed among the various newspaper offices where it was prominently displayed. Fortunately for the peace of mind of newspaper readers it was not published in the columns of the morning and evening newspapers. Had this been done it is to be feared that many readers, not knowing the good nature underlying it all, would have arrived at the conclusion that only the sternest action on the part of the police could have prevented worse than the letting of a little blood."[12]

The election was held on January 28. "After a furious campaign meeting and supper at the St. Charles, which added materially to the gaiety of nations, the members of the Toronto Press Club last night made a selection of the officers for the ensuing year. The campaigning was kept up till the very moment when the result of the polling was announced. No such excitement has been produced in the history of the club, and the voting for all offices was close and exciting. . . . It is significant that most of the candidates who were successful at the polls have had experience in running elections in different parts of the country, but so far no charges of ballot-stuffing have been made."[13]When the results were announced in the *Star,* the article's sub-heading was "Conclusion of a Strenuous Campaign Among Young Journalists"![14] One of these young journalists, James Scroggie of the *News,* was elected as an auditor. But there were at least four other young journalists, or so-called cubs, who had been members of the TPC since 1909, and likely threw themselves into the TPC campaign and the election hi-jinks. The shenanigans of these young journalists marked the beginning of this very interesting year.

In 1910 the wealthy Canadian financier, Sir Henry Mill Pellatt, commanding officer of the Queen's Own Rifles planned two events to celebrate the semi-centennial of the founding of the QOR: the first was a multi-day pageant in June to celebrate the history of Canada and the regiment, and also serve as a reunion for current and hundreds of past members of the QOR; the second was a fall visit to England of over 600 QOR men to train with the British military for a month.[15] Both of these events were to be subsidised by Pellatt. The overseas adventure was called "the English trip." For the young men on the journey, many who were humble office clerks, it was an incredible opportunity and an unforgettable experience as likely "very few of the 600 men . . . [had] ever been in the old country."[16]

Newspaper coverage was an important means to bring praise to Pellatt, the QOR, Canada, and England. There was substantial interest in the military and social details of the trip, so Toronto newspapers arranged for their own exclusive coverage. In 1910 there were six newspapers published in Toronto, the *World*, the *Globe*, the *Star*, the *News*, the *Telegram* (or the *Evening Telegram*), and the *Mail & Empire*. Each of these papers had a particular bent when it came to reportage: the *Globe* and the *Mail and Empire* produced "quality journalism" with a British-oriented world view; the *Telegram* and the *Star* focused on "people's journalism" with a local and US-style view; the *News* looked for sensationalism and local gossip; and the *World* was a popular local morning paper, which was "the darling of morning streetcar hordes."[17]

These papers needed reporters to accompany the trip, so who better to give this assignment to than young cub reporters, men in their late teens and early twenties, already in their employ? Some cubs were already members of the QOR, while others joined for the duration of the trip. In the end, there were six official Toronto reporters, five who served with the QOR, and one who accompanied the trip but did not enlist. The enlisted reporters were J.N.M. Brown for the *World*, Jim Scroggie for the *News*, John MacLaren for the *Telegram*, Roy R. Riggs for the *Mail and Empire,* and Ned Sheppard for the *Star*.[18] These men were sometimes given a dedicated space to write while in camp, a separate tent, but ultimately, they too were in the regiment just like the other enlisted men. The QOR journalists were all in the same company, H, and were assigned to the same tent where they were nicknamed "the press gang" by the regiment. Jaffray Eaton, of the *Globe*, did not enlist.[19] The editorial direction of each of the Toronto papers is reflected in the stories filed by these young men and their voices also inform us about their upbringings and personalities.

So it is that newspaper articles provide most of the story that is to follow; however, there are other resources, most importantly, scrapbooks of collected articles and artifacts from the trip. Pellatt employed a professional clipping service, and as a result there are several scrapbooks of articles from the United Kingdom (UK), where journalists provided coverage in several British papers.[20] But one of the youthful reporters, Jim Scroggie, kept a scrapbook of the trip; this included photographs (both published and unpublished) and his articles, which he often annotated with sarcastic notes and cartoonish drawings. It seems that he took a camera on the trip, as there are several small black and white photos in the album of the men in informal situations in camp and on marches.[21] Scroggie often directed his critical comments to his fellow reporters, and these highlight the interactions of these men with a humorous effect.

What is known about the reporters? Starting with the reporter who was not in the regiment, Jaffray (Jaff) Eaton (twenty-four) was born in Owen Sound.[22] He was educated in Owen Sound and then attended the University of Toronto. When he graduated from U of T in 1907, he began working as a reporter at the *Globe*, which his grandfather, the Hon. Robert Jaffray, and then his uncle, W.G. Jaffray, owned.[23] In Toronto, he lived with his grandfather and moved in the highest social circles of the city.[24] Eaton's father, Christopher, was English born and was not related to the Timothy Eatons of Toronto. Jaffray's interest in writing was encouraged by his family as can be seen in a poem he wrote when he was ten, titled "The Gong," which was published in the *Globe* in 1896.[25] He was an active member of the Toronto Press Club serving as the *Globe* representative on the executive.[26] Eaton did not enlist in the QOR regiment because he was active in the 147th Grey Battalion.[27] The *Globe* audaciously claimed that "Capt. Jaffray Eaton is representing the Globe with the Q.O.R. in England, the only exclusive press correspondent on the trip."[28] By exclusive, the *Globe* meant, as explained in a later article, "He is the only Toronto newspaperman who goes with the regiment as such, and not as a member of the corps."[29]

J.N.M. (Jim) Brown (twenty-one) wrote for the *World*. He was born in Aylmer, Ontario, a small farming community south of London.[30] By 1900 his father, Merritt A. Brown, a barrister, had relocated the family to Toronto. Brown attended high school at Jarvis Collegiate but apparently did not graduate. Beginning in 1909 he was employed as a reporter in the editorial department of the *World* when he published a humorous article, "Typographical Nature-Faking," in the Toronto Press Club Theatre Nights program.[31] Scroggie commented about Brown, "Distinguished also from other Browns by the initials J.N.M." His articles began with the words "From our man in the regiment," and there are fewer than ten articles on the trip in the *World*.[32] Initially, it was thought that Brown had no connections in the newspaper business in Toronto. That proved incorrect when it was discovered that his uncle, Walter James Brown, was the editor of the *Globe Weekly* and *Canadian Farmer*.[33] Since Brown had attended Jarvis Collegiate, he may have had some experience with the Jarvis QOR cadets but otherwise no involvement with the QOR.

John (Jack) Aiken MacLaren (nineteen) reported for the *Telegram*. MacLaren was born in Belfountain, Ontario, where his father was a stone mason. He attended high school in Orangeville, apparently not finishing Grade 10.[34] When he left Belfountain, he was hired as a messenger boy at John Ross Robertson's *Telegram*. According to Might's

Toronto directories, he worked for the *Telegram* starting in 1909. On his WWI draft form, July 1918, he was still employed as a journalist and listed his previous military experience as six months in the QOR. Seventeen articles appeared in the *Telegram* about the trip written "from the *Telegram's* special representative with the Q.O.R." or "from our own correspondent." He was not accorded a byline; however, based on his identification in Scroggie's scrapbook as the reporter for the *Telegram,* he is considered the official correspondent.[35]

Roy R. Riggs (twenty-one) was born in Toronto and at the time lived in the family home on Jarvis St., attending Jarvis Collegiate.[36] His father was a dentist. *Might's Directory for Toronto* 1910 lists his job as a stenographer.[37] The Toronto *Mail and Empire* newspaper has several articles authored by Riggs, who was one of their two reporters accompanying the trip. The second reporter is not accorded a byline and cannot be identified. Riggs had been in the QOR since 1908.[38]

James Scroggie (Jim or "Scrog," as he referred to himself) (twenty-one) was born in Simcoe County where his father, George E. Scroggie, was a school teacher.[39] Shortly after Jim's birth in 1888, the family moved to Toronto and his father began his career in newspaper advertising, where over several years he worked for various Toronto papers.[40] In 1910 Scroggie's father was advertising manager for the *Mail and Empire*.[41] Scroggie started working for the *News* in 1909, and was an actor in the theatrical performed by the Toronto Press Club at the Royal Alexandra in June of that year.[42] The family lived on Starr Ave., south Parkdale, near Lake Ontario and moved in the middle-class social circle of west-end Toronto, being members of the Parkdale Canoe Club, which, after 1905, became the Boulevard Club.[43] The *News* announced that he would be their reporter in the regiment stating that he "is a graphic writer, with a marked power of humor, and a knowledge of military work. He will send back by wire and letter complete descriptive stories . . . and the hundred and one vitally interesting features which will be a part of the journey."[44] Scroggie had been a member of the QOR since 1908.[45]

Edmund Culver (Ned) Sheppard (nineteen) was the "staff correspondent" for the Toronto *Star*.[46] Sheppard had attended Upper Canada College where he had been a member of the UCC cadets, 2nd

Regiment of the QOR. He had left his studies at the University of Toronto in the fall of 1909 to take a position at the *Star*.[47] His father was the well-known controversial journalist Edmund Ernest Sheppard, known as "Shep" and the "Don," who founded *Saturday Night* and was also briefly editor of the *News* and Toronto *Star*.[48] By 1910 Joseph E. Atkinson was publisher of the *Star*.[49] Under a photograph of Ned in the scrapbook Scroggie wrote, "Dashing young soldier as crease in trousers will denote. Photographed while lighting his own pipe with someone else's tobacco and match. Taken before the trip by the Star. Specimen of Ned's originality may be seen in roll of puttees."[50] Similar to Eaton and Scroggie, Sheppard was a son in a newsman's family and like them he was socially well-connected in Toronto.

Figure 1. Jim Brown's worn photograph of the English trip reporters; L to R, Brown, Jim Scroggie, Jaffray Eaton, Jack MacLaren and Ned Sheppard.

One photograph, kept as a memento by Jim Brown, showed five of the reporters.[51] A published version of the photograph was found in Scroggie's scrapbook with the caption "War Correspondents With the

QOR to England." According to Scroggie's notes, these photos were taken by the *Star Weekly* photographer in Ned Sheppard's backyard in downtown Toronto, just before the trip departure. Ned Sheppard's photo, cropped from a similar unpublished group photograph in the scrapbook, appeared on the front page of the *Star*, August 11, 1910, with the caption "MR. "NED" SHEPPARD of the Toronto Star Staff, who will accompany the Queen's Own Regiment to England. Being a son of 'Don,' newspaper work comes naturally to him, and his letters from 'the front' are sure to be interesting." The Saturday, August 13, *Star* mentioned that the Sunday paper would have "Some Snapshots of the Q.O.R. in their Going-Away Togs."[52] This is probably when the war correspondents photo appeared. The *Star* photographer was Fred H. Foster, according to the stamp on the back of Brown's photo.

Figure 2. Scroggie's artistically annotated photograph identifying the reporters' newspapers using their logos.

Just as Pellatt encouraged young reporters to join and train as privates with the QOR, another aspect of the publicity for the trip needed to be managed, and that was photography. Throughout the trip many photographs were taken of the officers, the men, their parades and marches, and casual activities. It is certain that media-savvy Pellatt facilitated the services of a professional photographer, but who was it? Several photographs of the trip were published and most had no photographer credited, but some *Globe* photos have the attribution "Photo by Gleason."[53]

In 1910 Arthur A. Gleason (thirty-two) was a freelance newspaper photographer based in Montréal.[54] In an advertisement in 1911, he identified himself as the official photographer in the Institute of Journalists, Canadian Division and wrote, "Newspaper Photography calls for the very best work and experience. You must have SNAP and Life in your pictures. Mine cover all these requirements and are up to the minute."[55] In 1908 he was hired by the *Globe* to photograph the Québec Tercentenary.[56] How he managed to be on this trip was explained when he was interviewed in 1958 for an article in the *London Free Press* about his career; 1910 "was a banner year for Art Gleason, a climax to 'shooting' the tercentenary at Quebec, attended by Earl Grey and Lord Roberts and the first tag day at Quebec. He was sent as official photographer by the *Canadian Courier* on the eight-week British tour of the Queen's Own Regiment."[57] Gleason took many of the photographs of the English trip, which appeared in the weekly *Canadian Courier*, and other papers, including the *Globe*, and these provide different, often informal views of the men and their activities.[58]

Probably many QOR men kept diaries of the trip, but only two are known, those of F.R. Henshaw and George W. Argue.[59] Frederick Robert Henshaw (nineteen) was a gentleman cadet, a corporal, at the Royal Military College in Kingston, who thought "The experience as a private would be very valuable especially as we would be taking part on the great manoeuvres. Besides I would have a chance to see something of London and part of England." George Argue (twenty-two) kept a pocket-sized day-timer in which he recorded the minutiae of the trip: reveille, times of meals, and time to bed, as well as other observations about his experiences. What is interesting about Argue, considering the newspaper focus of this story, is that his father, William L. Argue, was circulation manager for the Toronto *Star*. Argue was friends with Ned Sheppard, whom he mentions in his diary.

For the trip, all of the reporters were in the QOR's H Company, and there were two other reporters identified in this company, Rudolph Brazill and A.V. Corbett.[60] Rudolph Frank Brazill, (twenty) was a reporter for the *Evening Telegram* from 1908.[61] At the time of the trip he had been a member of the QOR since 1908.[62] Arthur F. Corbett (twenty-two) was listed in *Might's City of Toronto Directory*, 1910, as a travelling reporter for the *World*.[63] Corbett was in some of the photographs in Scroggie's scrapbook, where he was called "Papa" and "Corby." Since Brazill and Corbett are not identified as official reporters for the trip, and no articles published under their byline have been found, they are not discussed further.

These young newspaper men were all at the beginning of their careers, working in a large city during exciting times, when new inventions appeared that would change the world, such as wireless cablegrams and airplanes. By the personal banter of commentary on Scroggie's photos it appears the men knew each other, either meeting at reporting assignments or at the Toronto Press Club, where four were members.[64] They were probably the young journalists involved in the raucous elections of the TPC in January of 1910. For four of the cubs, their family connections led them to jobs as reporters in Toronto newspapers, but for all the cubs this trip would give them the opportunity to report under their own names with bylines for the first time.

In this book, the words of the reporters, diarists, and others, when quoted, are verbatim. It might seem to the readers that the spelling is inconsistent because it alternates English Canadian vs. American spelling, and with some words accented in French, while others are not. In 1910 the spelling conventions were different than those of today, specifically American spelling was used, and French words had no accents. Also, spelling of words varies from the past to the present, for example in 1910, it was grand stand, not grandstand. The spellings in the quotations are accurate and reflect the spelling of the time.

The trip was only one part of the semi-centennial celebrations of the Queen's Own Rifles of Toronto; there were other events for the QOR. But even before 1910 there is the story of Sir Henry Pellatt's history with the QOR, and other military and historical celebrations that led him to formulating his plans for the anniversary festivities.

CHAPTER

2

Pellatt and the QOR

For some two years or so, Sir Henry has intended sending a contingent from his regiment to have actual experience among British soldiers at home. [65]

The events of 1910 were the result of the ambitions and dreams of one man, Sir Henry Mill Pellatt. Pellatt was born in Kingston, Ontario in 1859. At the time, his father, Henry Pellatt Sr., a bank employee, was experiencing financial difficulties, which resulted in the family moving to Toronto to reinvent themselves. After declaring bankruptcy, Pellatt Sr. became a successful stockbroker and insurance agent, leading to his children, including his son Henry Mill Pellatt, having a well-monied upbringing as members of Toronto's newly affluent upper class. Young Henry and his father formed a stockbroker firm in 1883, and Henry's business career thrived. [66] One company Henry owned was the Toronto

Electric Light Co., making him one of the wealthiest men in Canada in the 1910s.

Henry Mill Pellatt's love of and lifelong commitment to the Queen's Own Rifles of Canada began in 1876 when, as a teenager, he enlisted as a rifleman of F Company. (In rifle regiments officers first serve in the ranks.) Then, over the years, Pellatt continued his commitment to the regiment, eventually being named commanding officer in 1901. The Queen's Own Rifles was formed in Toronto on April 26, 1860, and as the oldest militia in Canada, their history was worth celebrating, so much so that on their fiftieth anniversary Sir Henry Mill Pellatt planned and paid for lavish celebrations.[67]

Pellatt's respect for the QOR was closely aligned with his veneration of the British military and monarchy and the pomp and circumstance of the royal world. He attended Queen Victoria's jubilee celebration with a QOR contingent in 1897, and then, at his own expense, sent the QOR Bugle Band to England in 1902 for the coronation of King Edward VII. Pellatt was ambitious for royal honours, and in 1904 he lobbied to receive a Knight Bachelor, which was awarded to him in November of 1905, and henceforth he was known as Sir Henry Mill Pellatt, or informally, just Sir Henry.[68]

After the turn of the twentieth century, Canada had a military force of 3,000 regulars and a militia of nearly 30,000. Militias are a citizen's volunteer, part-time military unit. There were both urban and rural militias. Urban militias were more prestigious, offering enlistees access to a higher echelon of society and the opportunity of upward mobility. For city officers it was sometimes seen as membership in a private club.[69]

According to the Militia Act (1904) only Canadian-born and British-born men over eighteen were eligible for membership.[70] In cities, enlistees were often white-collar workers who, if they had attended high school in Toronto, had a compulsory cadet experience.[71] Once enlisted in a militia for a three-year term, there was an expected twelve hours of service every year. Duties involved drilling, parades, summer training exercises, and mock battles between competing regiments for the entertainment of the community; these latter events were often held over Easter and Thanksgiving weekends. In Toronto, the mock manoeuvres were often held in High Park or the Don Valley, where onlookers would watch while enjoying picnics. The summer training camps were hard work, with arduous military exercises under the hot summer sun, but there was plenty of food and fun activities such as picnics, sports competitions, performances, singing; drinking alcohol, usually beer, was allowed.[72] In return for their service, the men were given drill pay of fifty cents a day, from the Department of Canadian Militia.[73]

Traditionally, "City regiments demanded an entry fee and required officers to purchase detailed uniforms from British Military tailors. Toronto's Queen's Own were certainly not elitist, but the expense and the time commitment of joining the regiment proved a deterrent" to those less financially established.[74] In Toronto, dress uniforms were made by local tailors, including Austen Workman; Henry Pellatt and his son Reginald, favoured the bespoke Toronto tailors Beauchamp & How.[75] Officers and members paid into the regimental account, and these fees, with additional support from wealthier members, like Pellatt, supported costs of travel and the purchasing of uniforms for those who could not afford them.[76]

In 1902, as the preparations for the coronation of King Edward VII progressed, the Canadian government planned for a military contingent to be sent. Soon it became apparent that there were not the government funds to send a band to precede the troops in the parades. Pellatt understood that a band would herald the troops as a distinctive Canadian force and offered to send the Queen's Own Rifles Bugle Band to attend at his expense, an offer which the Canadian government accepted. By June 7, 1902, the band (with forty-nine members) and the others of the Canadian contingent, some twenty-six officers and 603 men, were in London in advance of the coronation, which was scheduled for June 26. However, due to the king's illness, the coronation was rescheduled to August 9, and regrettably the QOR buglers did not attend as their return was booked for July 3.[77]

Another significant travel experience for the QOR was the spring 1906 trip to New York City to take part in a military tournament. Over 800 men departed from Toronto on the evening of Thursday, April 26 and arrived in NYC the next morning when they paraded to the Twelfth

Regiment Armories, where they were being billeted.[78] Two evenings, Friday and Saturday, were spent performing regimental manoeuvres before audiences of the tournament, which was held indoors at Madison Square Garden. The US government had to provide special permission for the QOR to bring their rifles into the country.[79] Free time was spent being tourists in the city, and some QOR men had difficulties because Canadian money was not accepted for transactions.[80] The tournament was a great success, and after leaving on Sunday at 1.00 p.m., an overnight train brought the regiment back to Toronto on Monday morning.[81]

From the experience of the 1902 trip, Pellatt realized that it was possible to send a group of men to England, and more importantly, if the Canadian government would not pay to do so, they were not averse to allowing someone else cover all the costs. The advantage for the government was that in the end the praise and glory for the trip would be recognized for all of Canada. These trips were minor events for the QOR. The next major event for the Canadian military and militias was a significant experience, one that likely opened Pellatt's mind to think about other more ambitious celebrations and trips for his beloved regiment.

In 1908, between July 19 and July 26, with the support of the government of Canada, tercentenary celebrations were held in Québec City to mark the founding of Québec by Samuel de Champlain in 1608.[82] As a celebration it was one on a grand scale, with theatrical elements, including elaborate costumed pageants, which were enacted over several days before grandstands filled with thousands of paying visitors. There were Catholic Masses, Anglican services, nighttime firework displays, formal military reviews, and elaborate electrical illuminations of the battleships and the other British, French, and American navy ships in the St. Lawrence River.

Historical pageants were very popular in Edwardian England, becoming more common after 1905.[83] Costumed performers, often local dignitaries, portrayed historical figures in scripted vignettes, appearing in large and complex presentations where often hundreds of men, women, children, horses, guns, and cannons were involved. They performed on elaborate stages with customized painted backdrops before grandstands, often custom built, which were filled with thousands of paying visitors who eagerly watched the panoramic presentations.

Figure 3. Québec Tercentenary Fireworks and Electrical Display on the St. Lawrence, Québec.

Putting on these pageants required a skilled theatrical producer, actors, a playwright, or a director with large-scale pageant experience; the Québec Pageant, through Governor General Earl Grey, hired the well-known and respected British pageant master, Frank Lascelles.[84] After spending a weekend in Ottawa with Grey in March of 1908, likely to inform him of highly sensitive French-English relationships, Lascelles moved to Québec to begin planning the event. Lascelles asked the National Battlefields Commission for $155,580 to pay for big items, like the building of the grandstand on the Plains of Abraham, fencing, costumes, wigs, uniforms, and lesser costs, like $5,000 to cover the salaries and expenses of the "Indians."[85] In the end, Lascelles was given $109,000 to stage the event. The script was developed by a local historian, who consulted with historical committees. Performances were divided into "epochs" starting from the earliest up to the War of 1812. Epochs and acts in epochs were punctuated by musical interludes, which set the mood for the historical scenes that followed. Actors were selected, costumes fitted, and rehearsals held. Due to the large size of the cast, Lascelles communicated by calling through a distinctive, large megaphone; his assistants in the field relayed messages as required.

The pageants were a huge success and when the last one was over, a unique event capped Lascelles' time in Québec; the Huron Iroquoians, whom Lascelles had befriended, made him an Indian chief with the name Tehonoikonraka, meaning, "The Man of Infinite Resources." This was an honour that moved him and which he treasured for the rest of life, even to the point of having it mentioned in his obituary many years later.[86]

Apart from the flashy showmanship of the tercentenary, there were at the time significant underlying political issues in Canada concerning the development of the Canadian military and the ongoing relationship between French- and English-speaking Canada. Early in 1908 a Canadian, General William Otter (a QOR veteran), assumed command of the Canadian Department of Militia, and under him, government appropriations for the military increased. The tercentenary was seen as an opportunity to muster Canadian troops. As well, the presence of the prince of Wales and the British military would legitimize the Canadian government's militarization efforts. It was initially planned that 150,000 military men would attend, but because of the reluctance of the federal government to cover the salaries of so many men, it was scaled back to 13,000, including 1,500 regulars and Royal Military College cadets, the rest being members of Canadian volunteer militias.[87]

At the time, French and English Canadians co-existed in a tenuous détente, and this uncomfortable relationship was also apparent in the Canadian military. The tercentenary was seen as an opportunity to combine forces and demonstrate to Britain that Canadians could support their own military, which could defend their borders, if required, and could support the Empire in the foreseeable future.

Arriving in Canada for this gala was Prince George, the prince of Wales, as well as Lord Roberts, commander-in-chief of the British Forces, who was also an honorary colonel of the QOR and the Royal Canadian Artillery.[88] Other attendees were Prime Minister Sir Wilfrid Laurier; Earl Grey, the governor general; and US Vice-President Charles W. Fairbanks.

The Toronto brigade included the QOR, the Grenadiers, and the 48th Highlanders. In all, nearly 1,300 Toronto men attended.[89] The regiments from Ontario, being the most numerous, were given the best campgrounds at Savard Park on the St. Charles River; other regiments were on the south shore of the St. Lawrence. Capt. Walter J. Brown, an adjutant of the Canadian Field Artillery, (and Jim Brown's uncle) wrote, "We encamped at Savard park on the St. Charles River about two miles beyond the city limits. The camp grounds were very pleasant, in spite of the distance they were away from the points of attraction. We had owing to the limited ground at our disposal very little chance to do much in the line of drill however, we managed to get enough work done to enable us to make a good showing on the day of the Review."[90]

The military aspect involved parades through the streets of Québec City and the royal review on the Plains of Abraham. This review, on July 24, was additionally significant because it also heralded the establishment of the National Battlefields Commission by Parliament. At this, the prince of Wales presented a cheque for $450,000 with the deed for the purchase of the lands of the Plains of Abraham and the battlefield of Ste-Foye to Lord Earl Grey. Field Marshall Lord Roberts had inspected the QOR at Savard on July 21 and he also led the QOR regiment as it marched past the prince of Wales on the Plains.[91]

At its conclusion, the tercentenary was a success because of the Canadian military's general staff, and their capable handling of the organization of what was, at the time, the largest military event in Canadian history. It also demonstrated that the Canadian Armed Services Corps could sustain "the entire force, providing a pound and a half of fresh-baked bread to each man every day, a quantity amounting to 56 tons. In addition, 90 tons of meat, ten tons of bacon, 35 tons of vegetables, six tons of cheese and many other foodstuffs were prepared and delivered to different camps during the celebrations."[92]

In an eyewitness account of the tercentenary, Capt. Brown wrote glowingly of his experience:

> I saw the pageants on the Plains, was driven over and through most of the city, was entertained at the Garrison Club, had an invitation to lunch on board the H.M.S. Russell, was shown through the battle ships, saw the illuminated fleet several times, visited Montmorency Falls and had dinner at Kent House and returned to Montreal by boat the evening of the 25 of July. I was home a week ago to-day and at work by 9 a.m. Everyone I meet wants to know all about Quebec and I tell my story over and over day by day and evening by evening. I am so glad now that the chance came as it did and I took advantage of it.[93]

The tercentenary celebrations were heralded as a political success, and a reporter from the *Globe* wrote, "past bitternesses are forgotten, and that the two races in Canada and the great neighbouring republic intend to go on together in peace, seemed to be the lessons of today's mammoth spectacle."[94] Experiencing the glory of the pomp and circumstance of the tercentenary doubtless gave Sir Henry Pellatt the idea that such an event, with historical pageants and military reviews, could be planned and held in Toronto, and with his even greater ambitions, such a celebration could be combined with an overseas trip to the United Kingdom to show support for the military of the mother country.

Pellatt was so proud of the QOR and his experience at Québec that he commissioned a stained-glass window of the review on the Plains of Abraham to be installed at Casa Loma. This window was later discovered, still in its crate, and installed, after his death, in the QOR Officers' Mess at the University Avenue Armouries in April of 1939.[95] It is thought that it was destroyed when the armouries were demolished.[96]

CHAPTER

3

1910 and the QOR Semi-Centennial

Anniversary of Formation of the Regiment a Memorable Event in Annals of Canadian Militia.[97]

What was Toronto like in 1910? Lest one assume otherwise, Toronto in 1910 had a year much like most other larger North American cities, and a review of the front page of the Toronto *Star* for the year reports murders, drownings, fires, collisions involving runaway horses, cars, street cars, and accidents to riders, drivers, and pedestrians, resulting in maiming and deaths. Poverty and public health, especially concerns about typhus from contaminated food and drinking water, were major issues. Then too, Torontonians loved their football teams, and the University of Toronto Varsity Team won the first Earl Grey Cup in 1909, which, because the cup was not ready, was finally presented in March of 1910.[98] Some events stand out, and these help to form an impression of the social and civic fabric of Toronto and what was happening in the world in 1910.

The headline from the *Globe* on January 1 captures the mood: "1909 Was a Good Year –May 1910 Be Better."[99] In January Toronto elected a new mayor, G. Reginald Geary for his first one-year term, and in his inaugural address he made it clear that his goal was to make Toronto a "healthy place to live." [100] Then, on January 15, there was considerable astronomical excitement at the appearance of a bright comet over the Pacific, which became visible in the city on January 24.[101] However, this was not the anticipated Halley's comet, which appeared in April. Such was the interest in Halley's that there was a daily column devoted to updates through April to May in articles on the front page, informing Torontonians when it would be visible in the daytime skies.[102]

The increase in the enrolment of women students at University College also made front page news in January when it was reported that one-third of the one thousand students at the University were now women![103] Women's suffrage came unexpectedly to the fore in March when an unknown young woman spoke aloud at the Ontario Legislature from the Speaker's Gallery, "You have done nothing for the causes of women. I hope that in your future meetings you will do something to do justice for women."[104] When she started speaking, "Everyone was so thunderstruck that she was allowed to finish her statement."[105] The young woman, Olivia Smith, was an experienced English suffragist, who as it turned out was Canadian.[106] Her speech did not go over well with Premier Whitney's Conservative government, which opposed suffrage, and the coverage of it in the *Star,* can be described as perfunctory. On the other hand, the Toronto *World* unequivocally supported suffrage, tracked her down for an interview, and then wrote an article repeating her speech and heralding her considerable suffrage credentials.[107]

Torontonians had a reason to celebrate when on April 19, local Joe Corkery won third place at the Boston Marathon. In a race with 186 competitors, Canadians could be proud that first place was won by Fred Cameron of Amherst, Nova Scotia, with a time of 2.28.51, which was still "four minutes behind the peerless Longboat."[108] Later that week, the literary world was saddened to hear of the death of the beloved American humorist Samuel Clemens on April 21, better known by his pen name, Mark Twain.[109]

As the spring season developed, worrying news from England concerned the poor health of King Edward VII. His death was announced on May 6, and George V was proclaimed as king.[110] A large outdoor commemorative observance was held on May 21 in Toronto's Queen's Park, where the rain made for a striking photograph of an endless sea of black umbrellas on the front page of the *Star*.[111]

On Tuesday, May 24, British General John French, who had led the cavalry against the Boers in South Africa, unveiled a monument on University Avenue to honour those who had fought and died in that war.[112] A photograph of General French speaking shows several newsmen seated at a table in the front, writing down his words as he made his remarks. In 1910 there were no microphones, so journalists were important witnesses and recorders of these ceremonial events.

Figure 4. Unveiling of the South African War Memorial, University Avenue and Queen Street West.

On June 7, the well-known, controversial English-Torontonian Goldwin Smith, who supported Canada's annexation by the United States, died at his home, The Grange.[113] His wife, Harriet Smith, had died the year previously, and it was her generous donation of their home to the City of Toronto that would become the city's art gallery.

On June 16, the *Star* reported that Toronto-born Mr. Charles S. Wright had departed with Captain Scott on his expedition to the South Pole.[114] Wright, born in 1887, a former member of the QOR, had attended Upper Canada College and then the University of Toronto. He was at Cambridge University when he famously applied for a spot on the expedition by walking to London to entreat Scott, in person, telling him he had made a mistake by not including him. Scott, impressed by his physical and intellectual fervor, changed his mind and Wright became a physicist on the trip, not a physician as described in the *Star* article. He was twenty-three years old, and as an old boy of UCC he was doubtless known to other young men of a similar age and social standing, including Ned Sheppard.[115] Wright's position with Captain Scott was front-page news, stirring the desire for adventure among Toronto's young men. For those who did not have the opportunity to go on such an expedition, the QOR trip to England provided a similar, if lesser, but no less exciting adventure.

Following the example of the successful celebration of Québec's tercentenary, Pellatt planned events in 1910 to celebrate the fiftieth anniversary of the Queen's Own Rifles. The first part was the reunion in Toronto in June, including several functions for the thousands of past and current members of the QOR and the citizens of Toronto; the second part was Pellatt's ambitious plan to take over 600 QOR men to England to train with the British military during their fall manoeuvres.

The reunion celebrations officially began with a garden party on June 18 and ended with a grand ball on June 24. The plans for the reunion and the trip had been generally roughed out and were presented to the officers and men of the QOR at a meeting on Saturday December 10, 1909.[116]

Had Toronto previous experience in planning a large-scale celebration? It had indeed, in 1890 the July 1 Dominion Day, was a "monster carnival pageant!"[117] Various military regiments fell in at the drill hall and when the bugles sounded, "one of the largest military displays ever seen in Toronto before began to march" from City Hall to Exhibition Park. Over 3,000 men marched and the "last regiment of the active militia of Canada was the parade favorite the Queen's Own Rifles of Toronto, 475 strong" including one Capt. Henry Pellatt. The day was filled with athletic events, regattas, tug-of-war competitions between regiments, and a popular performance by over 1400 school children, over one-third being young girls all dressed in white. The evening ended with fireworks displays at Exhibition Park, Queen's Park, and Riverside Park. "Some beautiful set pieces were given at each place, and a profusion of rockets, shells and pyrotechnic bombardment filled in the interstices." The *Globe* concluded that "Hundreds of residences in all parts of the city were lit up with Chinese lanterns last night. . . . Seldom have the streets of Toronto been more densely crowded than they were during the procession yesterday."[118] The impression of Toronto neighbourhoods glowing with charming lanterns on a warm summer evening evokes a wonderful image.

To assist in the considerable work required in planning the 1910 events, Pellatt hired a "permanent secretary [George I. Riddell] . . . with an office down town [36 King St. E.], with whom all wishing to take part, especially those out of town, may communicate."[119] One of the first responsibilities of the secretary was to make an application to the City of Toronto to settle the location of the June festivities. On January 21, a report was received by the city from the QOR:

> . . . asking for the use of the Exhibition Grand Stand and grounds in front thereof for a Historical Pageant in connection with the 50th anniversary of the organization of the Regiment, beginning Monday, June 20, and lasting for three days; also for permission to rehearse on the grounds for a few days before, and to remove the properties a few days after; also for the use of the Transportation Building for a ball, to be held on June 23. It is recommended that the application be granted, and the use of the buildings and grounds to be under the direction of the Park Commissioner.[120]

One of the costs paid by Pellatt included salaries for groundskeepers at the Exhibition.[121]

However, at the same time, the QOR was also exploring holding the pageant at the Rosedale Athletic Grounds with access provided by the Toronto Street Railway Company, a company of which Pellatt was president.[122] Over the next several months, the TSR company applied to the City to have the Church streetcar line and tracks extended north over the Glen Road ridge to the park at the company's expense. The City delayed its permission, with the result that "the representatives of the Queen's Own Rifles are thus forced to make other arrangements . . . [and] . . . the company hereby withdraws the proposition made for the . . . extension."[123] The location of the jubilee festivities formally became the Exhibition grounds, and in light of the grand scale of the event, it is inconceivable that it could have been staged anywhere else.

To advise those wishing to attend the reunion, a brief pamphlet was printed and distributed to former and current members of the QOR; this explained what events would be held, where and when they would occur, dress codes, prices for seats at the pageants, and fees for tickets to the grand ball.[124] A commemorative medal was struck and was available for purchase in either bronze (sixty cents with mailing) or silver ($1.10 with mailing). Gold medals were also produced and likely given as gifts to dignitaries or purchased by officers.[125]

Reduced railway fares were negotiated for those members travelling from far away, places like California ($95.70 return) and British Columbia (summer tourist rates), as well as those travelling from eastern Canada, New York State, Chicago and Detroit. To encourage people from around Toronto to go to the evening pageants there were reduced local rail fares, and return rates were offered as well. Throughout 1910 ex-members contacted the reunion office, which co-ordinated their attendance.[126] However, the attendance of QOR men was just one aspect of the Toronto celebrations, the most challenging commemorative event, the historical pageant, had to be planned.

The highlight of the Québec tercentenary was the historical pageant about the founding of Canada, involving hundreds of participants, with Indigenous Iroquois, costumed French and English explorers, kings and queens, even including military battles re-enacted on the Plains of Abraham. Earl Grey, the governor general, had been able to hire the English pageant master Frank Lascelles. Lascelles was in high demand in Great Britain and was only able to do the Québec pageant due to a cancellation in his schedule. It is likely that Pellatt tried to hire Lascelles for Toronto, but because of Lascelles' popularity was unsuccessful. The respected actor and playwright John Henderson, another well-known British pageant master, was hired instead.[127]

What were the intentions of a pageant? As written by Henderson in the official programme, "The Story of the Pageant" under the coy byline "'By a Spectator from the Grand Stand.' . . . A Pageant is a series of historical events, regal or homely, grave or gay, heroic or simple, in a country's history, depicted by living representatives passing before us in processional review, accompanied by such music and suitable scenic embellishments as the theme or occasion may dictate."[128] The theme or occasion for this pageant was to celebrate the founding of the Queen's Own Rifles. Henderson wrote, "The Pageant of Ontario, given by the Queen's Own Rifles of Canada . . . [this] . . . will be the first Pageant to be held in the Province of Ontario, and as such deserves some place in the hearts of old and young alike, as a prominent factor in bringing before our very eyes living representatives, heroic and simple, who have been the makers of our country's history-makers of our great Dominion of to-day—the proudest jewel in the Crown of the British Empire."[129]

Henderson arrived in Toronto some two months before the pageant and his first task was to write the script, a copy of which has survived, titled *The Dramatic Story of the Queen's Own Toronto Pageant*.[130] This was likely approved by Pellatt, and it provided the outline, which was followed for the final programme. Briefly, the pageant began with Epoch I, that being the arrival of the United Empire Loyalists, Governor General Simcoe, the founding of York (to the tune of "Rule Britannia"), and Joseph Brant and the Six Nations Iroquois. Epoch II, was introduced by a comic interlude, with a wedding and a chivaree party, to lighten the mood, then it shifted to the War of 1812 (music included "Yankee Doodle Dandy"), battle scenes of the war, Brock's death, the Battle of the Thames, Tecumseh's death, and a vignette about Laura Secord in her house, including her leading a cow (music being QOR's own, Alexander Muir's "Canada, Land of the Maple Tree"). In Epoch III, Henderson's script included the story of Josiah Henson and escaped African American slaves fleeing to Ontario; however, this was removed in the final programme to focus instead on the military exploits of the QOR in the nineteenth century, the Fenian raids, the Battle of Ridgeway, the North-West expedition, and the Riel rebellions, which were significant engagements in the QOR's history (music regimental march of the QOR). Epoch IV was the current-day Dominion of Canada beginning with a procession of English kings and queens and the return to the stage of all performers of previous epochs. With this outline it was now up to Henderson to make it happen, which was quite a challenge with only two months of preparation before the first performance on June 20.

According to one newspaper of the day, it's estimated that the pageant cost over $30,000 to stage.[131] Henderson earned $200 per week, other office staff and pageant staff were employed, grounds people at Exhibition Place were compensated, and the thirty-six Iroquois from Six Nations were paid $2 a day (the chief was paid more) for a total of $4,000 in all salaries. The Garden Party cost $2,000 and the smoker in the armouries cost $1,000; advertising, rents, car rides, printing tickets, pamphlets etc., amounted to $5,000. The hundreds of costumes, which would have been a huge expense, were, according to a *Star* article, borrowed from England, and had to be insured at a cost of $2,500.[132] By far the most expensive feature of the pageant was the production of the scenic backdrops, and the erection of the scaffolding to hold the panels; this amounted to $13,000.

With the script and funding in place and commissions sent to England for costumes and scenery, it now fell to Henderson to produce the extravaganza. A pageant of epic proportions required a lot of people, not paid actors, but amateurs, hundreds of citizens willing to give up time to commit to rehearsals and several evenings of performances. Fortunately, Henderson had access to the hundreds of members of the QOR regiment, and they received the call to participate in the pageant at their Wednesday night drill on April 20.[133] For the pageant, the questions asked of the men were: "Have you a strong voice? Can you sing? Can you ride? Clean-shaven or otherwise? [And the last one]

Have you acted?" It was made clear that be they would be "under the direct control of the pageant master, and will take their orders from him." And why would they want to participate? Because "if plans are realized it will be the most spectacular function of the kind ever seen here!" Men from the QOR signed on for all major roles, but there were also parts for women and children, and these were recruited from the wives and daughters of members of the regiment.[134]

On Thursday, May 5, in a meeting at the St. Lawrence Market, Henderson assigned 300 parts, the other 500 were to be assigned the following Monday.[135] It was possible to inform men of the QOR about the schedules of rehearsals at their weekly drills, but to contact the women it was necessary to publish announcements in Toronto newspapers; the pageant master "desires to meet the ladies who have kindly consented to take part in the Pageant of Ontario, in the officer's lecture room of the armories on Thursday, May 5 at 3pm."[136]

One special aspect of the pageant was a performance of 300 children, the penultimate act in the fourth Epoch, as described by Henderson:

> Enter 'The Daughters of the Regiment' 300 girls up to the age of 15, children whose parents have in any way had connection with the regiment, either present or past members- preferable children on the spot, who can be called upon for frequent rehearsals as the singing and evolutions are intricate and require constant practice to make a perfect show. The 300 girls would be costumed simply, all in white, shoes and stockings to match, only the simple hood and short capes to place over heads and shoulders, would denote colour – which in due proportions of Reds, Whites and Blues, would provide the necessary contrasts. This attractive item in the last Epoch would be tabulated thus, The Daughters of the Regiment in Empire folk-song and exercises, special formations and patriotic emblems—the properties to be used by them will consist of sprigs of Maple Leaves. Garlands of flowers and flags of the Red Ensign of Canada.[137]

In the end, some 400 children, both boys and girls, participated in this very popular scene of the pageant.

Henderson's script included scenes where actors had lines to perform, for example in Epoch II, Laura Secord and her dialogue with her husband and American soldiers. But with no means of broadcasting their words to the viewers in the grandstands, these scenes would have appeared as vignettes, almost pantomimes, since no one could hear them. The viewers in the grandstand followed these small scenes, and the action portrayed in each of the Epochs, by reading the official programme.

Considering the size of the cast and the large scale of the performance area, how did Henderson communicate his directions? He used a large, bright-blue megaphone, which would have amplified his voice somewhat.[138] More importantly, he had four assistants; one, Collie Ross of the QOR was the chief of staff and stage director, and three stage managers of the epochs, all QOR men.[139] These men took their cues from Henderson, and then directed the cast through the scenes of the script. A lot of precise teamwork was required to assure a successful performance. In a photograph from the *Star*, Henderson can be seen with the QOR band at the front of the bandstand situated directly in front of the performance stage and the Exhibition Place lawn.

TORONTO SOLDIERS TROOPING THE COLORS *June 20 - 23 1910*
The trooping of colors by companies from the Queen's Own, Highlanders, and Grenadiers during the last epoch was one of the prettiest things of the pageant. This photograph was also made by the electric lights of the pageant during the performance, a novel feat in photography, which has very seldom been accomplished successfully.

Figure 5. Henderson and the band at the far right in front of the pageant stage.

Rehearsals were an important step to produce a successful pageant, in all there were ten; Henderson drilled the men of Epochs I (May 23) and II (May 24) and Epochs III and IV (May 25) in the St. Lawrence Arena. Rehearsals with women occurred in the arena; Epoch I (May 30), Epoch II (May 31), Epochs III and IV (June 1), and Epochs I and II again (June 6). A full rehearsal was held on June 8 at the armouries, including all characters, bands, and the children. Two dress rehearsals were held on June 16 and 17 at Exhibition Park. The children also had many dedicated rehearsals because their routine was the most complicated.

The most expensive and dramatic element of the production was the scenic backdrop painted by London set decorator Leolyn Hart Co.[140] Henderson commissioned two settings, the first a Canadian woodland, and the second, a painting of the Queen Victoria Memorial and the Canada Gate outside Buckingham Palace.[141]

Introducing the first epoch, Henderson dramatically wrote:

> The night deepens. The band of the Queen's Own, whom we have not noticed until now, seated in front of the green-swathed enclosure of the grand stand, suddenly assumes an attentive attitude. A shrill whistle is heard, a bugle sounds, and lo! As though by a magician's wand a flood of splendid light from arc and calcium suddenly envelopes the scene and shows to our expectant gaze a wonderous picture—a rich Canadian woodland, distant hills, lakes fringed with a rich wooded glade and dell, bright in autumnal color. Even as we gaze in wonder at so stupendous a result of the open-air scenic artists' work, our admiration increases. The music strikes up its martial and inspiring old-time airs, and the 650-foot [198 m] long picture, with its 56,000 square feet [5203 sq. m] of painted canvas, becomes instinctive with life and action.[142]

Figure 6. The setting for Laura Secord's story in the pageant.

The *Globe* reported on June 8 that "The monster canvas at the Exhibition grounds for the Queen's Own pageants is being raised, and it is splendid work."[143] Building and erection of this scenery:

> ... an extensive wall of Ontario landscape, rising some sixty feet [18 m] into the air and forming a beautiful and effective background against which the epochs could be worked out. This scenery, wonderfully contrived, was broken here and there by a cave-like entrance, from which Indians or soldiers made their appearance.... To the right stood a heavy piece of forest, apparently solid, but with the pull of a rope was turned into a brilliantly-lighted house. At the left was provided another ingenious device, namely a revolving piece of scenery, on one side of which was a piece of woods, and on the other the furnished interior of a house. The latter was used for the

Laura Secord episode with the American officers. The beautiful Queen Victoria gates was another attraction and like other massive 'set pieces' was moved on and off the scene by means of a railway track. Wonders in the pageant never ceased.[144]

The backdrop was nearly two football fields in length! Seeing the Victoria Memorial and the Canada Gate to scale would have been quite exciting for pageant-goers and performers alike; the gate was not officially dedicated until a year later, in 1911, so the pageant backdrop provided a thrilling preview.[145] The photographs published in the dailies showed the scale of the set, and the lights strung above the performance area allowed for night photography, which was quite innovative at the time.

Of the 1,200 participants in the pageant some 800 needed costumes. The first fitting was held early in June, and when the fittings were done a photograph was taken of Mr. Henderson's "theatrical battalion".[146] The costumes were apparently borrowed (rented?) from the British Government, and provided by the well-known London costumier and wig maker, William Clarkson.[147] Historical pageants had been popular in England since 1905, and companies like Clarkson's were able to provide wigs, hats, shoes, dresses, suits, and uniforms according to the well-known historic British, French, and American epochs on demand, and once the script was finalized the costumes could be ordered. One set of costumes might have challenged the British pageant master, those of the Indigenous performers played by Iroquois from the Six Nations in Brantford, fortunately these men self-costumed.[148] As well, the QOR riflemen wore their own uniforms.

Thirty-six Iroquois had arrived on June 15 by train from Brantford, detraining at Parkdale station, which serviced the Exhibition grounds. From there they had a short walk to the tents provided for them, which were located behind the grandstand.[149] As far as being able to perform in the pageant, Chief Atkins told the *Star* reporter that "Some of them [the Iroquois] were in Berlin with me last year and know how to be actors."[150] The performances of the Iroquois, although scripted to represent Joseph

Brant, were typical of "Wild West Shows" of the time, and were overly dramatic and theatrical, definitely not respectful of the Iroquois peoples.

Two dress rehearsals were held, and the *Star* reporter commented that there were, "Groans, sighs, and other remarks" of a comical and embarrassed nature when the costumes were first put on, but that "When the costumes and uniforms were all on, the effect was magnificent. The wearers appeared to be a little nervous about it at first, and stepped warily out from the dressing room. Usually this was greeted by a howl of joy from someone outside and caustic comments were passed for a few moments. Then another would step out to be looked over, until finally everyone was quite used to the regalia and the laughter ceased."[151]

Figure 7. Performers with Lady and Sir Henry Pellatt in front of Victoria Memorial with Canada Gate.

The Thursday rehearsal was for the first and last epochs, and even though the rehearsal went quite late, all performed well, including the children, who, the *Star* reported, "are excellently trained, and they are going to be one of the most pleasing features of the pageant."[152] The

World reported that "400 singing children, arrayed in red, white and blue, and arranged in lines accordingly. The martial music of 'The Red, White and Blue,' the lines were formed like three ribbons, stepping in perfect time."[153]

The *World* reporter sang the praises of the pageant: "People will not be disappointed with the spectacle, provided in the fourth epoch. It promises to be the most brilliant display ever viewed in Toronto. It was witnessed in its nearly finished state by a good thousand people who were interested in one way and another, and who will whisper its magnificence far and wide. There were 1200 brightly costumed and uniformed characters on the platform at one time."[154]

The pageant was performed on four nights, beginning at 8:00 p.m. Tickets were sold at Bell's piano store, at 416 Yonge St. Prices were: admission twenty-five, fifty, and seventy-five cents; with reserved seats $1.00; and box seats $1.50.[155] To help with the volume of ticket sales, Dr. Orr, the secretary of the Exhibition, "placed at the disposal of the Reunion Committee the ticket-selling staff of the Exhibition."[156] Apparently, after expenses for the reunion had been paid, any profits were to go to the Queen's Own chapter of the Daughters of the Empire.[157] It is not known if there was any profit. But before the pageants, there were other events planned for the QOR reunion.

By the evening of June 16, nearly 1,000 men had registered for the events.[158] The QOR had requested "the city for leave to hang a banner across King street east to show the old members of the QOR where the headquarters are at 36 and 68 King east, during the coming semi-centennial celebrations"[159]

The semi-centennial officially began with a garden party hosted by Sir Henry and Lady Pellatt on Saturday, June 18, on the lawn in front of the grandstand at Exhibition Place at 3:30 p.m. "For the garden party to-day, 1,500 medals were sold. These medals or a uniform are the only things that will gain admission to the grounds."[160] The *World* reported that some ten thousand attended the party. This might be an exaggeration, of these past members of the QOR it is likely only a few hundred were presented to the Pellatts, those of more senior rank received a personal invitation.[161] The receiving line was in the centre of the lawn, where there was a marquee with "an awning, with palms, chairs and rugs" at either end of this area the "bands of the Q.O.R., the 48th Highlanders, and the Royal Grenadiers were stationed."[162] The Pellatts were "guarded" by eight men costumed as Beefeaters and these can be seen in a photograph of the event.[163] Lady Pellatt "looking remarkably well in a mauve shade of silk, silk lace coat of the same shade, and large black hat with white plumes, wore an honorary badge for the occasion, and a very magnificent Q.O.R. crest in diamonds, rubies and other stones."[164]

Figure 8. Sir Henry Pellatt (left) and Lady Pellatt receive guests at the garden party. A ceremonial Beefeater is to the right holding HR sign, and in the background is the painted canvas backdrop.

Entertainment had been planned for the garden party, likely to provide a preview of the pageant, and as described in the *Globe*, "the Pageant Master was marshalling about 400 children, dressed in red, white and blue, across the platform in flag formation. At the first patriotic note from a band stationed in the front they broke into song. Ten large flags were carried in the centre, and at certain passages individual small flags were violently waved. The ensemble was very effective and the childish voices sweetly clear and in excellent time. After various manoeuvrings, which displayed careful drilling, they filed off in time to hearty cheering."[165]

A second entertainment at the party was provided by the Iroquois, who presented a formal "war dance" on the stage, and then after this dance the Iroquois:

> ... headed by their chief, in full war paint, and carrying their murderous-looking tomahawks, marched in single file and formed a circle around where Sir Henry stood among his guests. The old chief then in a short speech conferred first an Indian name on him, which signifies 'the dawn of morning,' explaining the reason they had chosen this particular name, he said it was that as Sir Henry was a colonel of a regiment it was necessary for him to be up early to look after his soldiers. Then he placed on Sir Henry's head a wonderful head-dress of scarlet satin embroidered with gold, green, blue, and yellow stones, and edged with eagles' quills. A stole of the same was placed around his neck.[166]

The *News* published two photographs of Lady and Sir Henry Pellatt laughing, with the caption "When Colonel Sir Henry M. Pellatt was being initiated on Saturday as a chief of the Mohawk tribe, he had placed on his head a gorgeous headdress of feathers. The adjustment made Sir Henry for a moment appear ridiculous, and Lady Pellatt broke into laughter, which provoked the broad smile that appeared immediately on the Colonel's face. Then the *News* snapped the camera."[167]

Figure 9. Sir Henry Pellatt in Queen's Own Rifles uniform and
Mohawk clothing.

Chief Atkins gifted Sir Henry the name Tawyunansara; Pellatt thanked him: "He had always been an ambitious man and had many desires in his life, but in his wildest dreams he had never thought he would become a chief of a tribe such as theirs."[168] The respect that Pellatt and the QOR had for the Iroquois was well known. Dr. Oronhyatekha, a Mohawk, had been a member of the QOR and had fought at the battle of Ridgeway in 1866.[169] However, local pundits, never losing an opportunity to opine, wrote the *Star*, "And pray, also, can you tell us, when Sir Henry Pellatt is wearing his feather headdress as Dawn of the Morning, what becomes of his night hood?"[170]

The last event of the first day was a "smoker" held at the armouries and attended by some 2,000 men. Smokers were informal events where military bands provided the music, and tobacco, a souvenir clay "dabber," and a pipe with the QOR crest were given each man.[171] Pellatt was given a gold medal by the QOR officers as "a token of the esteem in which he is held."[172] When he replied to receiving this gift, he took the opportunity to allay fears that there might be unruly behaviour of the men on the upcoming trip to England: "I can tell you that I do not feel worried, because I know that when I leave Toronto with 600 officers and non-commissioned officers and men, every one of them will feel they have a responsibility; that they have had the honor and credit of the regiment at stake. I know that . . . [people in Canada] will watch the work and behavior of the regiment while in England and will have no cause to be ashamed."[173]

The next day, Sunday, June 19, was also an important day for the QOR reunion. There was a massing of the past and present members of the regiment at the armouries, then a parade through the city to the University of Toronto quadrangle lawn for a church service. Alternative arrangements had been planned for the church service to be held in the armouries if the weather was inclement. More than likely the weather would have been a worrying factor in the planning of the semi-centennial, as several significant events were planned to be held outside: the garden party, the parade and church service, and the evening performances. As it happened, the weather forecasts predicted clear weather "fine and decidedly warm" for the week ahead.[174] In fact, the weather was blisteringly hot, well into the high 30s on many days, with the temperatures for the evening performances starting at the somewhat cooler mid-20s.

The Sunday parade was the first opportunity for all the QOR men to show their pride in the history of the regiment. "According to the official count there were 835 members of the regiment in line, one of the largest musters the Queen's Own has ever had."[175] The *Globe* estimated nearly 2,000 ex-members of the QOR attended the parade, one of the largest ever held in the city.[176] Detailed instructions on mustering were given in the programme: ex-members met at 2:00 p.m. and were to be led by the ex-members' band, then ex-officers, ex-members of the regiment who were in other Corps, then veterans beginning with those of 1866, 1885, and up to 1910. At 2.30 p.m. the current members of the regiment joined the muster. A photograph in the Toronto *Sunday World* shows several lines of men from 1866, seventeen were expected to attend.[177] These men from the Battle of Ridgeway, which had occurred some forty-four years earlier, were likely in their seventies, eighties and older.

The title of an article in the *Star* made it clear that the march was especially difficult, saying, "Veterans March Under Torrid Sun," and further that "Under the scorching sun of yesterday in the heat and dust, the biggest parade ever held by the Queen's Own Rifles marched off from the Armories, and swinging up Spadina and across to the University lawn, held its jubilee religious service under the open sky."[178] The march was gruelling. "It was a day to test the stamina of an experienced campaigner, but not a man dropped out. . . . Although in the ranks of the ex-members was many a grizzled head, many a man to whom the long tramp in all the heat of the day must have been a severe strain . . . [and once at the University] one by one the veterans broke ranks and sat down on the grass. . . . [where] A space had been roped off for the soldiers."[179]

One solemn feature of the service was the roll call of those members of the regiment who had died in service, Sir Henry read their names.[180] A sermon was given by Reverend Llwyd, the chaplain of the QOR, where he emphasized the loyalty of the QOR to England: "It is our aim to build around the world a rampart of Anglo-Saxons who love their fellow-men, and whose aim it is to defend and never defy. Q is for Quietness, O for Obedience, and R for Righteousness."[181]

After the service, the men marched through the eastern entrance of the university grounds to Queen's Park and then south on University Avenue, returning to the armouries.

The men in the parade complained about the lack of bunting and flags decorating the stores and downtown buildings. One caustically remarked, "When it comes to flying flags, it seems as though the citizens of Toronto had to have a dead King or a live American President before they get their bunting spread out."[182] The *Star* reported that "There were no decorations on the streets as was requested, and only 5 flags were in sight from the corner of Queen and Yonge."[183] However, the Toronto City Council did "fly flags on all civic buildings."[184]

The *Sunday Toronto World* of June 26 had several photographs of the week-long festivities and published a rather lyrical dramatic piece on the first page, the "Men of '66." It is quoted in part here: "They had fought side by side, years ago. They were good comrades. War forges a chain of friendship that is invincible, unbreakable….Time traced furrows in their faces, frosted their hair and warped their figures, only with the thoughts of old, striving days the spirit of youth and assurance came back to them. They met again, the other day. They walked, side by side, in the old veterans procession, shoulder to shoulder, hand touching hand."[185]

The first event planned for Monday, June 20, was the unveiling of the memorial stained-glass window at the University of Toronto in the afternoon.[186] Located in the East Hall of what is now known as University College, on the second floor, it commemorated the three university students who had died in 1866 at the Battle of Ridgeway during the Fenian raids. This was a replacement window for the one lost during the fire that destroyed the building in 1890.[187] This seems to have been a small U of T-focused event, with the men from '66 invited, and music provided by the QOR Band. Dignitaries in attendance included Pellatt; Ontario Lieutenant-Governor J.M. Gibson, who was also the president of the U of T Alumni Association; and Byron Walker, the chairman of the board of governors of the university.

The most important event of the day was the first performance of the pageant. The reviews in Toronto papers the next day were glowing. The cast included 1,200 people and "The platform in front of the grand stand last evening at Exhibition Park was a blaze of lights, brilliant uniforms and quaint costumes, Indians in war paint and a maze of moving figures."[188] The newspaper articles explained in detail the four epochs, and encouraged Torontonians to attend as there were still three more performances. All reporters commented on the 400 schoolchildren who "sang songs of the Empire, very sweetly, and after performing a fancy drill, formed a living Union Jack."[189]

FORMATION OF THE UNION JACK.

Figure 10. The "Living" Union Jack made quite an impression.

The *Star* reporter, who seems, based on his style of informal repartee, to have been Ned Sheppard, went behind the scenes to describe the "fun and laughter. . . . [where] Everybody wanted to get into the wings and see what was going on in front. And as a rule they got there, to be chased back every now and then by an official or a policeman."[190] Sheppard wrote of the humour of the occasion, "The uniforms which look so fascinating from the grand stand, look merely funny when you are close to them. For they were not made to measure. Men playing the roles of great and historic personages and dressed in full panoply of the role, wandered around behind the scenes, smoking pipes or cigarettes. . . . Kings hobnobbed with private soldiers, queens with dairymaids."[191]

Unfortunately, the first evening's performance was marred by an accident that resulted in the death of a young QOR rifleman, Pte. John Reginald Thorn. Thorn, twenty years old, was an actor in the scene portraying the Upper Canada Rebellion. It was planned that he would ride in at the end of the second Epoch as one of Mackenzie's rebels, Joseph Sheppard. While he was waiting in the wings for his scene, the fusillade for the battle of Queenston Heights startled his horse, which reared and fell down, rolling over him. His injuries were not thought severe at first, but after being taken to the medical tent and then the hospital, it was discovered that the pommel of the saddle had seriously and gravely injured him. The Thorns were a QOR family; his father, Sgt-Major J.O. Thorn, was the quartermaster.[192] Young Thorn had been studying architecture at the Toronto Technical school and had planned to join his father at the Metallic Roofing Company.[193] His funeral took place the afternoon of Thursday, June 23. A service was conducted at the family home, on Davenport Rd., after which the members of QOR's L Company, led by Capt. Reginald Pellatt, somberly escorted the casket to the place of interment in Mt. Pleasant Cemetery.[194] Tragically, young Thorne's last words, inscribed on the cenotaph were, "Tell Mother I'll be all right in the morning."

After this unexpected accident, there was serious consideration given to cancelling the grand ball scheduled for Friday evening; however, it was decided that since nearly 500 tickets had been sold, and more were expected to be sold, it would be best to continue with the plans.[195] It is assumed that the Thorn family was consulted on making this decision. Later, Major Thorn accompanied the young men on the English Trip. This would have been a bittersweet experience as undoubtedly Private Thorn had planned to take the voyage. In some of the photos of the trip several officers are wearing black mourning armbands, possibly in respect for young Thorn's passing.

One other person was injured the first night of the pageant when he was burned by powder from a rifle.[196] Actually, considering the number of persons involved on the stage, the presence of horses, the firing of rifles during battle scenes (with blanks, obviously), and the controlled chaos of the procession of the epochs, it's a wonder that more people were not injured.

The review of the pageant in the *News* was enthusiastic: "The picturesque and stirring story of old Ontario was written last evening in the characters of fire. Across the field facing the grand stand of the Exhibition grounds was assembled the most gigantic pageant spectacle which it has been Toronto's fortune to see."[197] They were the only paper to mention sing the praises of the pageant master: "Whether a stranger to pageants or familiar with the best in England, the great drama as given by twelve hundred people was a complete surprise, the perfection and extent of the production being altogether unsuspected. Not one perceptible error crept into the evening's work. Director John Henderson, with his assistant, Mr. D. Collie Ross having so carefully prepared the intricate action, the entrance and exit of small regiments of actors, and the novel and magnificent scenic effects."[198]

On Tuesday afternoon, June 21, there was a free streetcar ride through the city for QOR veterans. It started at 2:30 p.m., leaving Church and King Streets, and it did a circle tour around the city heading east and then north to the Rosedale loop, then west along Bloor, north along Avenue Road, circling south to end downtown, where it had begun. One of the old-timers said, "When I was here last, longer ago than I care to think, there were farms where the cars now take you past beautiful homes and tremendous factories."[199] Tuesday evening was the second performance of the pageant, no doubt a more sombre event due to the passing of Private Thorn. There was also a dinner for the 1885 North-West Field Force with General Otter. The performances on Tuesday, Wednesday, and Thursday were without incident.

The final scene of each pageant involved all the performers appearing on the stage and in the grounds before the grandstand. From a photograph in the *Globe,* the scale of the event can be seen: the imposing architecture of the Canada Gate, the Victoria Memorial, and the 1,200 men, women, children, and bands. As Henderson wrote in his script, King Edward VII would arrive on his steed through the Royal Gateway (the Canada Gate), there would be the QOR regimental march, the combined forces of the 48th Highlanders and the QOR, a royal salute, a rousing chorus of "God Save the King," and then the grand finale, the singing of "The Maple Leaf Forever." As King Edward had died in May, he was replaced by King George V in the programme. Concluding, Henderson wrote, "And reforming in order and presidence of Epochs, March past affording at once a magnificent object lesson to the young and the patriotic people of the History of their great and growing heritage- God Bless Canada."[200]

"Toward the close, the entire body of twelve hundred actors gathered on the field, under the strong glare of lights. Two companies each of the Queen's Own, the Royal Grenadiers and the 48th Highlanders undertook the impressive ceremony of the King's colors, assisted by the Queen's Own Bugle band and the band of the Grenadiers."[201] Barnard wrote about this in his history of the QOR, "The finale 'Trooping the Colour' . . . is unique as it is the only time that the regiment ever took an active part in this colourful military ceremony, for, as is well known a rifle regiment does not carry colours."[202]

The performance on the second night seems to have been a somewhat magical experience, as described by a *News* reporter: "The success of the first night's performance aided materially in drawing a crowd, no doubt, while even the sullen looking clouds failed to scare many thousands of people. As a matter of fact once the performance started the sky directly overhead cleared off, while the full moon appeared hot and red through a haze to the south. This formed a more striking finishing touch to the scenery than the hand or brain of stage manager could have devised."[203]

The *Mail and Empire* wrote on the day of the last performance that 12,000 had viewed the pageant on the third night, and that although many wanted to have another performance added it was considered too time-consuming for the cast of volunteers, so the last pageant was on June 23.[204] Thousands of Torontonians saw the pageant, and hundreds participated in it, and it had an impact on all of those people. The editor of the *News* wrote, "The pageant once more impresses upon the public the need of a readable Canadian history for use in the public schools. The dry-as-dust works heretofore employed omit all that romance with which the national history is full, and imbues the youthful reader with disgust for the subject."[205]

On the last evening, after the final performance, Pellatt hosted a dinner for the Iroquois participants. This event was described in the Toronto *News* as "a rather unique affair" and although no author is named for the article, the language of reporting reflects Jim Scroggie's informal style.[206] The dinner was held quite late in the evening in a dining room under the grandstands where there was a large, cavernous dining space.[207]

The *News* wrote, "Chief Tayoughsara, President of the Six Nation Agricultural Society, and his band of chiefs and warriors, consisting of chiefs of the Mohawk, Seneca, Onondaga and Cayuga tribes and twenty-five . . . braves who are not chiefs, were entertained very early this morning by Chief Tawyunsara, alias Dawn of the Morning, alias Sir Henry M. Pellatt, Colonel of the Queen's Own Rifles, in the dining hall . . . at the Exhibition grounds." Speeches were made and gifts exchanged, with the Iroquois Chief Tayoughsara giving Sir Henry a landscape oil painting, which "Sir Henry said he would always esteem it as one of his most valued treasures." At the conclusion of the dinner, in the wee hours of Friday, the *News* reporter commented that for the Grand Ball, to be held that night, the streetcars would run until 3:00 a.m. the next morning, adding wistfully, "There are those who wish they had been running to that hour this morning."[208] Pellatt's respect for the Iroquois is reflected in their daily remuneration of $2.00, which was quite generous for the time. In contrast, the riflemen privates of the QOR were paid only fifty cents per diem.

The last event of the reunion was the ball held in the Transportation Building on the Exhibition grounds; the *Star* and the *Globe* sent social reporters to cover the evening. Their articles published on Saturday, June 25, are brief on the details of the ball and long on the list of who was there and what they wore: "Mrs. Albert Gooderham, white embroidered crepe and diamonds."[209] Those attending were described as members of the "Military-Social Set" and the bored impression given by some of the reporters was that balls of this nature were not uncommon among that set. However, the reporter for the Toronto *World* wrote breathlessly, "[the] Spectacular Ball Brings To Brilliant Close Week's Jubilee Reunion."[210] This article positively glowed with excitement about the grandeur of this "costume ball. . . .The scene was one of wonderful richness of color, the wide range of costumes being responsible for the effect which might be best described as kaleidoscopic. Being essentially a military ball, the dominant note was struck by the army uniform, but the mingling of the participants of the pageants made the picture appear like a survival of a court function of several centuries ago, recalling the days when knights were bold and gallants wrote sonnets on milady's eyebrow."[211]

The Transportation Building was arranged so that refreshment areas were at either end of the hall, leaving the central area free for dancers, some seven hundred at a time: "The spectacle presented during the promenade and the lancers, with which the ball opened, was one which was strong in appeal to the sense of the picturesque."[212] At ten o'clock there was a grand march, led by Sir Henry and Lady Pellatt, consisting of 250 officers and costumed performers marching in step with the tune of the regimental band, concluding in the Pellatts arriving at the centre of the dance floor. The dance area was so large that "In all there were fifteen different sets with eight couples to a set, and this dance marked the opening event of the ball."[213] The ball ended in the early hours of the morning. It was indeed a successful and flamboyant end to the weeklong reunion of the Queen's Own Rifles, truly a highlight of Toronto's summer season for 1910.

The City of Toronto Council passed a commendation on July 14 to thank Sir Henry for the week's celebrations, the city:

> . . . moves that this Council on behalf of the citizens of Toronto desires to offer their hearty congratulations to Colonel Sir Henry Mill Pellatt, Commanding the Queen's Own Rifles, upon the success of the pageants recently presented to commemorate the Fiftieth Anniversary of the formation of the regiment, and to express its

appreciation of the public spirit and loyalty which prompted him to prepare so splendid a series of scenes depicting leading events in Canadian history which aroused intense patriotic interest and appealed most strongly to the loyalty and pride of all Canadians who had the pleasure of witnessing them. The citizens of Toronto are naturally specially interested in the welfare of the Queen's Own Rifles. They remember the part the Regiment has taken in past response to calls for active duty, and refer with pardonable pride to these occasions when members of the regiment proved themselves worthy successors to the gallant men who, in the War of 1812, under Sir Isaac Brock, repelled the invader and saved half a continent to the British Crown. The Council would further express the pleasure and satisfaction with which it has learned of Sir Henry's intention to take the regiment this year to the annual military manoeuvres at Aldershot, England, and believe that this undoubted evidence of loyalty and attachment will aid not a little in cementing the ties which bind together the Dominions of the Empire. The Council also deems this a fitting occasion to express its appreciation of the value to the community of the present effective Volunteer Militia and to cordially acknowledge the untiring efforts of Sir Henry Pellatt to secure this most desirable condition of the service of this City.[214]

These laudatory words gave credit to Pellatt and the QOR, but most telling about the City's reception of such an extravagant historical pageant was the establishment of a committee to celebrate the centennial of the War of 1812.[215] Mr. Henderson, the pageant master, "informed the committee that the Exhibition Grounds in Toronto afford ample scope for a great pageant."[216] This celebration never happened, in fact, the likes of the historical pageant extravaganza of 1910 seem to have never been repeated in Toronto's history.

With the reunion successfully concluded, the QOR and the citizens of Toronto could look forward to the next major event of the semi-centennial, the English trip.

CHAPTER

4

Toronto To Lévis, Québec

*The men . . . who are going to England under Colonel
Pellatt are apparently to enjoy that happy combination of
work and pleasure which prevented the famous Jack from
being a dull boy.* [217]

After the QOR reunion, Toronto news was dominated by other events;
on Saturday, June 25 the front page of the *Star* was full of pictures of
Canada's first aviation meet. Held in Montréal it showcased the Wright
brothers' biplane and the French aviator Count De Lesseps and his
Blériot monoplane, named Le Scarabée.[218] In July, the second Canadian
aviation meet, the first for Toronto, was held at Trethewey Farm,
Weston, northwest of downtown. All the Toronto newspapers were full
of accounts of the aviators, their planes, and their daredevil exploits.[219]
The Toronto *World* covered the meet extensively. A photograph taken on
July 11, 1910, labelled on the back "aviation meet," shows two dapper

Figure 11. Jim Brown, (R) and an unknown reporter at Toronto's first
aviation meet.

young men, wearing fashionable straw boaters, both sporting **PRESS** ribbons. The man on the right is Jim Brown, for the *World*, the man on the left is unknown.[220] Did newspaper editors assign youthful, new reporters to cover these innovative and quite exciting meets because they thought they might better comprehend this new technology?

There were two other major news stories: one of national significance, the Grand Trunk Railway strike, and the other, of both international and local interest, was the case of Dr. Hawley H. Crippen of London, England. Crippen, along with his girlfriend, Miss LeNeve, were fugitives who were sought for the suspected murder of his wife, the actress Belle Elmore.[221] His wife's partial remains had been thought to be discovered in Crippen's cellar in London.[222] Crippen, an American, had lived in Toronto for several years before settling in England.[223]

For the QOR, focus shifted to the trip to England. Since the 1908 Tercentenary celebrations, ideas for the English trip had been gestating in Sir Henry's mind, but was he the first to propose such a venture for the QOR? Apparently not. In 1863 a letter to the editor of the *Globe,* written by a member of the QOR, submitted under the penname, "A Full Private," outlined a several weeks-long trip to England for the regiment.[224] This never happened, probably due to lack of money. Thirteen years after this letter was published, Pellatt joined the QOR as a rifleman. Perhaps the "private" who penned this letter still voiced the dream of an overseas trip, and for young Pellatt this became his aspiration as well.

The plans for the trip had been roughed out the previous year and had been presented to the officers and men at a meeting in December 1909.[225] At that time, Pellatt declined to discuss the cost of the trip, except to say that he was financing it and had "not figured it out in detail."[226] The Toronto *Star,* drawing upon expertise of military men, estimated that the trip would cost about $65,000. "All arrangements have been made by Sir Henry with the War Office in London, Eng., through the Governor-General and the Militia Department at Ottawa."[227] The role of the quartermaster, Major J.O. Thorn, was paramount for this stage of the anniversary and his experience had been proven on the trip to New York in 1906. At that time the *Star* reported that "In a long trip . . . with a large body of men, a great deal of arduous work falls to the lot of the supply and transport officers. Captain J.O. Thorn, the regimental quartermaster, was a tired man when he reached home."[228]

Although not directly contributing to the costs of the trip, "The Militia Department is supplying the Regiment with a new Khaki uniform, which will be substituted for the present drill uniform. With the Khaki will also be worn black waist-belts and boots, but the puttees and headgear will be Khaki also. For full dress the ordinary uniform will be worn. A white duck uniform is provided for wear on board the ship."[229] In an article published later, when the men had just arrived at Aldershot, the *Times* of London specified in detail what the Canadian government had actually provided to the corps: " Each man has a new outfit, including the traditional dark-green serge uniform, a uniform of khaki, full-dress tunic, green linen service shirt and trousers, caps, boots, canvas shoes, puttees, haversack, kitbag, and even arms, 700 brand new Ross rifles and bayonets having been served out just before the regiment sailed" at a cost to the government of £8,000.[230] The Toronto *Evening Telegram* republished an article from the *Times* on September 10 updating the cost to $40,000 in Canadian dollars. This decision by the Canadian government to provide the "QOR Special" uniform was made the year before.[231] By the end of the trip, the contributions by both the Canadian and British governments in goods and services would be substantial.

A senior military source spoke to the *Star* stating, "It will be a soldiers' life as seen on active service and Sir Henry is right when he says it will be no picnic. However, it will be a splendid training for the men, and as only fellows in the best of physical condition will be taken there should be no trouble."[232] The official programme of the June pageant gave more specific details: "All the men going must pass a thorough medical examination, and have a satisfactory military record. During the trip the men will be under pay, and will be free of any expenses of any kind whatsoever. The accommodations provided will be first-class in every respect, that on board ship being quite equal to ordinary second-class. Officers supply their own uniforms and servants, but otherwise their expenses will be defrayed. The trip is to be a generous contribution by the Officer Commanding to the development of the imperial idea amongst colonial militia."[233]

On June 29 a delegation from the QOR, led by George Hope, asked the City of Toronto for "a contribution towards a fund to pay $1,800 in insurance premiums on the lives of the members of the members of the Queen's Own regiment from the time they leave Toronto for England until they return."[234] The City reserved its decision, and no record of this motion was found in the council minutes, so the cost of the premium was possibly raised by public subscription.

Apart from preparatory months of light drilling in Toronto, the away portion of the trip lasted for seven weeks: August 13 to October 3. In return for their voluntary service, the young men had all their expenses covered. This included transatlantic crossings, train travel through Canada and England, and a salary while serving, as well as a guarantee that their jobs would be waiting for them when they returned home.[235] Initially, it was thought the men would not be paid, but then it was announced that they would receive twenty-five cents per day, as well, the men would receive pay from their employers.[236] Although most of the young men were probably not yet married with families, many were, and the continuation of salaries meant that their families would not be without income. This made the trip more economically feasible and attractive.

It was reported that the ten or twelve civic employees would receive full pay while on the trip, but that was changed and they received "half pay."[237] Even though James Simpson, the chair of the Toronto Board of Education, did not support militarism, five staff members of the board were paid full salaries and given extended holiday time to go on the trip.[238] Twenty-five post office staff applied to accompany the trip; they were granted leave to go, with full pay, and in their absence twenty-five replacements filled their positions. On their return the post office announced that the substitutes would become full-time employees, adding twenty-five new men to the staff.[239]

In England, later on the trip, Sir Henry speaking from memory, told the *Canadian Gazette* that "The detachment, consisting of 608 men and 36 officers. . . . We have among the men 33 university students, 20 bank clerks, several men from stores such as Eaton's, which supplies us with 17, [as well as] 50 accountants, 6 post office clerks, a number of clerks employed by the City Corporation, and 7 school teachers." [240] The number of men on the trip was usually vaguely described as over 600.

Enrolment was underway by February 1 and continued through the spring and summer. Recruits were chosen for their height, five feet, eight inches up to six feet (1.7-1.8m) and good physical condition.[241] The February enlistment form made it clear that the dates for the trip were still being worked out: "Leaving Toronto about August 13th, returning about September 30th."[242] This form also made it clear that by joining the regiment the enlistment period was for three years as was expected for men joining the regular QOR militia. However, this enlistment period was not on all the forms signed by the men, and many of the men joined just for the trip and did not remain in the QOR after the trip. The QOR and the Toronto *Star* called this a "Provisional Battalion."[243]

Many men on the trip knew each other because they had been in the QOR for years. Scroggie and Riggs had been in the QOR since Québec in 1908.[244] Other reporters, Brown, Sheppard, and MacLaren joined for the trip.[245] MacLaren, in his WWI enlistment document, states that his prior military experience was six months in the QOR, basically the duration of the trip.[246]

Five cadets of the Royal Military College in Kingston enlisted; they had to receive special leave to join the regiment as privates. F.R. Henshaw joined with his fellow gentleman cadet, C.M. Horsey, both from Montréal. Henshaw thought it would be good to experience the army as a private and, coincidentally, see London and England. Henshaw was one of the diarists on the trip.

Jim Scroggie signed up to go on the trip on June 15, and men were still being sought to make the numbers. His form stated that "A few vacancies in each Company are being reserved for good men. Should any of your friends desire to enlist, have them present with you on the 29th June."[247]

Notable Torontonians on the trip included Capt. Reginald Pellatt (twenty-five), Sir Henry's son; Lieut. Roy M. Gzowski (twenty), grandson of Sir Casimir Gzowski; Lieut. C. Vincent Massey (twenty-three), son of Chester Massey, of the well-known and very wealthy Massey family; and Lieut. Harry Eden Smith (twenty-eight) who, with his father, the well-known Arts and Crafts architect Eden Smith, was a practising architect at Eden Smith & Son, Toronto.[248]

The companies were organized on June 29, when those enlisted for the overseas battalion were separated for training from those of the QOR who were staying home.[249] "The first organization parade will be held at the Armories on Wednesday, June 29th and there will be weekly parades until further orders. These parades will be mainly for organization purposes, no hard drilling being undertaken until Quebec is reached."[250]The railway strike delayed delivery of equipment from Ottawa, "by being tied up somewhere between Toronto and Ottawa during the strike. It has arrived safely."[251] Uniforms were issued on July 13.[252]

The grooms and batmen were Pellatt's staff: two groomsmen (for the horses) and the batmen; two coachmen, his valet and chauffeur.[253] On the eastbound SS *Megantic* passenger list these men bunked in the same cabin in third class. The professional photographer, Arthur Gleason, was not listed on the QOR Nominal Roll for the trip; however, he is on the *Megantic* passenger list as a private in the QOR, bunking with the grooms and batmen.[254] Being with these men would have afforded him the freedom to be able to move freely about the ship and take photographs of the regiment when they were training.

On the trip, the QOR had eight companies lettered A through H. All the reporters were in H Company (sometimes also called No. 8). Over the course of the trip, K Company was mentioned frequently. K Company of the QOR traditionally drew its members from the University of Toronto (and was originally called the University Company). K Co. men were a significant presence in the 1910 H Company, twenty-one men in all, a fact which they proudly acknowledged by working together in such activities as singing and performing.[255]

There were eight men to a tent, the five reporters were together, and a handwritten list in Scroggie's scrapbook gives the names of all the men in their tent. The other three men were all university students, M.R. Helliwell, R.B. Johnston, and C.E. Molland.[256] Maurice R. Helliwell (nineteen) and Robert B. Johnston (nineteen) were from Toronto and had been in the QOR since 1908. Charles E. Molland (nineteen), was a Chinese-born British citizen who was studying in Toronto.[257]

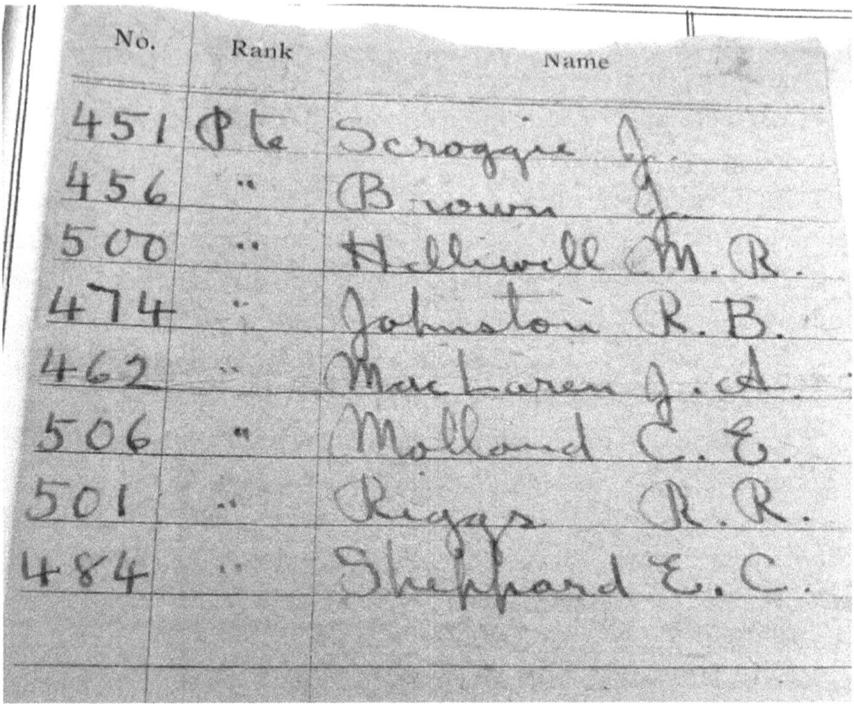

No.	Rank	Name
451	Pte	Scroggie J.
456	"	Brown J.
500	"	Halliwell M. R.
474	"	Johnston R. B.
462	"	MacLaren J. A.
506	"	Molland C. E.
501	"	Rigas R. R.
484	"	Shephard E. C.

Figure 12. The list of names and their numbers of the men in the press gang tent.

As reported in the *World*, "Confusion in baggage arrangement has been avoided by an ingenious system of numbering devised and worked by Sir Henry Pellatt himself. Each man in the regiment will be given a number from 1 to 600 and each piece of baggage will have his number. Each berth on train and boat will also be numbered and each man will know exactly where to go. By this arrangement, it should take only five minutes to entrain or embark."[258] Scroggie's list of names also included the numbers each was assigned.

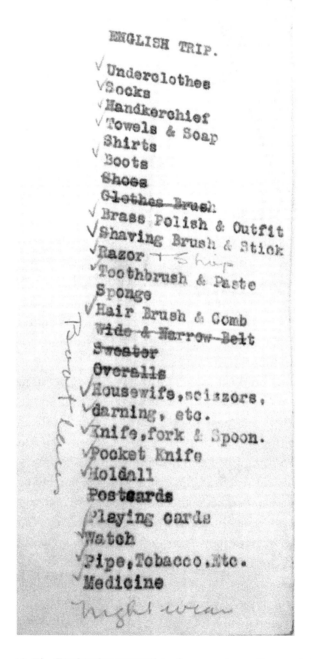

ENGLISH TRIP.

√ Underclothes
√ Socks
√ Handkerchief
√ Towels & Soap
  Shirts
√ Boots
  Shoes
  Clothes Brush
√ Brass Polish & Outfit
√ Shaving Brush & Stick
√ Razor
√ Toothbrush & Paste
  Sponge
√ Hair Brush & Comb
  Wide & Narrow Belt
  Sweater
  Overalls
√ Housewife, scissors,
√ darning, etc.
√ Knife, fork & Spoon.
√ Pocket Knife
√ Holdall
  Postcards
  Playing cards
√ Watch
√ Pipe, Tobacco, Etc.
√ Medicine

Figure 13. The ENGLISH TRIP list of personal supplies needed for
each private.

To make certain that the men had sufficient clothes for the seven weeks, a typed list was drawn up and distributed.[259] The *Evening Telegram* expanded on the items required. "Small list of articles which will be squeezed into the kit-bag: four pairs of socks, two pair of boots-one of them tennis-handkerchiefs, three shirts, a quilt, if one is wise, underwear, countless little articles, knife, fork and spoon, etc. Then beside this load there is the coat, water bottle, cooking outfit, and many other articles that go to make up a complete Oliver equipment, heavily loaded." [260] Although this information might seem trivial, it was exactly these kinds of details that Toronto newspaper readers, family and friends, wanted to know about.

The final "kit" was distributed on August 8 and included the Ross rifle, which the men took home. One enlistee, Fredrick Wright of Galt Ave., immediately, after receiving his rifle, pawned it in one of the pawn shops on Queen Street for five dollars. Wright had intended on redeeming his rifle in time for the trip departure and when caught out said, "I presume I was intoxicated."[261] It seemed that Wright, an ex-soldier from the British military, looked upon the English trip as a ticket home. Obviously, he did not join the excursion.

The farewell send-off was held on Wednesday, August 10, at the armouries, and was attended by nearly 3,000 friends and families, where the men stood in full gear for the entire ceremony. There were many speeches. The first was given by Hon. J.M. Gibson, Ontario's lieutenant-governor, who reminisced about his time in the QOR in K Company some fifty years earlier. Next, Sir James Whitney, premier of Ontario and Mayor Geary gave speeches with a response followed given by Pellatt. On behalf of the government and the people of Ontario, Whitney thanked Pellatt and the men for their "spirit of self-sacrificing patriotism."[262] Sir Henry "urged the men to behave themselves as gentlemen and soldiers wearing the King's uniform and expressed his assurance that all would do their duty throughout."[263] The *Times* of London sent a correspondent to Toronto to accompany the trip and his first article, wired by marconigram to London, appeared in the paper on August 12.[264]

The actual departure was on the evening of Saturday, August 13. The night before was busy at the armouries, with men "religiously going over the lists to see that nothing had been left out."[265] The expectant mood of leave-taking was captured by the *Evening Telegram*: "Every man is bubbling over with happiness. It is an occasion which could not help but bring joy in many respects. However, there isn't a lot of elation in leaving fond parents, brothers, sisters and friends. But it's only for seven weeks and nothing worth crying about. Possibly some parents are glad to get a few weeks rest as the daily grind of getting the boys ready has been pretty strenuous."[266] The anticipation and excitement felt by these young men was palpable, and the citizens of Toronto were equally enthusiastic. It was not Scott's expedition to Antarctica, but for these young men it was just as exciting an adventure, notwithstanding.

On departure day, the *Globe* published the names of the men on the trip, excluding Pellatt's staff and the photographer Gleason.[267] The men were expected at the armouries at 9:00 p.m. so they could assemble and then march to the train station. Instead, due to "surprise parties" held by families and friends for some of the men, it was 10:30 by the time the regiment left the armouries and 11:30 by the time the trains departed.[268] Waiting in the armouries in full kit, in the heat of late summer, was stifling, and after a few speeches, "The boys were 'wilting' their martial determination dripping from their foreheads, or running down inside the pretty green-faced collars of their jackets. The new Ross rifles, handy and light as they are, felt heavy as a 20-foot oak beam. So they pressed these rifles into service. They stood the butt on the ground, the muzzle under the kit bag—part of the Oliver equipment—thus easing the strain on the tired shoulders that could not droop because the straps of the Oliver held them erect. . . . A little bunch of men in a rear rank crooned softly, 'Oh! Oh! For some bee-ah: beautiful, beautiful bee-ah!'"[269] This article, written by Scroggie, described the men in the rear, which included the members of the press gang, and the refreshment they longed for—beer! For the day, this reporting in the *News* verged on scandalous, which was what the *News* was known for.

One man in the regiment, Robert Tunstead, was walking to the armouries in full QOR gear for the departure, and he came upon two men fighting. When he attempted to stop the fight, the two men turned their attention to him, beating him severely. Due to his injuries, he was unable to make the trip, and the public shock over this story was such that it made it on the front page of the *News*.[270]

Before leaving the armouries, Lady Pellatt was presented with a gold and diamond medal with the QOR crest; above the crest was "a bar bearing the letters Q.O.R. and Lady Pellatt's initials, M.P. all in diamonds."[271] Lady Pellatt, also wore a QOR badge of gold and diamonds at the garden party, and it's likely she owned several custom QOR pieces of jewellery.

The ride to Montréal was an overnighter. A feature of this portion of the trip was singing. The *Evening Telegram* wrote, "Competition is rife among the companies as regard warbling. Each is under the impression that it has the best, so men are incessantly training. Many quartettes have been formed already. Many companies have parodies on popular airs ready to belch forth on the unexpectant officers and outsiders."[272] However, conscious of unbridled boyish enthusiasm and potential hi-jinks, "Two men-- one at each end of the coach-- will be on guard throughout the noisy and long night. The 'non-coms' will see that the privates take turns in performing this tedious and weary task."[273] Ned Sheppard, seemingly used to traveling under better circumstances, complained about the train ride and the lack of porters and their service using language that shows the racism of the times and his entitled snobbery: "The seats [pulled] out and making very realistic beds. But there was no bell to push with the resulting ebony colored and obliging gentleman with the significantly deft hand. There were mattresses, but no blankets or sheets. There was no chance of undress and climb into cool pyjamas and above all there was no walking around the trains permitted."[274]

Sheppard reported about the train songs, "Spirits liquors, fermented under the all embracing title of 'booze,' formed the subject matter of the many, many songs and parodies that were either perpetrated or sung during the railway journey. . . . A pathetic and most often sung ditty is entitled 'How Dry I am.' When sung in properly doleful accents it would make a drowning man's mouth water. University yells and popular songs went a long way towards keeping gentle slumber at a distance."[275] They had a brief stop in Cornwall for "Light breakfasts, [which they had] carried in the knapsacks."[276]

Figure 14. Gleason's photograph of the QOR marching in Montréal.

After the break they continued to Montréal, where they paraded through the city to the armouries for lunch. Ned Sheppard described the march: "There was a general consensus of opinion among the Toronto boys that they were a better-looking outfit than their hosts. They did not say so, but they looked it. The 65th men wore the old rifle green uniforms and were all small men. The Q.O.R. in their new khaki, looked like giants compared to them. Every movement was performed with clockwork precision, and for once, the officers wore absolutely contented smiles."[277] At the armouries they were welcomed by Colonel Labelle, who complimented Pellatt on the appearance of the regiment. Col. Roy, the Commanding Officer of the permanent force, said in his speech, "Permanent militia officers are apt to scorn the effort of volunteer corps, yet, never have I seen a militia company, either permanent or volunteer, who presented as good an appearance on the street as the Queen's Own of Toronto did today."[278] This theme of tension between the regulars and the volunteers (known as militia in Canada and territorials in the UK) would be repeated again on the trip.

Sheppard observed that once at the armouries, "Everybody went where fancy led them, and that was invariably over the shortest route to grub. . . . Down in the basement the corporals and private soldiers were fed. Large quantities of various brews were on tap, and healthy-sized sandwiches were available to all."[279] After lunch they had a friendly game of basketball, which the QOR won, and they departed the city at 3:00 p.m., arriving in Québec at 9:00 p.m.[280]

Then in the dark and fully loaded with their kit, they marched to the camp in Lévis, where, to their happy surprise, they found that the tents had already been pitched and dinner was ready to be served. The *Evening Telegram* reported that "Sure enough there were some fagged out boys when the camp was reached. The burden carried on the backs is a slow torture. The harness, which holds everything in shape felt almost like knives, especially after much standing and walking. . . . About one hundred tents had already been pitched. . . . Orderlies, a man from each tent, which accommodates eight men, serve up the rations. Last night, the hungry, half-starved boys had roast beef and new potatoes and coffee."[281] Scroggie wrote about the tents, "Each one looked like a canvas covered heaven. . . . Supper was waiting in the mess tent, but it had no time to get impatient. Then came sleep in blankets, on the ground, with all the lumps under me, one of [for?] each sore shot [spot?]. It was good."[282]

Lévis, on the south side of the St. Lawrence River, was where they found "Ninety tents in regular military order dotted the grassy plain. On a slope to the west were the officers' tents, and to one side was the large dining tent."[283] MacLaren, in the *Evening Telegram,* thought of the history of Canada when he described the camp as being opposite the "Gibraltar of America. . . . [with] The view . . . magnificent. The Q.O.R. boys are in the midst of it, a handsome addition to the scenery. It was from the heights of Levis that the English bombarded Quebec in 1759, and it was down the valley of the Chaudiere swarmed Arnold and his brave men, and on the banks of the river they first looked upon the city which eventually proved their prison or grave."[284] Brown, in the *World,* took a more rural view, and noted the seigneury land system:

"In the opening of the valley can be seen the waters of the river and the farms, still retaining the same elongated formation in which they were first laid out in the infancy of Canada, the Montmorency Falls, and in the distance the Laurentian mountains."[285]

Figure 15. Ferry terminal, from Lévis to Québec City, 1908.

The day's schedule was outlined by MacLaren; up at six o'clock, then breakfast, eight o'clock fall in, drill to 9:30 then. "There was an investigation of all offences and reports of any nature," 10:15 staff parade until 12:00, 12:15 to 1:00 dinner; 2:00 to 2:45 lectures, 3:30 another parade for a distance of five miles, 5:30 supper, 9:30 first post, 10:00 last post, and 10:15 lights out.[286] There was no singing or yelling after lights out, but from somewhere "comes the music of men's voices as harmonious as a certain blacksmith. . . . Softer, softer the notes become as the tired singers drop off into slumberland to dream of the big ship Megantic, the mighty ocean, the old land, and the cheering crowds that see one of Canada's finest regiments pass by."[287]

Brown wrote that "eight of the most competent drill sergeants in the permanent corps of Canada . . . will accompany the regiment to Quebec, where one sergeant will take charge of each company and drill them for five days."[288] These men did not accompany the regiment to England. The drilling began in earnest on Monday, August 15, as Brown wrote, "The men, unaccustomed to physical labor, got up stiff and sore . . . but they had to drill, nevertheless. . . . [Most grumblers] were well satisfied with their physical condition before they came."[289] The reality was that the men of the regiment were "Office clerks, university students and others whose activities in civil life are largely mental [and who] are being given the treatment meted out to recruits for the regular army."[290]

There was instruction on the Canadian-made Ross rifle, and the reviews on them were mixed, with the *Mail and Empire* reporting, "The new rifles are accepted favourably by all, and will soon be handled as readily as the Lee-Enfields were."[291] On the other hand, the *World* reported negative comments: "The Ross rifles came in for criticism owing to their being hard on the hands of the men."[292] In September, once in England and on the manoeuvres, the criticisms of the Ross only increased, but for now the men were just getting the initial feel of the rifle.

Figure 16. The QOR's 'A' Company getting rifle instruction
from a Ross rifle expert.

By Tuesday, Brown reported somewhat optimistically that "The march was greatly enjoyed by the men. All are in good shape and are becoming accustomed to military life. . . . The route march was also a choir practice. The boys sang as they marched, and generally enjoyed themselves."[293] Sheppard wrote more realistically, "While it is no longer a dream of pastoral bliss for the 600 soldiers, they are making it go pretty well, but it is still a silent camp and the songs and yells are heard no more. Everyone has settled down to the hard work that has to be gone through with before the regiment can hold their own in England. . . . Extreme weariness is still one of the chief characteristics of the camp, and it is not hard to explain. These men who are to represent their country in England, are practically all office workers, bank clerks, architects, everything but day laborers."[294] Tuesday's march ended with an hour's skirmishing and attacking—exhausted, the men returned to camp. "Slowly and sadly, but keeping perfect step, they marched in at six o'clock. Suddenly the band appeared and started a lively march. The pace smartened instantly, tired arms began to swing, and steps smartened up. They marched the rest of the way in as though they had just been promised a million each."[295]

Ned Sheppard wrote that the QOR officers were pleased with the training: "The proof is in the fact that they came in from a six-mile march under the eyes of General Otter, and the even keener ones of Capt. Butcher feeling better than when they started out. Their boots and uniforms were white with dust, their faces black with the same commodity, but their knees were coming high, and for the first time since leaving Montreal they sang regimental songs. And this was not bad for the second day in camp, and both officers and men were delighted with the result."[296]

Scroggie quipped, "From a military standpoint it was good business, oh fine; but from the honest to Grandma feelings of an ex-police reporter, arising from protests that come from hitherto unnoticed portions of one human body, it was like General Sherman's pointed opinion of the soldiering game, multiplied by two or three and then squared."[297] MacLaren noted, "The fact that one month's drill is being taken up in four days will show the men's friends at home that the trip is by no means entirely one of pleasure." [298]

Scroggie relished taking jabs at the other reporters: "Signal honor has been shown The News in camp. Four other newspaper writers, in uniform, ungainly creatures and very loth to be obedient, have been placed in charge of your representative, who has been elevated to the proud position of squad commander. . . . The first time a good news item blows into camp, they will be put on fatigue duty while some 'leaps in the dark' are pulled off. Thus far, no complaints have been heard, except from The Star representative, concerning the food and other supplies." [299]

The quirks of the reporters' personalities and reporting styles became more pronounced as the trip continued. Scroggie's acerbic and jousting style of commentary about the other reporters left no one unscathed, but he did take glee in going after Sheppard who returned his own volleys. Ned commented on the bossy nature of "the men in charge of the tents, many of them newly appointed, had troubles of their own. They are held responsible, so they struggled madly to make their charges get out of bed. It was hard work. Bed felt good, and the morning air was chilly. Then came the packing up of kits and the hanging up of stray articles of warfare. 'For heaven's sake, fellows, if this tent falls down we will never hear the end of it,' came in a muffled tone from the centre of the swaying mass of canvas. The tent didn't fall all the way down. But it was touch and go." [300] Brown, MacLaren, and Riggs kept their reporting focused on covering what the men were experiencing, not engaging in personal jabs.

Meals were served in the mess tent: "The first meal was spread out on ten long tables, one for each company, and soon the appointed waiters were busy with porridge, beef, potatoes, bread, coffee and tea. The fare was very good and the men are not suffering on that account." [301] The *Mail and Empire* wrote, "Contrary to the general rule in a military camp, there is no grumbling about the food. No camp has ever been fed better, and to-night an agreeable surprise awaited the men (whose appetites are constantly growing) in the shape of raisin pudding and fancy biscuits." [302] However, the opinions about the quality of the food were, as one might expect, varied. Brown thought the food was fine but noted that others did not: "The food is much better than usually found in military camp, but, because it is not as good as home fare, they grumble. Large numbers of them went without supper and ate in Quebec to-night." [303] One of Scroggie's article's lede was, "One Gastronomic Wonder in Press Complains Unjustly About the Food—Not Enough of It" which he clarified by adding, "Thus far, no complaints have been heard, except from The Star representative, concerning food and other supplies . . ." another friendly dig at Sheppard.[304] Perhaps Ned was more interested in the food served to the officers and the non-commissioned officers as Sir Henry had arranged a caterer for them, while other cooks were hired for the men, apparently not up to the standards Ned expected.[305] As the trip unfolded, that the men had a different caterer than the officers was a good thing.

The reporters didn't discuss hygienic matters much except to write that the men were able to have a shower after drilling. "Talk about camping in luxury; shower bath after every drill. Yes sir, after a gruelling hour in the field the boys go out and water their skins until they glow, and at the side of each shower there's a tank of sea water in which their tired feet are washed."[306] Before tea, and before going to Québec City, they had to have "a barefoot parade. . . . This was a sad blow, and even might have taken as an imputation of uncleanliness. But it wasn't meant that way, as the officers took pains to explain quickly. It was to see if any of the men had sore feet . . . there were very few who could show anything worse than a pet corn."[307] Eaton, of the *Globe* commented "There is a pond near the camp, where the bathing is good, and shower baths have been provided in a small house outside the lines . . . it is imperative that the men must wash their feet at least once every day in sea water, and sea water has been supplied by the purchase of one hundred pounds of rock salt, which is dissolved in tubs of water."[308] This was to make the soles of their feet leathery, but really there was too little time allowed to develop callouses. The problems with delicate feet, used to being in offices and not long marches in new boots, would prove a serious issue while on manoeuvres in England.

Sheppard noted that the health of the men was fine and this was important since typhus was a concern in Canada at the time: "There has been no sickness, the drinking water is in the same class with the proverbial liberty, as far as freedom from germs is concerned, and the men are so tired at night that old Mother Earth looks like eiderdown."[309] The drinking water was tested by Québec officials regularly to be certain it was safe.

As emphasized by Pellatt during the farewell parade at the Toronto armouries, these men were expected to be gentlemen and soldiers and to that end there were lectures on their expected behaviour. "Sobriety and a strict moral tone are two of the most pronounced features of this camp."[310] Although not mentioned in the newspapers, due to the delicacy of the subject matter, conversations were likely held about loose moral behaviour and the evils of venereal disease.[311] Instructors "gave the men . . . Some valuable points on how to behave in the barracks and camp with the real 'Tommies' in England."[312] Tommy, Tommies, and Tommy Atkins referred to the slang name given the British soldier and appears in several articles over the next couple of weeks.

Scroggie wrote that the instructors "gave the men some straight talk about their conduct in camp and the street."[313] Sheppard reported that "The Queen's Own men enjoy their little parties into Quebec at night, and have conducted themselves excellently, with the usual rule-proving exceptions. The guard house has not been found necessary though."[314] The *Mail and Empire* confirmed the behaviour in Québec: "The obedience and duty lectures are apparently having good effect. The men have been very orderly, and no arrests have been made for even minor misdemeanors."[315] Good behaviour notwithstanding, "Men misbehaving themselves are not given much consideration. One was sent home today."[316] The reporter for the *Evening Telegram* explained, "A little cloud fell over the camp yesterday. A member of No. 5 Company went back to Toronto. He had consigned Capt. Kirkpatrick to a sulphurous place beyond military jurisdiction, and in turn was consigned to his home."[317]

Pellatt's honour and the honour of the regiment and Canada was at stake. Not risking the possibility of hijinks at night, "The military iron hand of discipline already hovers over the camp. Guards all night long in turns, saunter up and down the passageways between the rows of tents."[318] But this patrol was not entirely effective as was soon apparent.

Wednesday August 17 was a long day, chronicled by Sheppard's chatty commentary, which added significant colour to the activities of the men. "There is one very serious malady that everybody has got badly, and that is sunburn. They are sunburned good and proper, necks, faces, and above all, noses. . . . Nevertheless, it is more than a man's life is worth to slap a pal on the back and come within six inches of his neck. Lynching is considered too good for this offence. If raw beefsteak could be termed 'animals' the S.P.C.A. would have reason for stepping in if any neck in camp was deliberately slapped."[319]

Ned pointedly observed that group dynamics were strained: "Many old friends are going by the board and new ones are being taken on. One amateur psychologist, who would probably pronounce it 'fish,' explained it quite simply. He was at out's with a friend of long standing. 'I guess it's like being married. I have been friends for a long time, but I've seen so darn much of him, that he makes me tired. He's grouchy, too. Gee, it's funny what sleeping in the same tent with a fellow does.'"[320] One wonders if it was the interactions with Scroggie that were being recounted?

Sheppard continued, in fine form, going on about the activities of the camp:

> The different tents are being christened in accordance with the recent riots of the owners. There is about eight men to a tent, and a hot rivalry is beginning. The "Scouts" and the "Runts," are two that make a large amount of noise. The former got their name because they liked it; the latter had it thrust upon them owing to the small size of its inhabitants. Their main object in life is to make Art Scott, the tent master, wish he were not too short. Other tents are named "Oh, so Easy," "The Knockers Klub," "All the Time," the "Hive," "Mebbe," and there is "The Press" tent, where the newspaper men would sleep if they had time.

Sheppard's mention of the scouts' tent being noisy could be perhaps because he seems to have been at times an occupant of that tent, George Argue (a scout) lists Ned as one in his diary.

Sir Henry and the officers were invited to the Garrison Club, Québec City, by officers of the 8th Royal Rifles for dinner on the evening of Wednesday, August 17. The *Evening Telegram* described the evening: "The scene was grand. The furnishings are in mahogany and leather and the rich walls are hung with oil paintings of old warriors who have helped to make Canadian military history. Lt.-Col. Davidson presided, with Col. Sir Henry Pellatt on his right side and the Hon. Col. Wm. McPherson on his left."[321] Col. Davidson toasted the QOR: "I know of the achievements of the past and we look forward to great achievements when you meet should to shoulder with Tommy Atkins. . . . Beaming on his hearers, Sir Henry replied with much feeling. . . . He had been doubting the success of this undertaking several months ago, but was leaving the shores of Canada on Saturday assured that the hearty support of the whole Canadian Militia was behind him. Ringing cheers and the clinking of wine glasses and shouts of 'Queen's Own' echoed through the halls of the club as the colonel of Toronto's finest sat down."[322] Jaffray Eaton, of the *Globe,* was also at the Garrison Club dinner and recorded Pellatt's comments: "We are not undertaking this trip to England as a mere picnic. It has long been under consideration by us, as a serious piece of business. It is our object first to learn from a practical point of view, and we believe it will be to the best interests of the Canadian militia generally. In the second place, our idea was that something might be done to help the mother country. It will be an object lesson to the other countries, as it will show something of the underlying power that Britain possesses in the assistance of overseas dominions."[323]

A bone of contention about this regiment of the QOR was that it was comprised of men from other units, the "suggestion has been made that . . . Q.O.R. provisional battalion is composed of men picked from other corps. Col. Sir Henry Pellatt to-day denied that, the battalion was composed entirely of Queen's Own men, not a man being enlisted from any other regiment."[324] This was reported by Jaffray Eaton, the one journalist who did not enlist, probably for the very reason that he was in another regiment. Continuing this theme, the correspondent for the *Evening Telegram* commented that the officers were sore that an article was published in Québec stating that some of the men have jobs. "That statement would lead men to believe that privates could do as they like, and that this is a sky-larking expedition. I can tell that this camp is being run on strict lines as any I know of."[325] Throughout the trip there was this back and forth about the men of the QOR not being regular soldiers, and although all were enlisted members of the QOR militia, the fact was this English trip regiment was indeed temporary. The QOR was a voluntary militia, and all the men had jobs or were students. When they reached England, the battalion officers wanted the men to be respected as soldiers, equal to those of the British regular army. This required constant reinforcement with the men so that no bad behaviour would damage the QOR reputation.

Thursday the camp awoke to a wet rainy day that dampened not only spirits, but it seems, everything else in the camp.

> Shakespeare's old friend, "the gentle rain from Heaven." Has struck the camp in large wet bunches, and any fool idea that tents keep the rain off has been dispelled forever, for 600 sadder, damper people than the 600 at this camp couldn't be found anywhere. . . . Anybody who had thought for a moment that it was more fun lying in a tent all through a rainy day soon discovered that they had just one more thing travelling in their direction. The rain had just made a good start when the usual late ones discovered that they hadn't any trenches dug, and the rain trickling peacefully under the tent side aroused in many minds the same thought.[326]

The men were trying to make light of this demoralizing experience by singing, "one half clad young soldier, wearily bailing out the floor of his tent, sang 'Showers of Blessings There Shall Be' at the top of his voice . . . other mariners chanted 'One More River to Cross,' or 'Pull for the Shore Sailor, Pull for the Shore.'. . . The more sarcastic and heart embittered went in for 'How Dry I Am.'"[327] As Scroggie told it, "As soon as reveille sounded this morning the rainstorm that has been brewing for days butted into camp without even waiting to be introduced, and then proceeded to make up for lost time. With cheers and songs the boys tumbled out and got busy to batten down the tents."

It seemed that drainage trenches had not been dug around the tents and the rainwater freely flowed through the tents, thoroughly drenching all inside and their belongings. Adding to the problem, there were very few shovels available to dig trenches, furthermore, the lack of interest of the tent occupants to remedy the flooding situation led Scroggie to write sarcastically, "It is with regret that I feel obliged to write that neither the Star, Evening Telegram, World or Mail and Empire representatives would dig an inch of trenches. They calmly deserted their lance corporal and slid into the dry spots." Then, to provide the men with some warmth, a soup was served, which was not well-received: "The staff executed some strategy. . . . They executed a flank movement on the soup and dropped several pounds of pepper, the stomach being the most accessible point. The general opinion of the mess was not printable."[328]

On Thursday evening, the sergeants of the garrison entertained in the Sergeants' Mess: "An elaborate and varied program was put on in the big mess tent by members of the regiment. It included selection by the band, songs, recitations, burlesque, prize fights, and a band-conducting contest open to officers only. . . . The climax was capped by all singing to the tune of 'Has Anybody Here Seen Kelly?' [with adapted words] 'Has anybody seen Sir Henry? Henry, Henry, Has anybody seen Sir Henry? Canada is his home. Sure, he's an Indian chief and who knows what? And we're following him to Aldershot. Henry of the Second Queen's Own.'"[329] The *News* reported on the entertainment put on by the "Disturbance Committee," led by Cully Robertson, who was not going overseas: "He brought with him a box of costumes and 'Charlie.' The latter's real appendage is Charlebois, but nobody minds that much. The two of them rigged up the band in fool costumes and gave an imitation of Sousa's band."[330] Charlie was Walter J. Charlebois, (A Company), and he was assisted by Sgt. Joseph Salvaneschi (Quartermasters' Stores).[331] Charlebois was "a valued member of the entertaining staff of the

Queen's Own Rifles."[332] He had also performed at the smoker held in the armouries for the reunion in June.[333]

Figure 17. The Disturbance Committee. Sixth from left, Salvaneschi (?, holding a baton), third from right Charlebois (?).

The *Star* reported that "Last night the band got right out . . . and marched around the camp playing every kind of lively tunes. It was the first lively party since Montreal, and it was decidedly so. Then the band grew tired, and struck up 'God Save the King.' Without a word every man of the crowd drew himself stiffly to attention and stood silent. A week ago it would have been called affectation, now it comes as naturally as anything."[334] The *Mail and Empire* added that the men "roused out the band, which played all the well known, popular airs. To the tune of 'Harrigan' 300 men did the lockstep around the whole camp, marching to the tent of one of the instructors, who had gone to bed at the ridiculous hour of 8.30. They serenaded him until he made a speech. The singers went back to their own lines, where the men had a chance to war dance and yell."[335] Evening hijinks were also recorded by Argue in his diary, with what he called shirt-tail parades, these were conga-line dances, led by the band, parading around the camp in undershirts both before and after lights-out.

Each day the march route was extended: "The regiment was taking a long cut through bush, and blistering feet tell the tale. Tactical exercises were held the day before camp was to be broken. They did skirmishing drills and practised an attack. The men who are in pink of condition, stood the work without flinching, but The Evening Telegram saw fewer faces in the Quebec post office last night, and a whole lot of mothers and sweethearts must wait another day for their picture post cards."[336]

In the *News*, on the editorial page, there were often poems, just bits of doggerel, with pointed political or social sarcasm, led with a cartoon drawn by a staff illustrator. Scroggie's first about the trip was "Concerning Private Scroggie" with a cartoon of him sitting, in uniform, on a rock, the first stanza read: "The soldier of the legion was sobbing in his tent, / With fearful energy he said: 'I'm sorry that I went, / I thought it would be bread and jam to go to see the King, / To loaf about at 'Haldershot' and never do a thing, / To make a trip to Britain at another man's expense / Appealed to me as something which was certainly immense, / And so I grew a small moustache at regimental call / And some on-horse reporter goes to 'do' at City Hall."[337] In this poem one can see the sentiments of many of the young men—who could resist the opportunity and fun of an all-expenses paid trip to England? even if it meant sore feet, aching bodies, and the "order" to grow a mustache! Scroggie, although he could not have known it at the time this was written, was also prescient about meeting the king as it would turn out.

The last night in Lévis was the scene of a near-disastrous event that could have derailed the whole trip, no doubt caused by anxiety of the preparations for leaving for England, and possibly fueled by alcohol. The fracas was reported in the *Star* and the *Evening Telegram*, but by none of the other papers. An article titled "Wild War" described a QOR private being hit with a plank by a drunken French-Canadian soldier in Lévis: "The fuse was lit. Five minutes later Capt. Alley [Allan?] brought the colors down to 'K' Company and the bugle sounded. In an instant every man was out of his tent. Sleep be blowed. Let's have war."[338] The *Star* elaborated: "The story flew around camp that the garrison at Quebec was laying for the Queen's Own. A picket of 100 men were called in to go out and arrest the trooper [the "Tipsy Trooper" who attacked the QOR man], no matter if they had to go right into Quebec after him. In the interval he came back near the guard tent to look after his cap, without which he could not get back to the barracks. He was put under arrest [by the French-Canadian guard].[339](Pickets were soldiers tasked with policing duties.)

To complicate matters, at the same time there was a rumor concerning the QOR band, which:

> . . . was playing at the Dufferin Terrace, Quebec, and the boys feared that the troopers' friends might punish them, so at half-past ten a call went out for pickets to go into Quebec and Levis to see that all was right. At that, the camp went right up into the air, and before a minute 200 men had piled out of bed and were ready to start. It was a three-mile march into Levis, and they made it in less than half an hour. They were all armed with bayonets and looking for trouble. It was decidedly lucky that none of the garrison men started out to recapture their comrade, or to hinder the Q.O.R. As it was, at Levis all was quiet, and the band arrived on the next boat safe and unharmed. They had been having a royal time. Feeling rather silly, the boys returned to camp, but not to sleep. Everybody was on edge, and there was little sleep to be had until later in the morning.[340]

This paragraph of the article in the *Star* was titled "Brave But Foolish." The copy editor who wrote this subheading seems to have immediately grasped the gravity of the actions of the men. They were lucky that nothing happened, as it might have ended the trip and caused immense embarrassment for Pellatt, the QOR, and Canada. In his diary, Argue also briefly describes this event, saying once back in camp there was a shirt-tail parade and then in bed at 1:15 a.m.

On Saturday morning, departure day, the tents were struck and there was a march to the ferries where heavy kits and baggage to be put aboard SS *Megantic* were deposited. Then they paraded "about five miles through the city, visiting the Plains of Abraham, and finishing up on Dufferin Terrace. They will board the steamer ready to sail at 7 o'clock."[341]

Ned Sheppard wrote:

> A week ago they left Toronto, an almost inexperienced bunch of men, men with office pallor on their faces. To-night at seven o'clock they embark on the Megantic, a sun-blackened regiment of real soldiers. A week has made all the difference in the world. They have had bushels of fresh air, no worry, large meals of the 'plain but healthy' variety, plenty of hard outdoor work, and strict military discipline. All of these things would turn Bowery loafers into real men, and when you take in mind that the Queen's Own is emphatically not of that class, and that the trip is a holiday for them, the change is easily understood.[342]

In Lévis the articles written by the reporters were mailed to Toronto and published the next day. They provided detailed accounts of the hard work of being a soldier, the fun and anticipation of being on an adventure, the clashing of different personalities, and the camaraderie of these young men working together to form a cohesive force of the Queen's Own Rifles, one that the citizens of Toronto could be proud of.

CHAPTER

5

The SS Megantic

Surely, a never more enjoyable voyage was experienced. Not much rougher . . . than Lake Ontario was the broad Atlantic until the next to last day.[343]

The QOR boarded the SS *Megantic* in Québec City on August 20, and the ship departed at 7:00 p.m. The Québec City-Liverpool route was the usual run for the *Megantic*; her maiden voyage was in June of 1909, making her a new ship for the White Star line. She could accommodate 230 first-class, 430 second-class and 1,000 third-class passengers. For the eastbound trip: "The men will travel third class, the whole part of the steamer, which has accommodation for 1,200 being for the Q.O.R. exclusively."[344] In total there were 738 passengers on the *Megantic* for this voyage.[345] There were a few other passengers in first and second class, such as businessmen and teachers. There were Canadians, Americans,

French, Germans, comprised of husbands and wives, infants and children, but all the third class were the QOR men.

"The accommodations provided will be first-class in every respect, that on board ship being quite equal to ordinary second-class."[346] Sheppard reported that second and third class was full of soldiers, "just plain Toronto soldiers, clad in brown overalls and enjoying their first sight of the Atlantic Ocean."[347] The distribution of the men in the compartments was quite generous, as the *World* told it there were "two men to each stateroom, which can accommodate four, the upper berths to be utilized for baggage."[348] MacLaren added that "The bunks were comfortable but for a few exceptions. Many of the companies had outer ones. They were fine, but others had inner sleeping quarters, fresh air was hard to get. Second-class staterooms were occupied by a few. The officers, of course, travelled first-class."[349] Actually only the Pellatts, both father and son, and their wives, Major Arthur Peuchen and his wife and two children, and the wives and children of Major Thorn and Dr. Winnett travelled first-class. All the other officers, including Thorn and Winnett, travelled second class.[350]

There were a few other notable first-class passengers, including the British Metropolitan Inspector of Police, Walter Dew, Detective Charles Mitchell, wardresses Sarah Foster and Julia Stone, and their prisoners Dr. Hawley Crippen and Miss Ethel LeNeve. The whole world had been following the hunt for Dr. Crippen over the summer—it was a sensation. At the end of July, a marconigram was received by the westbound SS *Montrose* to be on alert for the couple, who had likely left Europe with LeNeve dressed as a boy. They were identified as passengers on this ship on route to Montréal. Scotland Yard was notified by the ship's captain and Inspector Dew left England on the SS *Laurentic*, a faster ship, which overtook the *Montrose*. Dew was able to board the *Montrose* from Father Point, Québec and arrest the couple on August 2. They were being returned to England on the *Megantic*. Apparently, Dew chose the *Megantic*, for although she was not fast, the complete charter of the ship by the QOR meant she offered the privacy needed to shelter his prisoners from the insatiable and melodramatic American and British tabloid journalists.[351] The couple were sequestered on the ship and the QOR men had no interaction with them.

Once onboard, there was consternation among the stewards as the QOR men in the second- and third-class moved freely between second- and third- class promenade decks, and some men even visited first class! Brown wrote that the stewards were "astonished when they saw men in evening-clothes walking around in the third class part of the ship. . . . [and] The stewards in first-class were disgusted when they found that some of their passengers had been receiving third-class passengers in their staterooms and had been feeding them."[352]

"After being two days out of Quebec the boys were given the privilege of promenading the deck used by second-class passengers, which was from one end of the steamer to the other."[353] The reporters in "The crack company of the regiment K, [were] quartered in regular second-class cabins, much to the disgust of the more unfortunate. The meals were bully, and although it was hard to get used to the good British custom of no butter with midday dinner."[354] Privates Henshaw and Horsey, the cadets from RMC, were also in a second-class cabin.

Jaffray Eaton, who travelled in first class, observed that the men were billeted according to their companies, and every man was familiar with the fire drill and his lifeboat assignment: "Fortunately there has been neither fire nor shipwreck."[355] Ned Sheppard of the *Star* said about the *Megantic* voyage: "It was a happy trip for all concerned. The men and officers were absolutely comfortable and well treated."[356]

With the voyage underway, this week-long journey was seen by some as a needed break after the week of intense training in Québec. "Rest, spelled with an extra-large-sized capital R was the one best bet during the week that the QOR spent on the salty wet."[357] But exercises and drills continued on board, reveille was at 6:30 a.m., a half hour later than Québec, breakfast at 7:45, "and everybody rushed into the dining-room with ravenous appetites," first post was at 9:30, last post at 10:00 and lights out at 10:15.[358] The *Globe* described: "Morning and afternoon parades have been held regularly. Those morning parades were great. They consisted of physical drill and free gymnastics . . . [the men] enjoyed this, and especially the concluding runs around the lower promenade deck, which necessitated their jumping the hatchway at the forward end, and sent blood tingling in the ends of every man's fingers. The afternoon parades consisted as a rule of arm drill and kit inspection."[359]

Regimental sports were on held Wednesday and Thursday: "The pioneers pulled over No. 8 company in the tug-of-war . . . boxing matches were witnessed . . . and provided endless amusement. Real science was shown by some of the contestants, but it was the most unscientific of the bouts which called forth the greatest enthusiasm on the part of the onlookers."[360] Lieut. Roy Gzowski was a popular wrestler and "excelled in the games held on board."[361]

Figure 18. Wrestling match on the *Megantic.*

One particularly fun event was when Sir Henry tied the rope around his waist, as anchor in a tug-of-war, as described somewhat gleefully by Jack MacLaren:

> Isn't it fun to see a man, a big, fat man, with a rope tied around his waist, standing anchor in a tug-of-war contest, especially if the aforementioned personage is

your boss? Col. Pellatt was in a tug-of-war game in the regimental sports on Wednesday. It was the officers against the sergeants. The latter didn't have a peep at the laurels. The officers, all husky individuals, merely played with the 'non-coms.' Guess if the whole five had been against Col. Pellatt he would have yanked them off their pedals. Anyway, the big guns just pulled the sergeants along the deck like they would a long ribbon.[362]

The Disturbance Committee was responsible for entertainments held every evening while on the *Megantic*. The main instigators were Private Charlebois and Sergeant Salvaneschi. "Every night there was some kind of performance. Some would-be or thought-to-be vaudeville artists were permitted to stay aloof from the military fun during the day so they would get up a programme to entertain the boys at night."[363] Music was welcomed and "The band was the life of the trip."[364] Choirs and singing were common: "Number eight company, formerly the University aggregation, which boasts of a corking good choir, entertained the passengers in the first and second-class dining-rooms every night."[365]

There was a big performance on Monday evening called the "Shine," held in the third-class dining room, the largest on the ship:

K Company sang wonderfully [and] Sergt.-Major Brittain then delivered a little oration comprising chiefly nothing with a fringe around it. Someone sang a little ballad entitled "She Sleeps" or something like that. That she should have slumbered earlier was the opinion of all. "The great 28-cent shooting act by Snakebite Bill" was next on the calendar. He hit a biscuit, but the bullet never made a dinge, it being so tough. The Raz-ba-tay band with Helme Kipporpalick as conductor followed. A Limburger waits, a beautiful dreamy thing, and several other German airs made up their repertoire. . . . Sir Hank was wreathed in smiles. It was greatly appreciated. Then Pte. Young gave a classy little buck and wing jig

on a two by four slab. With various other skits followed
by a silver collection in aid of the Seaman's Charities
of Liverpool and Montreal, the burlesque broke up.[366]

As the *Evening Telegram* reported: "That was not the only concert which
was held. Every night something of the same character was enjoyed by
the regiment."[367]

The entertainments were held in the different classes of saloons on
the ship. Eaton mentions one held in first class where the Hon. Rodolphe
Lemieux, the post master general of Canada, "acted as chairman of the
concert . . . and in the intermission made a delightful address, with the
choice flow of language and finished French-Canadian polish that is
characteristic of him."[368] Then at a concert in third class the "Hon. Mr.
Lemieux "got in right" with the men of the regiment. . . . One number
that particularly took his fancy was the reciting by Private Charlebois
of several of Drummond's poems in the real habitant dialect."[369]

Dr. Drummond's poems were humorous and considered quaint; they
often told stories with a moral recounted in the accent of a Québec-
Canadian habitant. These were very popular in the late nineteenth
and early twentieth century, and the men of the QOR would have
been familiar with them.[370] Undoubtedly Drummond's best-known
poem, "The Wreck of the *Julie Plante*" was recited by Charlebois, a
Francophone from Penetanguishene, Ontario, which was delivered
in the "real habitant dialect." The topic was sensitive, considering the
venue for the recitation, after all the poem was about the power of
storms and a ship's sinking, its concluding moral was: "You can't get
drown on Lac St. Pierre, So long you stay on the shore!" Fortunately,
the eastward crossing of the Atlantic was calm until the last day, when
doubtless many men of the QOR were remembering the words of Dr.
Drummond with considerable trepidation. In those times, men often
dressed and performed as women on the stage, as Charlie did in this
act; however, more socially complex and racially charged, Charlebois
performed in blackface. Although this form of entertainment was
common for the time, it was not universally considered appropriate and
Black community leaders had requested that such performances not be

allowed in Toronto. There was at least one Black rifleman on the 1910 trip: Col. Sgt. Robert E.E. Moore.[371]

One of the entertainments held in Lévis at the Sergeants' Mess involved dressing up the band in fool costumes and performing as Sousa's band. This was also done on the ship and was captured in a photograph taken on board. (The name of the band seemed to vary according to who was writing about it.) As Shepard reported: "The regimental band, called for the moment the 'Raz-ha-daz,' attired in tight-fitting burlesque Dutch costumes, wigs and false noses, peeled off all the discords they could find within their bosoms."[372]

Figure 19. The Raz-ba-Tay band, made up as fools, with long noses, beards and berets.

On Sunday, a church service was held, led by the QOR Chaplain Reverend Llwyd. As Eaton wrote in the *Globe*, the reverend "does more than preach" as he was a leader in all the deck games.[373] For the service "A handful of other passengers, there being very few on board, lined the upper decks. Col. Pellatt and the other officers stood alongside the minister. The band, which was grouped in the centre, rendered the music to several hymns, and the Toronto soldiers sang lustily . . . with soldiers on all sides as an audience is a picturesque ceremony."[374] Brown reported on the sermon given by Llwyd, in which he focused particularly on profanity: "He asked the men to remonstrate with anybody who used profane language in their presence."[375] This conservative message was very much a part of the tone of the lectures given to the men throughout the trip. Since this was a protestant service it is likely that Roman Catholic and Jewish members of the QOR were given permission not to attend.[376]

Apart from the accommodations, the food, the training, and the entertainments, the greatest impact on the young men of the QOR was the thrill of that first experience of leaving the comforts of home and going on a transoceanic voyage. It cannot be understated that this excitement was bolstered by the knowledge that there were no unexpected worries for these travellers; they knew where they were going, they knew what they had to do, they knew that they had money for their adventure, and finally, they knew that they were returning home where their families and jobs were waiting for them.

Figure 20. The QOR men on a boom of the *Megantic.*

It's apparent from reading Ned Sheppard's reporting in the *Star* that this was not his first crossing, but he was aware that for most of the QOR this was not the case: "There is something solemn in a first ocean voyage, and most of these six hundred, in spite of their host of new found adjectives, were putting the water between themselves and home for the first time."[377] He described the experience of being on board as not unlike that of being on "one of Hanlan's Point ferry boats."[378] The weather of this crossing proved to be marvellous, "much as other ocean voyages have been. Only one day, the last, was unkind enough to cause any seasickness."[379] Scroggie penned a "ditty" about his experience on board: "I would I were upon the sea / To watch the billows bounding free / And Scroggie, working at his drill / While feeling rather pale and ill."

Many natural wonders were spotted: "When some distance out an iceberg was noticed and everyone rushed to the starboard where it could be seen. Further out sprays were seen shooting from the surface, and soon whales were seen, and many had never seen them before so enthusiasm was rife."[380] Eaton reported: "Tuesday an iceberg was sighted. Wednesday some whales were attracted by the strange contortions of the men at physical drill, or perhaps by the penetrating voice of Captain Butcher shouting 'Stand steady, you the man in the corner.' And approached almost within hailing distance of the vessel. Thursday several shoals of porpoises came and disported themselves for the benefit of the Canadian soldiers. Friday, more whales."[381] Brown reported: "Several large fish were disporting themselves in the waves some distance ahead of the ship. 'Whales, whales!' arose, and after taking a look men ran to tell their friends. A large crowd collected in the bow of the ship. The ones learned in piscine lore saw immediately that they were porpoises, but many are swearing yet and will continue to assert that they saw a school of whales."[382] Scroggie wrote, "we passed a large iceberg and since that time have seen some whales and dolphins. . . . We have seen the Northern Lights regularly and have had some sunsets that make you feel very far away from home and absolutely without friends."[383] George Argue wrote, "We saw a whale and I also got a peek at Miss Leneve." The latter declaration might have been an exaggeration since Miss LeNeve was quite inaccessible.

Minor details of the voyage were written about by Brown, one being that "There was a candy and cigaret [sic] famine after Thursday noon. . . . The ship's salesman did not know what was coming when they stocked up. All soldiers are strong on both sweets and tobacco. There was a large enough supply of both to do for two ordinary trips, but not half enough to keep a regiment going for a week."[384] The *Megantic* offered the chance for the men to have a much-needed wash-up after their week at Lévis. "Opportunities for washing clothes were practically nil at camp. On the boat there was fresh water and those willing to assume the duties of washer-woman buckled down. Some preferred to hire the stewards or other members of the crew to do it."[385] In the weeks to come, occasions to wash both their persons and their clothes became exceedingly few and far between.

At night: "The 'lights out' alarm didn't work very well, though. The salty breeze was way too alluring and many liked to stay in the open and enjoy it . . . they fairly licked it up. You could see in the moonlight the dim outlines of human beings stretched out in every available spot on the decks. They lay everywhere. No one was particular about cushions."[386] The men became familiar with the ship, and during free time stayed on deck to soak up fresh sea air and enjoy the view.

The weather on the last day was unpleasant. As Eaton wrote, once the lights of Ireland had been spotted, the men cheered, they were "glad to land tomorrow. Such a voyage it has been!"[387] The *Evening Telegram* wrote that the last day was a corker: "The waves were wild and angry. The liner rolled and pitched forward and backward, and the khaki-clad soldiers walked about like drunken men."[388] The last night was the captain's dinner, which because of the poor weather was not well attended, and the evening's entertainment, "the Shine," was cancelled.[389]

The men from the QOR really gave Dr. Crippen little thought as the voyage continued; it was impossible to see him (or Miss LeNeve) as they were billeted in cabins that no one, except the police or the captain, could access. One soldier thought, "I wonder what the poor son of a gun thinks when he hears this bunch talking and singing, and laughing, while he sits in his cabin? I bet he feels pretty rotten."[390] They jokingly called themselves "Crippen's Own Regiment."[391] Scroggie wrote, "This trip of the Megantic will go down in her history as one of the most eventful, for onboard are not only the Queen's Own Rifles, but also Dr. Hawley Crippen and a News reporter."[392]

The *Star,* in an opinion piece, not by Shepherd, observed that the ship was not without journalists: "If Inspector Dew had been reading the Toronto papers he would know that there was little to be gained in privacy by sailing on the Megantic, for while he may succeed in keeping the English correspondents off the vessel, several 'war' correspondents of the Toronto papers, members of the Queen's Own Rifles, are on board, going to Aldershot, and they will be keen to learn all they can about the doings and experiences of the famous prisoners. They are bona fide newspapermen as well as militia men, and have been sending lengthy accounts of the regiment's experiences while in camp at Quebec."[393]

In fact, apart from the press gang, there were five journalists in first class: Jaffray Eaton; three English journalists, Bernard Grant, A.P. Hallam, Percival Phillips; and a fourth, S. McK. Brown, who was colonial born (Canada). Bernard Grant was for the *Daily Mirror* and Percival Phillips was for the *Daily Express*—these two were specifically assigned to the Crippen case. Stanley McKeown Brown, the correspondent for the *Standard Empire,* was covering the QOR expedition beginning from Toronto.[394] There was also a journalist for the *Times,* who had been assigned to the QOR starting from Toronto. This person's name is not known with any certainty, but it might have been Hallam. [395]

Bernard Grant was a photographer for the British tabloid, the *Daily Mirror*. Later he wrote about his time on the *Megantic* in pursuit of photographs of Crippen and LeNeve.[396] The story was that while on his way from London to Canada, he connected with another journalist, his old friend Percival Phillips, who was working for the *Daily Express*.[397] While trying to find out when Dew intended to transport his wards to a ship going eastbound, they determined that the ship likely to take them was the *Megantic*. In his dramatic account of the transfer of Crippen and LeNeve, Grant describes waiting on a tugboat in the St. Lawrence for the *Megantic* to pass by to permit the transfer of the prisoners. An account of this also appears in the *Times*: "The Megantic had received wireless orders to slow up between Sillery and Cape Rouge to permit the party to go onboard. The transfer occurred shortly after 11 a.m. in midstream. . . . Some journalists and photographers chartered a tug, which followed him [Dew] to Cape Rouge, where they lay-to for three hours until the arrival of the Megantic."[398] At the moment of the transfer, Grant was able to get photos of Crippen and LeNeve crossing the gangplank and boarding the *Megantic,* then he and the other journalists rushed back to Québec City to board the ship. While Grant was on the St. Lawrence, Phillips had purchased two first-class tickets so they could join the voyage east.

Figure 21. Dancing to the music of the regimental band.

Grant wrote in his memoirs: "Onboard there were six hundred and twenty officers and men of the Queen's Own Rifles, a Canadian Volunteer regiment under the command of Sir Henry Pellatt, who for patriotic reasons was bringing them to England at his own expense. I could not help but wondering what must be the extent of a man's wealth to carry out such a project."[399] He did glimpse Crippen on the *Megantic*, "silhouetted in the pale moonlight," and as "The wind whistled through the rigging, and the distant strains of a dreamy waltz, played by the regimental band at a dance on the deck, seemed to add a touch of uncanniness to the scene."[400] Grant took two photographs of the trip: one of the men lying on the deck seasick on the last day of the journey and one of dancers on the deck.

S. McK. Brown was an experienced war correspondent, who had written for Toronto's *Mail and Empire* during the Boer war.[401] His war-correspondent experience would have provided interesting conversations at the first-class dinner tables. In the beginning of his Africa trip, described in his book *With the Royal Canadians*, there was a sea voyage full of young, enthusiastic men leaving Canada to go to war. It would have made for interesting comparisons with the current QOR voyage. However, the young men of the Boer War met with different fates, while in stark contrast the English trip was a lark, as S. Brown and other seasoned military men on the *Megantic* knew.

The unnamed *Times* journalist (Hallam?) sent telegrams to London describing the trip. He wrote, "The voyage had been smooth enough to allow for daily training . . . . every day there was physical drill, without arms, followed by a sort of expeditionary march round decks and over hatches. There were boxing contests and obstacle races, not to speak of concerts at night."[402] The *Times* also wrote that due to the sudden change of weather off the Irish coast: "For the last day of the voyage the men were content -or profoundly not content- to lie still while the ship did all the exercise and the storm howled, the only music."[403] Stabilizers on ships, which make ocean voyages so endurable in modern times, were a technological development some twenty years later, in the 1930s, thereby rendering the rough seas of 1910 particularly difficult and unpleasant.[404]

Getting ready to disembark on the morning of Saturday, August 27 was a rude awakening for the QOR men who, as much as they wanted to get ashore, were accustomed to the daily ship routine. "The sound of a horrid bugle was heard. 'Fall in!' croaked the officers—no, not in the drink, but into company formation. The harness was thrown on broad shoulders. The burdensome kits, filled with wearing apparel, were attached thereto. The straps started to cut the shoulders—a slow torture. But what of that? We were military men now, and hard, and expect to class with the cream of the army."[405] MacLaren described the arrival in Liverpool best: "As the Megantic steamed into the harbor this morning, six hundred youths, ruddy and tanned, and feeling like young colts, waited expectantly to land. The khaki-clad boys, burdened down by heavy luggage in kits on their shoulders, were all a-flutter . . . as they came down the gang-plank in 'twos,' cheers upon cheers sounded through the air. Truly, it was an encouraging reception, and enough to arouse the spirits of the crack regiment from Canada-- the Queen's Own Rifles."[406] Landing was no easy step though, as the "The wharf seemed to sway to and fro . . . we were land-sick."[407]

Figure 22. Arrival and official reception, Liverpool.

The reception of the *Megantic* in Liverpool was overwhelming. It was attended by thousands of people and countless newsmen and photographers from all over Great Britain; however, much of this reception was for Dr. Crippen and Miss LeNeve. On arrival at Liverpool, they were escorted out through the baggage gangway quickly and efficiently taken to London for trial.

After official speeches, the QOR marched from the pier to the train station to continue the next part of the journey—training with the British regulars at Aldershot as the English part of the trip commenced.

CHAPTER
6

Aldershot and Balmoral

It was a great and glorious sham battle, with plenty of reality to it. Fifteen thousand men a side, plenty of ammunition, and loads of noise. What more could be desired to make six hundred Toronto boys feel good?[408]

The QOR arrived in Liverpool complaining about their unsteady sea legs, which were quickly forgotten as they were overwhelmed by the excitement of marching through the streets of Liverpool, cheered on by thousands of Liverpudlians, on their way to the train station. The British press reported nearly daily on the activities of the Canadians—their looks, their quirks and mannerisms—covering their presence in the UK as a sort of charming colonial oddity. The *Daily News* reported: "A hearty civic and military welcome, organized by the Liverpool City Council and the War Office, was given to the Canadians as they marched off the liner on to the Liverpool landing stage . . . the deputy Lord Mayor . . . made a speech of welcome, and speaking in reply, Colonel Pellatt pointed out that the sole object of the trip was to make a further study of the art of warfare."[409] Scroggie commented, "Somehow or other we marched over the humps and hollows of those wobbly Liverpool roads until we reached the railroad station. The photographs in the newspapers since showed we marched in some kind of order, but it did not seem to us like a serpentine slide. The best part of it all was that there were no speeches. After Toronto and Montreal where we stood under our kits for an hour or so, to applaud occasionally when given our cue, we rather dreaded the ordeal. It was pleasant to miss it."

Figure 23. Marching off landing stage at Liverpool.

Canadians had been forewarned about the uniqueness of British rail travel in contrast to that of Canada's railroads. In February, an article by Joseph T. Clarke appeared on page one of the *Star* titled "English Railway System Is a Source of Wonder."[410] Clarke wrote, "When a Canadian lands in England and leaves the boat to take the train to London he can see no sign of a train anywhere. What he does see is a long row of bob-tail street cars and when someone tells him that this is his train he suspects that someone is putting up a joke on him. It seems to be a toy train . . . [when one is] accustomed to the Mogul engines, long and high passenger coaches, and huge freight cars used in Canada." The coaches were divided into compartments with an aisle down the side, and the compartments, even third class, were spacious, just not as well-appointed as first class. Scroggie wrote, "The war office had two special London and Great Northwestern trains waiting, and it took but a few minutes to up anchor and away. The coaches were labelled third class, but were really luxuriously appointed. Different from our trains, they caused much comment. Their tiny engines with their high narrow wheels did not look powerful enough to pull a battalion, but they did, and at a rate that was a pleasant contrast to Canadian troop transportation." Sheppard added, "They were all compartment trains, but with aisles at the sides, and the men could pay friendly call. The seats were upholstered and comfortable."[411] Pellatt and his party travelled in the royal coach.

MacLaren wrote of the trip south. "The ride from Liverpool to Aldershot was truly delightful. Two special trains carried the boys . . . eyes staring at ruined castles, ancient churches, small and large estates, rolled fields, neatly trimmed hedges, which line the tracks, and numerous other things that go to make England so beautiful."[412] Jaffray Eaton wrote, "All were keenly interested in looking at the beautiful country they were passing through, as the majority of the regiment are in England for the first time. The train itself was very comfortable, and what pleased the men the most was the fact that the railway company gave to each man an individual lunch box neatly done up in a cardboard box."[413] Lunch "included two sandwiches, two pieces of cake, a soft drink and a glass and a souvenir menu card, bearing a photo of the colonel, and adorned with the maple leaf and flag."[414] In all, the trip lasted seven hours and outside London, after about four hours, the train engines were changed and they arrived at Aldershot around 9:00 p.m.[415] Walking through the flag decorated town they arrived in camp after 10:00 p.m. That night Sir Henry took the opportunity to address local dignitaries, and more importantly numerous British press reporters, under the glare of night lights.[416]

The reception at Aldershot was memorable, as reported in the *Daily Standard*: "It was, as one of the rifles said, as if we had arrived at a great crisis and had saved the town."[417] Locals lined the route to Camp Rushmoor where "On the line of the march soldiers and civilians crowded on the Queen's Own, clasped the hands of the Canadian visitors, calling them comrades. It sent a thrill through the heart of every man."[418] Brown of the *World* commented: "The welcome we got is one of the greatest that any regiment ever had, so we are told. . . . Decorations along the way, too, and half a dozen bands from the British troops now here 'to play us in.'"[419] Scroggie's comments were the most dramatic: "Good old mother England has opened her arms wide and taken into her embrace the 600 odd sea-sick and travel-tired members of the Queen's Own Rifles of Canada, who arrived on the steamer Megantic at Liverpool on Saturday night last."

After all day in transit, with little to eat, it was the dinner that proved the most significant part of the day. Sheppard said it best, "One meal did it. One large, soul-satisfying, genuine English meal decided the Queen's Own Rifles of Toronto, now travelling incog [incognito?] under the two sobriquets of 'Canada's crack regiment,' and 'Crippen's Own,' that they liked Aldershot and England, and everything in sight. They don't mind the rain, nor the drill, nor the long route marches; these don't count so long as the meals continue to be soul-satisfying." [420] As Scroggie described: "When the rifles [the men] entered the mess tent at camp after being pried out of those awful equipments, there was a howl of surprise. Tables with white cloths, jardinieres with potted plants, loaf sugar and benches, took the place of the long wooden structures that have been our lot, except on the Megantic." Ned Sheppard added: "There were two mess tents for the men, huge affairs. They were led in and given seats. 'Will you have roast beef or beef steak pie?' asked a polite waiter. Nearly dazed by the fact the there was a choice, everybody took beef. After that was cleaned up they tried the pie. . . . 'They're not treating us like soldiers—we're princes,' shouted someone. 'Look at the flowers on the table!'"[421] Scroggie exclaimed, "It was like waking up in a military heaven."

The men were exhausted from their journey and wanted to settle in. Having been in the camp at Lévis they knew what to expect for camp life at Rushmoor; however, much to their pleasant surprise the British accommodations were superb, and for the first night the men "slumbered peacefully in the luxury of comfortable straw ticks and three blankets, and, most significant of all, a straw pillow. Only six men occupy a tent, which accommodated eight cramped individuals in Levis. The tents are floored."[422] Eaton noted that "Each officer has a tent to himself completely furnished with a bedstead, bureau, washstand, table, chairs, even a bathtub, and matting on the floor."[423]Exhausted, but well fed and well-housed, the men were in bed by 2:00 a.m.[424]

Figure 24. Church service conducted by Reverend Llwyd on Sunday, August 28, at Aldershot camp.

Sunday, August 28, was a quiet day; a church service was conducted by Captain Reverend Llwyd and was attended by the men of the QOR. The massive size of the camp can be seen in the background of the photograph of the service. "The barracks, inclusive of the parade grounds, cover a tract 2 1/2 miles [4 km] in length by nearly a mile [1.6 km] in width . . . each barrack is named after a notable battle. More than 20,000 men and 4000 horses can be accommodated."[425] The *Globe* mentioned thirty thousand people and eight bands welcomed the QOR to Aldershot, the immense size of the camp would have been awe inspiring.[426] Needless to say, this would have been an incredible experience for the QOR men, having come from the camp at Lévis. The intensity of the military experience yet to come would soon be realized, but there was still time for fun.

Since it was Sunday: "An immense crowd of civilians and soldiers visited the camp, eager to get a glimpse of the soldiers from across the water."[427] MacLaren quipped, "Civilians from old 'Lunnon' arrive every minute to look over the Q.O.R."[428] In the afternoon many men explored the camp and its surroundings, visiting the grocery canteen where one could buy anything, making friends with the "Tommy Atkins . . . marching arm in arm with them [the regulars] down the Aldershot streets or even going for a visit up to London with them."[429] That first Sunday many took the opportunity to visit London "to obtain a first glimpse of the world's metropolis."[430]

Also on that first Sunday, Pellatt was visited by Major-General Mackenzie, and the two men worked out a plan for the training of the QOR. They would begin by "opening with a few days' drill and route marching to get the men fit for the coming manoeuvres."[431] This would take the men up to the London break, which was planned to start September 14.

First and foremost, for the men was the military training, which was the primary reason for the trip. As he did in Lévis camp, Jack MacLaren, seemingly one for logistical details, outlined the daily routine: up at 6:00 a.m., tent inspection at 6:30 a.m., roll call at 7:00, breakfast at 8:00, at 8:45 a.m., "in the ranks for three-hours heavy stunt- skirmishing, company drill, manual training, attacks, physical exercises and others.

Before you leave for the Aldershot rally to perform the latter work, one's rifle must be thoroughly soaked with oil, which is a trying job. Those who say military work isn't the limit for endurance are insane," parade, then lunch, parade again, then dinner at 5:00.[432] A photograph taken by the QOR photographer Gleason shows the men clowning around as they jostle to enter the mess tent. MacLaren added: "It's positively hard work, but it has its compensations in a trip of this character."[433]

Figure 25. Men entering the mess tent.

Monday, August 29, was a rainy day, but rain did not hinder the first day of training; it was a day to test the mettle of the QOR "soldiering in real earnest now. This morning, in spite of the pouring rain, they drilled steadily for three hours, and this afternoon went for a five-mile [8 km] route march. It was still raining, and the combination of rain and heavy mud was not a cheerful one."[434] Back at camp for lunch at noon they changed into dry clothes, "and afterwards during a bright twenty minutes started out in a light marching order on a five-mile route march, Colonel Sir Henry accompanying on foot."[435] It started to rain again: "Great coats were hastily unrolled on the march and were donned so that the men were able to save their good uniforms from a thorough soaking.

Sir Henry Pellatt 'stuck it out' to the end, and the men followed him. When they returned to camp they cheered their Colonel."[436]Although Sir Henry joined in the march on the first day at Aldershot, he remained firmly on horseback for all other military events of the trip.

Figure 26. Sir Henry leading the march the afternoon of August 29, 1910; rifles are at trail arms.

Days spent marching took their toll on their feet, but in return the men got to see the beautiful countryside around Aldershot. Often a British regular regiment set the pace, sometimes the Leicester Buffs: "We will give you boys a few hints on how to walk a route march."[437] One morning march, "We were getting farther away from camp. And the trees which surround Aldershot and the high statue of the Duke of Wellington were left in the distance. We had tramped for about four miles [6.4 km] out and had yet to get our second wind."[438] The officers called out: "March at ease. . . . We did, with the greatest of ease. Rifles were carried anyway, some on shoulders, some in the hands and others strapped across the body."[439] Walking and walking, getting no nearer to camp, "about half a mile [0.8 km] of soldiers on the dreary road, neatly

102

in 'fours' wending their weary way under the broiling sun."[440] Three miles [4.8 km] from camp, the officers commanded: "Trail arms. . . . [the response was] 'What for?' we asked. Why couldn't we walk at ease the rest of the way? It was soon explained. We were passing a Government house, and four red-coated husky-looking guards had turned out to salute us. They 'presented arms' with a snap. 'Eyes right,' commanded the Chief. . . . We did, they looked all right when looked over. The agony was over. We were allowed to walk at ease again."[441] The QOR band played them in to camp to the regimental air, and Colonel Mason spoke: "All I can say men, is that your work was well done."[442] When marching "trail arms," which is particular to riflemen regiments, the right arm is extended down by the side and the rifle is held perpendicular to the body, making a "T" (see Figure 26).

Figure 27. Hanging clothes to dry on the outside of the tent.

Adding to the record of the trip, a local photography studio and printing company, Gale & Polden Ltd., who were military specialists, had photographers document the QOR while in Aldershot over August and September. They took photos of route marches and the official photographs of all the companies. Each of the photos was numbered

Figure 28. H Company. The reporters are in the second row, beginning at fourth from the left to the right, Scroggie, Riggs, Sheppard, Brown and MacLaren.

and the numbering helps to determine when they were taken at what point in the trip. The first photograph, No.1, taken late in the evening shortly after arrival on Saturday, August 27, was of Sir Henry talking to press and dignitaries at Aldershot. Image No.15 shows Pellatt walking with the troops, which he did on Monday, August 29. It rained that day and image No.17 shows the men arranging damp clothes to dry, possibly later in the day.

Because of Gale & Polden, the Aldershot portion of the English trip is the best documented, while for the remainder of the trip the photographic evidence is sparse. At the end of the trip in Liverpool, prior to embarkation, each man was presented with "a pretty little souvenir of Aldershot by Messrs. Gale & Polden. . . . The souvenir is in the form of a booklet, containing a history of Aldershot camp."[443]This included photographs of all the companies and in the photograph of H company, the members of the press gang hold a place of prominence in the second row, centred behind the officers of the company.[444]

At Aldershot, the QOR's neighbours were the First Battalion of the East Kent Regiment, commonly called the Buffs, and: "It is a curious coincidence that forty years ago that famous regiment gave the Queen's Own permission to use their quick step. The Canadian band played it as the men tramped back to camp this evening."[445] On another occasion, after a long and challenging march: "The Buffs' band played [the QOR] in with the regimental. It was glorious." [446] That the Buffs band played for the QOR made a lasting impression on the men, such that it was remembered fondly for years.

The following week was spent drilling and marching, marches that got longer each day in the countryside around camp. "This part of the country does not boast the best roads, and plenty of English mud is gathered upon these marches and brought back to camp. The compensating feature is the beauty of the country, and the marches are being so arranged that by the time the men are ready for manoeuvres they will have seen practically all of the country within a radius of about ten miles from Aldershot."[447]The *Daily News* recounted one of the Canadian's marching songs; "We come from a land of bright blue skies, / Where fruit tree blossoms greet the eyes-- / A land where grapes in the open grow, / And we love our Lady of the Snow. / Here's to our land of the maple leaf, / Here's to the land of the golden sheaf, / here's to the Empire's flag unfurled, / Emblem of freedom around the world."[448]

The regulars' regiments gave demonstrations for the QOR. "The Buffs gave an exhibition of battalion attack. It was really only showing the Queen's Own a few things that they had been doing themselves for several days, but showing them how they ought to do it. They made a good job of it, but once again, it wasn't taken much to heart. The men felt that they hadn't been shown much that they didn't know before."[449] Then, the Yorkshire rangers did a shooting exhibition that was an eye-opener; there was none of the orderly lying down (which the QOR had been practicing). "They took short rushes and fired quickly at all sorts of moving targets, some to represent calvary charging and other skirmishers."[450]

The QOR men had identified two serious issues with their kit: the Oliver equipment belt and the Ross rifle. The problem of wearing the Oliver harness had been recognized in Lévis and only got worse in England. Jim Scroggie sarcastically wrote, "We were hitched up as usual to the antique Oliver equipment, which added to our joy."[451]Riggs also took a swipe at them: "The packs the men carry weigh a great deal. The Oliver equipment knocks. The straps bind a man so he cannot take a proper breath or stand erect, while the collar piece pulls the neck forward, tending to give a stooped position. The Webb equipment of canvas straps, worn by the British regulars, is far superior and it is unofficially rumored that the Queen's Own will be supplied with this before leaving."[452] Even the British minister of war, Lord Haldane, who inspected the equipment stated, "The whole system of it was wrong and that the QOR might go with some better outfit."[453] The unwieldly Oliver equipment continued as part of the Canadian equipment up to and including the Great War.

But it was the Ross rifle that came in for the most severe criticism; this too had been recognized as problematical in Lévis. Jim Brown commented they "are fragile and rust appears in all manner of places . . . in dry weather they become clogged with dust and sand. . . . It would not do for a man to hammer an enemy over the head with butt when at close quarters, because the butt would break off."[454] Scroggie's comments were scathing: "Just one more grouch. The Ross rifle. That little toy shooting iron should go out into the garden and eat worms for the rest of its natural life, which most of us hope will only be until we reach home. Nobody loves it. The Officers openly ridiculed it. . . . It took just one wet day to prove its worthlessness in its present form as an active service weapon." Ned Sheppard was also vocal in his disapproval of the Ross: "For active service it didn't make good for a minute. Apparently, it is an excellent arm for target, but it has made a bad impression as a service rifle. The breech is not protected sufficiently to keep the sand from getting in, and several doubts were cast on the rifles as to whether it was safe to fire them off. . . . They are little less than toys, and have been cussed more heartily than anything in camp. Several were put out of commission before the manoeuvres began."[455]

It was the criticism about the rifles that Jack MacLaren published in the *Evening Telegram* that caught the attention of Canadian politicians in Ottawa. "The first week in England has found the rifles in a terrible state. The barrels in some case are rusty on account of the damp weather. The intricate sights are twisted and altogether they hardly bear the appearance of a real rifle. . . . Practising the attacks put the rifles on the rocks, so to speak. . . . The officers ridicule it and the men curse it."[456] As a response to this criticism an article in the *Ottawa Citizen*, reprinted in the *Evening Telegram*, stated, "The Citizen today, commenting upon the denunciation of the Ross rifle by the Toronto newspaper men in England with the Queen's Own, says: Though the Government has accumulated 50,000 at something over $25 a piece . . . the QOR is the first regiment that has been fully armed with the weapon. . . . It would scarcely have done to have them appear [in England] armed with Lee-Enfield-rifles when it had been certified by superior military authority to the Bisley committee last spring that the Ross rifle was the military arm of the Canadian forces."[457] Furthermore, the *Citizen* article goes on, "About the only reason for reviving the Ross rifle discussion is to point out that on the first occasion in which a Canadian regiment has been armed with the weapon it has been pronounced a complete failure in the columns of a newspaper organ of the Liberal party, thus more than bearing out the severest criticisms that have been passed upon it by military men and by the Opposition in Parliament."[458] The rifles were manufactured in Québec City. The makers of the Ross rifle commented that the steel they used was the best quality, the sights were not made by Ross, but by another company (Sutherland), and that the wood used for the stocks "is the best quality of Italian walnut."[459] The Canadian Militia Department response was classic political-speak, saying only that as the Lee-Enfield rifles were becoming worn out they were being called in and replaced with Ross rifles.[460] Basically, all the reporters said the same thing about the Ross rifle—that it had the durability of a toy gun, and that "It is likely when the Queen's Own arrive home again there will be no Ross rifle, just a twisted piece of steel and a cracked stock."[461] As history would tragically demonstrate, all the comments about the Ross rifle were correct, and except for its use as a sniper's rifle, it proved unfit for battle in WWI.

Not only were the rifles a problem, but there was also the matter that the QOR were being charged to purchase the blanks for the rifles![462] As Jaffray Eaton reported, "It was feared at first that Colonel Sir Henry Pellatt would have to pay the British Government for the blank ammunition to be used during the manoeuvres. The attention of Hon. Mr. Haldane was called to the fact that they were being charged, and immediately the charge was dropped. The Queen's Own were supplied with 60,000 rounds of blank ammunition for nothing."[463]

As the week progressed the men were anxious for news from home and to facilitate letter writing, "A writing tent is provided where one can communicate to mothers and others."[464] The most common method of correspondence by the QOR men was the postcard. Views of Aldershot cards were chosen. Rifleman Chas. G. Winsor sent a postcard of Queens Avenue & St. George's Church, Aldershot, on September 1, 1910, to Toronto from Rushmoor Camp: "Dear Mrs. Rennie, I am over here with the Queens Own Rifles having a fine time with lots of hard work. We will go to London for four days in about a weeks time then start on a seventy mile march."[465]

Gale & Polden, with a thriving print shop in Aldershot, quickly produced postcards of the series of photographs taken of the QOR men at the camp. No. 18 showed the men walking in their uniforms in the

Figure 29. "The *Star Weekly* Arrives in Camp and They All Want to See It."

camp. Harry Wilcockson sent his sister Maude this card and wrote, "We are getting lots of drill these days but will be able to survive it alright. The camp grounds cover 22 miles and there are 50000 regulars stationed here all the time."[466] A photo postcard of QOR company No. 2 made it clear why postcards were the preferred method of communication, as a rifleman wrote on September 5, "We leave here tomorrow morning at 6.30 the war is started several Regiments have left today and some are moving now and will be all night long. There are about thirty thousand troops around here now, so you can see how busy it is around here. . . . I am afraid I will not be able to write a letter right now so you will have to excuse that and I will send you some postcards instead."[467] Obviously, a postcard does not allow a lot of text, but some postcards were very light on words and seem to have been solely to inform family back in Toronto of safe arrival. Willi Rossen wrote to his mother on September 16 using a Gale & Polden image of QOR men handling white packages: "Dear Mother, I hope you are keeping well. Best respect from Willi, goode-bye. XXXXXXX."[468]

For the men, it was most exciting to receive newspapers from home with pictures of the QOR on the trip and stories written about them by the press gang. The *Star Weekly*, which had just begun publishing on Sundays, and the *Sunday World* were photograph rich. Copies of these Sunday papers are rare, and since Brown's letters were published in them, only one of his articles in the *Sunday World* exists for the rest of the English trip.

The press gang had sent copy back to Toronto from Lévis, and it was their task to do the same from Aldershot; however, the circumstances of working as journalists had changed. With the reporters now off the *Megantic* and in England, stories which were written as letters or despatches, had to be sent back by ship to Toronto, so the stories were published with a turn-around of seven days or more after they were written. Marconigrams were used to send news quickly, but because they were expensive, the filing of long and detailed stories was not feasible. In fact, the Marconi cables filed about the trip were usually just one or two sentences at the most—bullet points of breaking news.

Shortly after the arrival at Aldershot, special accommodation was made for the reporters. A journalist from the UK's *Daily News* wrote:

> I learned from an officer of the Rifles this morning that practically all the men are on full pay during their seven weeks absence from the Dominion. There are one or two of them who are earning their salaries. The most noticeable of these is a little bunch of five reporters for Toronto daily papers, who, housed in one tent, have naturally been christened by their comrades "the Press Gang." During their first days at Aldershot their work was carried on under almost overwhelming difficulties, for, huddled up in a small bell tent, squatting on the

floor, and writing by the light of a candle, the five batches of "copy" were produced only by much painful exertion and mutual obligation. But the practical nature of the Canadians came to their assistance. Before they had been in camp two days they had erected a square marquee just clear of the regimental lines, and now, from behind its canvas walls, the clicking of five typewriters can be heard from tea time to "lights out."[469]

For these days spent at Aldershot the dedicated tent allowed the press gang to write about the men's daily duties and especially their night adventures. The journalists were even interviewed by other newsmen. The *Canadian Gazette* interviewed "Mr. Ned Sheppard," elevating him to "one of the Queen's Own journalist attachés."[470] Knowing Ned and his ego, it seems that he promoted himself from being a lowly journalist to a position with more gravitas! It's no wonder that Ned and Scroggie butted heads.

Over the days at Aldershot, as the marches got longer, one common complaint the men had was the state of their feet. Scroggie humorously wrote that six hundred men wished they had no feet or had been born with hoofs, after a "promenade . . . in a broiling hot English sun, we did our fifteen miles and at the end every man was still in his place, but almost all were limping." After dinner, the men did a goose walk to the wash benches, where those with blistered feet "were given a good ice cold bath". Ned Sheppard wrote, with bravado, "Everybody said the Buffs would walk the feet off the poor Canadians and reduce them to an apologetic pretence. Not for a minute. . . . After a good wash and brush they felt as well as ever. . . . Baseball, before a crowd of spectators, was the order of the day."[471]

On Wednesday, August 31, the regiment was inspected by the commander of the camp, Lieutenant-General H. Smith-Dorrien. "The inspection was a very close one, and at its conclusion the general expressed satisfaction to Colonel Sir Henry Pellatt . . . with the smartness and appearance of the battalion."[472] The Buffs and the QOR had a competitive march on Thursday, with the Buffs setting a quick pace on the twelve-mile march; "The Canadians are rather proud of their tramp . . . and the men of the Queen's Own would sooner have died than disgrace Canada in the eyes of the Regulars by dropping out."[473] Jim Scroggie observed that the men were getting lots of exercise; "Your beloved offspring is getting his, and is getting it good and plenty, if he survives he will tell the things that newspapers refuse to print."

Figure 30. Foot care at Aldershot.

While at Aldershot the men were free to visit London after dinner. "They feed and after that it's no more duties for the night. Hurrah for London or elsewhere!"[474] To make it easier to leave the camp, "Permanent passes have been issued to all members of the regiment to allow them in through the lines at any time up till half-past eleven. Late leave may also be had on application."[475] The trains ran frequently: "Each day, thirty-five trains go to the metropolis and there is a special theatre train which returns to Aldershot each night, leaving London at 12.15

o'clock."[476]Aldershot was situated some fifty-three km southwest of London and the one-hour trip cost "one 'bob.' It means a shilling, for the edification of the unlearned."[477]

Figure 31. The QOR at Aldershot.

Over the next nine days, until September 6, when the QOR left Aldershot camp for manoeuvres, the men spent the days training and the evenings exploring London and the surrounding countryside. While in London, the QOR men in uniforms with the distinctive Maple Leaf badges were recognized and feted. "Londoners know who the men with the Maple Leafs on their caps are, and where they come from. . . . They have been the cause of courteous reception they have been received everywhere."[478]

The worldly traveller Ned Sheppard described, with glee, arriving with fellow QOR, dressed as privates at "the biggest and sportiest restaurants in London, the kind where anything but evening clothes after six o'clock is welcomed with a frigid good bye, [where they walked] in calmly as if they owned the place, there is bound to be a sensation."[479] Sheppard, familiar with the etiquette of the London theatre scene, also recounted the story:

At the theatres not only the management, but some of the Toronto boys got a sensation. Three of the latter went up to the box office to book their seats. When they arrived, instead of going through the usual procedure of asking the price, they immediately demanded box seats and quickly. The box office man had great difficulty in keeping his heart pumping while he went to the manager about it. He didn't want to turn them down, but it is a never broken law in the better theatres that the only proper decoration for a box seat is either a large expanse of white boiled shirt, or an equally expanse of diamond studded neck and shoulders. It had to be done, and it was done gently, but the three were told that there were no box seats available for them, even if they had enough money to pay for the theatre. . . . Coming from a city where law suits followed fancied insults, and where they sat in boxes in any kind of clothes that they happened to have on, these three were sadly disappointed and a little bit sore, but the situation was explained to them with so much gentleness that they managed to get over it and enjoy the show from slightly less expensive seats. They are not going to law about it.[480]

Exactly what play Sheppard and friends saw was not mentioned, but as he wrote, "Most of them [the QOR men] have come to England with enough money saved up to take in a good meal now and then and see some of the plays that won't strike Toronto for many moons. . . . They will be able to put it over on their native city when they come back."[481] Ned thoroughly enjoyed causing consternation among the stuffy upper classes of London, bringing his iconoclastic colonial attitude. He searched out interesting stories to write about, and because of his life-experiences, he was often the source of them!

The most popular story that Ned reported, one which was repeated over and over again at the camp, was about the millionaires. An officer, dressed in mufti, was returning to camp on the late train from

London where he overheard several regular soldiers talking: "Do you know that all the soldiers in the ranks of the Queen's Own Rifles are millionaires? . . .Why do you know, they drive to and from the station and camp in taxicabs, and eat at the swellest restaurants in London. I've seen them going in."[482] Ned added, "It has now become a standing joke around the camp, and requests to cash thousand dollar checks are quite the thing."[483] The wealth of the men of the QOR became a common theme in the British press. MacLaren reported that "Lately one paper said we were gentlemen (everybody hopes so) and that we all earned from £1,000 to £4,000 per year. We wish we did . . . 'oh, here are the boys with all the money?' People said . . . it was certainly a great advertisement for the Dominion."[484]

The first week in England the members of the press gang were "made honorary members of the London Press Club, which has as members more famous newspapermen and artists than any other organization in the world," and also honorary members of the Institute of Journalists, which was currently meeting in London.[485] Canadian Journalists attending the conference included Mr. B. A. McNab of the *Montreal Star* and Jim Brown's boss, Mr. W. F. Maclean of the Toronto *World*.[486] As the *Daily News* reported about the young QOR journalists, "They are looking forward with relish to that trip to London. Most of them have cousins or relatives to visit; several have been made honorary members of the National Liberal Club, and the Press Club has extended a comprehensive invitation to all military journalists."[487] Scroggie pasted his membership cards of the British Empire Club, The Press Club, the National Liberal Club, and The Institute of Journalists in his scrapbook. MacLaren kept his membership card for the British Empire Club and invitations for lunch on September 10 with the Institute of Journalists Annual Conference, the annual conference dinner on September 13, and a conversazione for the journalists at the Guildhall on September 15.[488] The QOR were on the Aldershot manoeuvres until September 14, so the only reception the journalists could have attended was the conversazione at the Guildhall.

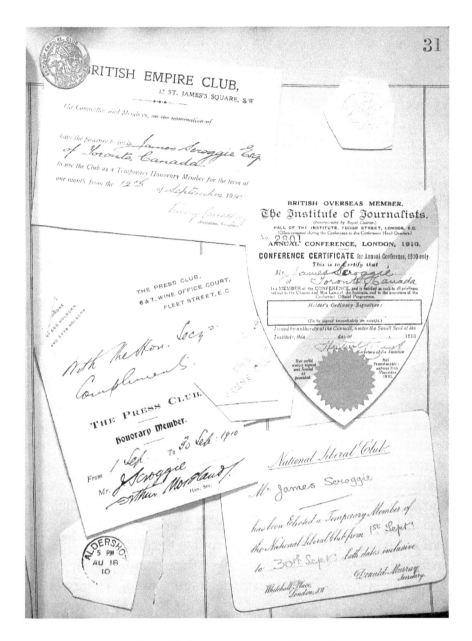

Figure 32. Scroggie's membership cards.

The camp was a place of intense interest for visitors. Scroggie humorously wrote, "The officers' quarters are jammed with dooks and counts

and one thing or another. Count de Lesseps, who startled Toronto out of its sleep for a few days by his flights in La Scarabee a short time ago, likes the meals fine and is out here most of the time. The 'dooks' don't mix much with 'us privates,' but we don't care. The other persons who come to camp are very much taken up with our Canadian game of baseball. It is a day's work to explain it though."[489] Correspondents from London visited the Officers' Mess and signed the visitor's book; F.J. Star of the *Times*, W.E. Grey of the *Daily Mail*, Stanley McKeown Brown from the *Standard,* and even Jaffray Eaton of the *Globe*.[490] Toronto people who visited have "Broad smiles wreath their faces most of the time. . . . A wonderful spirit of camaraderie has sprung up. They are all strangers on a strange land together, and if they have never spoken to one another before, they are glad to stop and have a chat, or at least exchange greetings."[491]

Some QOR men met relatives for the first time, leading to some embarrassing exchanges, "One party got in decidedly wrong, and picked up the wrong soldier for a cousin. After greetings of the most effusive kind were exchanged, including kisses from a decidedly good-looking maiden, the soldier managed to explain that he was 'Jack' but sorry to say that he wasn't the 'Jack' they were looking for. The girl was a fine specimen of English colouring when the explanations were over."[492]

Though the men's time at Aldershot might seem idyllic, there were constant reminders of the necessity to adhere to military discipline. The military police were called the "red-caps," and "If a man creates a disturbance in camp he is dealt with promptly and without ceremony. Whether he be soldier or civilian makes no difference. No civilians are allowed within the lines without passes, and in the carrying out of this order the other day an English newspaperman, anxious to obtain an interview with Sir Henry Pellatt, was challenged, and being unable to produce a pass was promptly apprehended."[493] The red-caps added that this "'is about the most orderly crowd we have had to deal with.' This is probably due entirely to the class of men that compose the regiment" but one or two "have in fact already been dealt with pretty severely."[494] Ned Sheppard wrote, "When a man leaves camp to go to town, he feels that he is the smartest soldier that ever went into Aldershot. . . . Their behaviour in most cases is exemplary, although there are exceptions who find their way into every community. These exceptions are looked after so well that they have little opportunity for disgracing the regiment's name. There are mighty few of them, and they are not of the younger men."[495]

On the morning of Saturday, September 3, the QOR was "witness [to] the review of two battalions of the Scots and Irish Guards" before Lieut.-General Sir Horace Smith-Dorrien.[496] Eaton wrote, "The troops did the march past in column in slow time, and the effect produced by the Guardsmen, nearly all six feet and over, and perfectly sized, was most impressive. The companies moved as one man, with lines absolutely unbroken. . . . As the saluting base was reached and the command 'Eyes right!' was given, the heads could almost be heard to click, so simultaneously and smartly did they turn."[497] Scroggie was impressed with this parade: "To see two regiments move about for an hour as one man, in their scarlet tunics and huge bearskin busbies was a sight that will never be forgotten by the Canadian boys."[498]

Ned Sheppard's thoughts on the display were of a more practical bent, the guards "gave them a lesson in really perfect work on the parade ground. . . . It was superb and an unforgettable lesson, but it wasn't taken to heart after all. . . . With their steadiness and general bearing there could be no fault found, but the Toronto boys wouldn't try for a minute to make this style of walking theirs. It's pretty, but what's the use? It wouldn't be any good in an attack, and for a retreat it wouldn't carry anybody away half fast enough." [499]

After the drill the QOR men, "Arrived back in their camp, [and] practised a march past by themselves before dismissing for the day. Then there was jubilation, for it was announced that they might all go where they liked, and need not return until . . . Sunday. By 2 o'clock the greater part of the regiment was away, most of the men going to London. They were to be seen everywhere in the streets of the great city, all of them taking in the attractions which appealed to them most."[500] The weekend provided locals an opportunity to visit the camp, but visitors were disappointed because "the Queen's Own were literally 'not at home.'"[501] There was to be a parade to a local church on Sunday morning; at "fall in" there were fewer than a dozen men at camp, so the parade was cancelled.

The Saturday and Sunday break of September 3–4, allowed the men their first opportunity to stay overnight out of camp and on return, "the camp was quite noisy with the recounting of first experiences with the people of the Old Country. One idea was unanimously endorsed. It was the custom of placing boots outside bedroom doors and finding them nicely cleaned when it was time to dress. Almost everyone had slept until noon."[502] Some of the men returned on Monday morning; they had visited summer resorts on the sea and "many journeyed to Felixstowe on the North Sea, near Harwich, where the liners to the continent dock. Others took boats to the mouth of the Thames. More went up to Windsor. Some went to Brighton, Bristol, Liverpool, and even two Irishmen travelled across the Irish Sea to dear old Dublin."[503]

George Argue arranged to go to London for the weekend with Rudolph Brazill, another reporter on the trip, but one who was not officially a member of the press gang. They stayed overnight at the Charing Cross Hotel and then, after breakfast at the Union Jack Club; "We walked to the Strand and met Shep [Ned Sheppard]. We walked up to the Florida, had dinner after dinner we took a motor bus around the city sight seeing." It's not surprising that these men, all with newspaper connections, were comfortable hanging around together.

Ontario's Premier James Whitney and the Hon. Dr. Robert Pyne visited the camp on Monday, September 5. "Three cheers and a tiger went up in all quarters, and a multitude of times, as soon as the men recognized their Premier and his Minister."[504] However, the day before while in London, Ned Sheppard had recognized Whitney, and he wrote, "It was rather funny to see the Premier, who is not noted for his softer feelings, standing on Trafalgar Square on Sunday when most of the boys were in London over the weekend. He stood there watching the khaki clad bunch as they walked past and never said a word. He was alone and wasn't recognized, but there was a look of pride about the Premier that showed how he felt about it."[505]

The visit of Dr. Robert A. Pyne, the Ontario minister of education, occasioned some wit's comment to the Toronto *Star*: "The Hon. Dr.

Pyne, has emerged from hiding in order to visit the Q.O.R. camp. His department's regulation to the effect that words ending in 'or' must be spelled with a 'u' doubtless led him to visit Aldershot in order that he might endeavor to persuade the regiment to make it 'Q.U.O.R!'"[506] Although Canadian newspapers continued with American spelling, the shift to English conventions was occurring in Ontario, apparently not without some cynical resistance.

Throughout their stay at Aldershot, the QOR received "invitations to 'smokers' and challenges to cricket. . . . The visitors, on their side, are looking round for the prospect of displaying their prowess at baseball if an English team can be found of sufficient daring to accept a challenge."[507] Eaton reported that "seven employees of the Toronto Post office who are in the Queen's Own Rifles were entertained at a small smoking concert by the post office employees at Aldershot."[508]

On return from the weekend away the men were happily surprised to discover "Two big fat bags of mail delivered by those in charge of the postal arrangements before they were settled down. Throughout the manoeuvres there will be two daily deliveries of mail to every regiment. . . . Letters to them need only bear the name, unit and the address 'on manoeuvres.'"[509]

As the QOR men prepared to leave Aldershot on Tuesday, September 6, to go on manoeuvres, the terrible news of the illness of several officers spread through camp: "Sickness had the officers of the regiment pretty firmly in its grasp before the camp broke up. . . . Among the private soldiers there was very little illness."[510]

A series of frantic cables to England from the wealthy entrepreneur Chester Massey (CM), Lieut. Vincent Massey's father, from Muskoka, Ontario, show his desperation to find out what exactly was happening with his son's health. Massey Sr. would have known about the illness affecting the officers through his newspaper connections; publishers John Ross Robertson of the *Telegram* and Robert Jaffray of the *Globe*, would have been aware of the illness of Lieut. Roy Gzowski, as Roy had been taken ill almost immediately on arrival to England, on September 1.[511] On September 8, CM received a telegram from a *Globe* reporter, (not Eaton) stating, "No one ill at Aldershot."[512] CM cabled the next day to his son "From Lake Joseph to Aldershot, Queens Own Canada Manoeuvres, Lieut Vincent Massey. [asking] 'How are you immediate, Father.'"[513] Cabling his son, he demanded an immediate reply, which he did not get.

As the week progressed this story developed, and the news became grimmer. But for now, the rest of the regiment "was busily engaged in packing up and striking some of the tents, for early to-morrow morning they leave Aldershot, not to return."[514] Ned Sheppard wrote "Starting on manoeuvres was no easy task. For over a week the regiment had been more than comfortable at Aldershot, treated like millionaires they were thought to be, and fed even better. The night of breaking camp, rations were handed out for next day's noonday meal. It, or they, consisted of three not overly large biscuits, and a small piece of cheese. 'Where's the rest of it?' was the first query, when this decidedly puny paper parcel was handed out. 'That's all,' was the answer, and consternation filled the camp. A wild rush took place at once for the stores, and before fifteen minutes there wasn't a bit of chocolate or biscuits left in the place."[515] The *News* was more descriptive, "hardtack, hardtack, hardtack and cheese!"[516]

The striking of camp involved taking down only half of the tents (leaving the remaining tents at Aldershot) and preparing them for travel to the next camp, with the number of men in each tent doubled. "Twelve in one little bell tent does not leave much room for moving around, but they have the consolation during the cold nights of feeling that they are warmer than when there were fewer in the tent."[517] There was only one tent for all the officers, whereas at Aldershot each had his own tent. "The company officers must sleep on the ground the same as the men, much to the delight of the latter."[518] A more sombre reason for the use of only one tent was to be revealed shortly.

As the manoeuvres progressed, there would be nights when "All will sleep in the open, with one blanket per man and one rubber sheet for two men."[519] Scroggie wrote wryly, "Tired to death of the luxury of camp life, we are off to the front at the bewitching hour of five to-morrow morning."[520] His thoughts about sleeping twelve to a tent were poetic, "It would be a touching sight to have Kipling entwine his little toes with ours amongst the cool barrels of the rifles stacked in the centre of the tent. We often long for Kip—with the same longing that the Tommy longs sometimes for his recruiting sergeant."[521]

The troops marched from Aldershot, southwest through Farnham, Bentley and Alton, halting at Chawton Park, where they camped at a park owned by a squire knight who had given permission to the government to use the grounds. Pheasants abounded in the woods "but orders are strict that no game of any sort is to be touched by the soldiers. This policy of billeting the troops in private property . . . will be pursued all through the manoeuvres."[522]

Jaffray Eaton had a unique opportunity to view the manoeuvres as an outside observer, while the other reporters were busily engaged as soldiers. Eaton wrote about the support aspects of the trip: "An analysis of the baggage transport column proved most interesting to The Globe correspondent, who rode with the troops on a bicycle." [523] There were two men from each battalion assigned to the wagon, and there was competition for this position as they were not supposed to ride the wagon, but "few of the baggage escort . . . walked more than a small part of the way."[524]

Roy Riggs described:

> Accompanying . . . are ten wagons, carrying tents, blankets, and officers' camp beds, besides two water carts and a cooker. The cooker is something quite new, and while the regiment is marching, it can be directly in the rear cooking a good hot meal for the men. As soon as it arrives in camp, the stew, potatoes, tea or whatever is the fare, is ready to be served. . . . A guard of two men to a wagon is detailed as the enemy might take away all the comforts and necessities, for once the transport is captured it means that the men sleep in the open with only a great coat for a cover and there is no meal coming until the country round about has been searched. As yet the Queen's Own men, who are accustomed to their "three squares a day" have not suffered in this way.[525]

The wagons and other carts were all horse drawn. Eaton observed that mobile water carts were fitted with water filters so that the water was potable and the men filled their thermoses while in the field.[526] Pellatt was so taken with the efficiency of the cook wagon he purchased one for the use of the QOR in Toronto.

Figure 33. Filling water bottles from a portable water cart.

After departing from Aldershot, "The first three days were occupied by the march to Winchester, the centre of the fight. And the much-dreaded sleeping in the open wasn't so bad, because the tents were sent on."[527] Arriving around 1:00 p.m. on Wednesday, September 7, the QOR camped at Avington Park, near Winchester, where they washed, but were not allowed to bathe, in the River Itchen. The Duke of Connaught, the king's uncle, was to review the QOR that afternoon. "There was some consternation among the officers as 4 o'clock drew near, as it was time for the regiment to be reviewed by his Royal Highness, the Duke of Connaught. The greater number of the men were down at the river, when the bugle sounded. There was some 'tall hustling' back to the tents, and into their uniforms. Everything was lovely, however, and the battalion was formed up in line ready to receive the Duke when he arrived."[528] As Ned Sheppard described it, the review when announced was not popular, "What the Toronto boys wanted was much rest, what they were going to get was to them but an empty honor. . . . In a cow pasture surrounded by magnificent and huge old trees the famous duke inspected the Q.O.R . . . [and] after his dukeship and six or eight stray generals had carefully inspected the Queen's Own, a short speech from the great man brought him right back to favor. He complimented the regiment from the commander down, and they purred accordingly."[529]

The duke had an historic attachment to the QOR, "I can never forget that I had the honor of taking part with the regiment amongst other Canadian regiments in the defence of the Canadian frontier in 1870."[530] He presented remarks on behalf of his nephew, the king. "In his Majesty's name I assure you of the very great pleasure and satisfaction that it is to know that you have been the first representatives of the armies over the sea to take part in the training of this country. . . . I thank you very much for your parade . . . and of the great pleasure it has been to me to see you".[531] As well, the duke brought an invitation from King George V for a representative contingent of the QOR to visit him at Balmoral.[532]

Rigg's account of the manoeuvres over the next few days, and the march across the countryside is detailed: "For the last week the men . . . have been engaged in an immense sham battle, that has been as realistic as war, and have covered over 100 miles [161 km] in marches in the last five days . . . [these days have] opened the eyes of every man . . . to see what trouble and expense the British Government has in maintaining its army and keeping it in fighting trim."[533] Along the march route the regulars had written messages in chalk: "Buck up, Queen's Own [and] Stick to it, Canadians."[534] The British Army knew that the men of the QOR were volunteers, not accustomed to the army life, and they respected their hard work.

Figure 34. Review of the Queen's Own Rifles by the Duke of Connaught at Avington Park, September 7.

The *Daily News* reported, "But they are a plucky lot these Canadian boys. To my own knowledge many of them are suffering silently with scarred and blistered feet, and last night I saw one Canadian officer whose feet were almost raw. He had borne what must have been intense agony without complaining, and to-day he paraded and marched with the regiment."[535] Henshaw makes a point of the serious condition of the men's feet, "Most of our men had blistered feet as our boots are not as good as the hob-nailed boots of the regulars. . . . Some of the men went to the doctor to have their feet attended to, and two of the sergeants fainted. Everyone was glad that they kept their fainting till after the halt and did not have to fall out on the line of march."

After the days of marching, the war manoeuvres officially began on Friday, September 9. Sheppard wrote, "War was declared at midnight; at four in the morning the Riflemen were pried forcibly out of bed, and left camp before six, to do or die—all metaphorically."[536] The Canadian

Associated Press despatch in the *World* reported that the QOR took prisoners "and immediately marched them to the rear, and regaled them with solid and liquid refreshment."[537] In the battle the Canadians also captured a horseman. "Catching a mounted infantryman's horse by the bridle, two of them prepared to lead the animal and its rider to the captain of their company. 'Hullo, chaps,' ejaculated the prisoner, 'are you the Canadians?' 'We are' replied his captors. 'Then shake hands, boys. It's the first time I've met you.' Generously responding to his advances, the Queen's Own Riflemen released the bridle and extended their hands only to see the captive put spurs to his horse and disappear, laughing down a precipitous lane."[538]

According to Ned Sheppard's account, the QOR captured two York regiment scouts on horseback, who, because there were no umpires about, resisted and returned to their regiment. The York scouts reported to their command that there was only a small body of QOR men who could be easily captured, not aware that the full QOR force was nearby. Then "an innocent-looking little girl on a bicycle, who was fascinated by the 'Canidians,' caused the downfall of the Yorks."[539] The young girl heard the York scout tell their command of the small group of QOR men, which she relayed to the Canadians, so that the York regiment fell into a trap and was surrounded by the rest of the QOR. "The Queen's Own Rifles started to pop, and pop quickly. It only lasted a few minutes, when an umpire ruled the Yorks off for the rest of the day."[540] The *Star* reported "By the war experts in charge it was considered almost unprecedented and the Q.O.R. came in for all sorts of glory. Besides that, they had more fun than anyone on the grounds."[541] In this encounter the QOR men also had hand-to-hand combat with scouts who refused to surrender, "They went at it hot and heavy, and came out of it dragging two unhappy prisoners. It was a glorious day all through."[542]

Meanwhile, in Toronto, on September 10, a cable from the Canadian Associated Press on the front page of the *Star* reported for the first time that several men of the QOR were ill with typhoid. Those who were ill included six officers and Sir Henry's secretary. The *News* also reported several serious cases of influenza with men in military hospitals.[543] The Massey family already knew that there were problems from a cable received by Chester Massey on September 9, which stated "Special to Telegram on sixth stated lieutenant Massey, and four others left Aldershot owing slight influenza not serious due to climate change. Globe cabling for particulars will advise upon receipt reply."[544] CM reached out to the *Globe* and the *Telegram* for current information: "Induced Globe to cable correspondent with regiment to give full particulars illness of officers. Globe say cabled twice already but no answer regiment on march hard to locate Globe think likely report exaggerated."[545]

But by September 10 a cable to CM wrote, "Despatches to Telegram state Capt Pellatt [Sir Henry's son] with six other officers down with typhoid. Pellatt seriously ill others slightly. J. Ross Robertson has cabled correspondent for full particulars about Vincent and if he is one of the six. Star Globe and other sources keeping me posted. Arranging to forward answer to cable immediately on receipt."[546] On September 12, in a cable to CM "The Globe special correspondent reports as follows, the influenza of several officers has developed into typhoid fever, this is regarded as somewhat remarkable since none of the privates have it. Capt Pellatt case most serious somewhat improved today Globe states all officers in London."[547] On September 12 another cable confirmed, "Following cable to you just received Vincent ill with mild typhoid."[548] This terse exchange is an example of one family's flurry of cables to find news about their loved one. It also demonstrates that the reporters, including those in the regiment, would have fairly quickly been aware of the seriousness of the health of the officers. There also seems to have been consternation that the men who were ill were of the "officer" class, not the "men," of the common class. Even in Canada during the Edwardian era there were not so subtle class differences.

In interviews, when asked about the typhus, Sir Henry said that some of the men had been ill at Lévis, and then the men had been ill on the *Megantic*, and therefore the likely source of the illness was the dinner that the officers had at the garrison in Québec City.[549] Eaton wrote "A decided gloom was cast over the Queen's Own Rifles when it was learned that the officers who have been unwell were suffering from typhoid fever instead of from influenza, as was first supposed. The remarkable fact that six should be seized by the same malady, from which none of the men were suffering, seemed at first inexplicable. A very few days after arrival at Aldershot . . . it is now thought that the disease originated while training at Quebec, and is connected by some with a dinner which the officers alone attended. The day after that dinner nearly everyone who had attended suffered severely from an attack of indigestion. It is all, however, mere conjecture."[550] Those suffering were; Lieut. Roy Gzowski, Lieut. R.K. George, Captain Kirkpatrick, Capt. Reg Pellatt, Captain Dr. Winnett, Lieut. Vincent Massey, and Sir Henry's secretary, George Riddell.[551] By September 12 another officer had also become sick, Capt. James George.[552] Much later, Lieut. H.G. Muntz was added to the list.[553]

These articles from early September were all wired by cable to the Toronto newspapers because of the seriousness of the illnesses and the necessity for immediate news coverage. The presence of typhus would have caused alarm among the Toronto families of the QOR officers and riflemen. In response to Sir Henry's allegation that the typhoid was the result of the dinner in Québec, there was a very rapid rebuttal published by the 8th Royal Rifles of Québec denying that the dinner was the cause. "It is simply foolish to say that dinner gave the men typhoid fever. . . . In the first place there were no oysters served, so that source of possible infection can be eliminated. The only other possible one that remains is the water. . . . The water did not have anything to do with it."[554] The article continued, "The time it takes typhoid to develop is from three to twenty-one days, and while it is within the realms of possibility that the officers became infected on the Megantic, it is in no wise likely." [555]

Time would show that the dreadful impact of the typhoid infections had yet to run its course on the officers of the QOR, and the answer to the mystery of the nature of the infection would only be revealed a month after the return of the men to Toronto. In the meantime, it was as Eaton had written in the *Globe*, a matter of speculation of how the men were infected, and it was more important that they recover. The illnesses did leave the QOR with fewer officers as they continued manoeuvres, thus requiring fewer tents.

The night of Friday, September 9 the men bivouacked in the open air, lying on rubber ground sheets, with a blanket and their great coats for cover; however, "a couple of courageous youths slipped out of camp to a near-by barn and were sleeping comfortably in a bed of straw when they were discovered by the detestable 'red caps.' Fair for one as it is for the other is the motto in camp life."[556] As Ned described it, "This part of manoeuvres no tents, but food and water. . . . It was a nice damp British night and everybody was chilly, but after the food was gone they were all ready to turn in. Bivouacking, it's called, this sleeping without tents, and the Queen's Own bivouacked . . . it was cold sleeping, but no boots were taken off nor pink silk pajamas slept in."[557] Had Ned's fascination with silk pajamas became a running joke with the men of the press gang?

In Riggs' account of that day and night he reported a rumor that spread among the QOR men that the accompanying transport and cooker wagons had been captured and:

> . . . the thought of a night in the open without blankets or tents was most discouraging. It was a critical march to see if the men had the right stuff in them. Most of the men by this time were limping with sore feet. They were tired, hungry, dirty and sore all over. Then the humor of the position came to them, "if mother could see me now." Pleasant memories of a hot bath, clean clothes and a good square meal came back, and before long a song broke out, and each company vied with each other to appear the happiest. At last the lights of a camp came into view, and they knew that there would be some kind of comfort waiting for them. The cooker was there, and the blankets, and the hot tea and stew warmed them up so it didn't seem so bad after all, but there was no chance to pitch a tent on such a dark night, so for the first time the men slept in the open with one blanket and their coat.[558]

Figure 35. On manoeuvres from Aldershot.

MacLaren wrote that the enemy was "waiting for our scalps, and we were waiting to get at 'em."[559] There was the sound of shots and "the roar of the cannons mightily ear-racking roars they were. The Queen's Own were wobbling on their feet. The march was a corker. 'Buck up, fellows' yelled the officers, who sat comfortably on their horses."[560] He added "We are indulging in nearly real warfare now at the manoeuvres. Blistered feet, sick headaches, hungry, choking for a swig of water don't count. These mere obstacles never hinder a soldier from working on the firing line, scouting and galloping across ploughed fields in pursuit of the enemy." After sleeping in the open on a rubber sheet, with a blanket and the great coat for warmth, there were more clashes on Saturday. "There was hard work with fun sandwiched in galore. It was the experience of a lifetime. The Good Friday Toronto sham-battle alongside of these is a complete farce, no mistake. They do it in a scientific way here, while in Toronto they do it—well, nuff sed."[561]

The most gruelling march started on Monday, September 12 and finished Tuesday, it was a march of forty km (twenty-five miles) and thirty-six hours of being awake. "After full day's rest [on Sunday] in their camp at Overton and Basingstoke, the Aldershot troops, with the Queen's Own Canadians are fit to undertake the task which lies unfolded as yet in the next twenty-four hours. So far, in the manoeuvres now in progress, the troops have practised convoy guarding and rearguard fighting, with, of course, their naturally correlated attack practises. To-night they are to get a taste of midnight marching and deployment, to be followed by a battle in which one side has made strong defensive dispositions, and the other presumably equally strong preparations for attack."[562]

Then the order was given to put coats "on over their equipment, giving them a camel appearance, as their coats bulged out at the back from the mess tins being placed there. . . . On they marched, arm in arm, for support . . . [at breaks] the men dropped to sleep on the road where they had stood."[563] The march was described by Henshaw:

> At 11 pm the column started, the Queen's Own leading the way, and that night march was the weirdest experi-ence I have ever had. The night was very dark and still, nothing could be heard but the tramp of the men's boots. After we had gone about a mile nearly everyone began to feel very drowsy and some went to sleep while walking. I did and found myself stumbling along in another company when I awoke. Horsey also was overpowered by sleep and woke up suddenly in a ditch. Whenever a halt was called nearly everyone dropped down on the road and went to sleep and when we had to move on again, the few who were awake had a hard time to arouse the sleepers.

MacLaren wrote quite simply, "Truly it was a nightmare march."[564]

After walking through the night, on Tuesday morning they were called to halt and had their breakfast, "but soon they were ordered to get into the firing line. With rushes of twenty-five or fifty yards and dropping fire, they advanced for a mile across country and through plowed fields. The enemy were forced to retreat after two hours' fighting. At 8.30 the

'Cease fire' was blown."[565] After the whistle the men marched several miles to Alton to entrain for their trip to London and the adventures of the QOR men, on their third week in England, continued.

At the same time the men endured the long and gruelling night march of Monday, arguably their worst experience thus far, the small contingent of men who had gone to Balmoral to meet the king had a luxurious experience. This invitation caused a good deal of excitement among the men. Who would go? How would they be chosen? Roy Riggs wrote in the *Mail and Empire,* "There was a whole lot of speculation among the men as to who would go, and the eight fortunate, needless to say, were well satisfied with the selection. They leave London on Sunday night and visit Balmoral on Monday, when the officers will dine with the King. They return to London Tuesday night."[566]

Sir Henry Pellatt led the delegation with a representative number of officers and non-commissioned officers.[567] For the riflemen, one private was selected from each company, so there were eight: H.M. Dunn, A Company; P.E. Newton, B Company; W.C. Hammond, C Company; J.A. McRae, D Company; W.J. Muir, E Company; W.J. Stickney, F Company; R.H. Forsyth, G Company; and Jim Scroggie, H Company.[568] Since Scroggie was a tent "commander," it's possible that the other men were also tent commanders in their companies, or possibly Scroggie was chosen because he was one of the journalists of the press gang. The reporter for *Evening Standard* noted, "Most of those who will see the King have previously seen him on the Plains of Abraham, when, as Prince of Wales, he visited Canada last year."[569] Scroggie had been in the QOR at those celebrations, and his rhyming doggerel published when training at Lévis had come true—he was to meet the king!

The men had been selected on Thursday, September 8, and they left Aldershot to go to London on Saturday, September 10, where they stayed at the Duke of York's School, Chelsea.[570] They were seen off at Euston Station Sunday night by a crowd, which included Ontario's Premier Whitney, who gave them "a hearty 'send-off.'"[571] One can only imagine Whitney's disappointment at not being included. The men travelled overnight in a private sleeping carriage and arrived at Aberdeen, where Pellatt entertained local municipal dignitaries in his saloon car, while the men "partook of the coffee [on the platform] . . . chatting affably with citizens and railway officials."[572] A local Scottish newspaper reported that "As the men stood on the platform taking their coffee, it was suggested by Baillie Taggart that 'a stan'in sack fou's best,' but the Canadians did not appear quite to grasp the significance of the remark. They thoroughly enjoyed the refreshments, however, and one of them declared that they were much appreciated. 'But we do not think much of the long journey,' he continued, 'for we are getting accustomed to them now.'"[573] Though many of the QOR men claimed ancestral connections to Scotland, it's doubtful that many could comprehend the meaning of Taggart's phrases in Scottish brogue, and no translation is attempted here.

Reporters interviewed the men while on the platform waiting for the journey to continue. "'Was there not some difficulty about you getting off for this visit?' [the QOR private] was asked. 'Well, I had some difficulty,' he replied, 'but my firm was really very willing that I should go, as is shown by the fact that they paid me three months' salary in advance, and were to the trouble to put three men in my place. Now that I have been selected for the inspection, I believe my employers will be doubly pleased.'"[574] According to the notes written on this article in the Scroggie's scrapbook, the private who replied was "Whitey Forsyth," a clerk at Manufacturer's Life Insurance Company.[575] Scroggie, or "Modest Scrog" as he described himself in his scrapbook was "Asked how he was fortunate in being selected for Balmoral, the Rifleman said he did not know, and that it was indeed a great surprise to know that he had been selected." When asked about the illness in the regiment he said, "Are there not some of your men down with typhoid fever? [Forsyth replied] Oh no, there are no men sick, but there are eight officers ill. It was dinner at Quebec that did it. They are getting well again, I believe."[576] This response is interesting since it again shows the clear dichotomy between the men and the officers. The reporter concluded with, "The detachment looked forward with pleasure to the visit to Balmoral, and they said they would always regard it as an honor to have been selected for inspection by the King."[577]

The stop in Aberdeen was necessary for "special coaches [to be] shunted and coupled to the Great North Deeside train to resume their journey to Ballater."[578] On arrival, Pellatt and the officers were taken in an open carriage to the castle. The men marched to the barracks where "After breakfast a change had to be made in dress before the men were ready to appear before His Majesty at Balmoral. The khaki uniform in which they had travelled north was quickly discarded, and soon they appeared in full regimental dress of rifle green tunics, and trousers with red facings, and busbies with red plumes."[579] At the review, "They will carry no-rifles, only side arms."[580]

Once changed, the privates were driven to the castle in an open cart while pipers played on the route. Then the king inspected the QOR. His speech started with, "Sir Henry Pellatt, it gives me great pleasure to receive you and this deputation from your regiment in my Highland home here to-day." To which Sir Henry replied, "Your Majesty, on behalf of the Queen's Own Rifles, I beg to thank you for this reception to the detachment of the regiment which I have the honor to command. . . . This day will be a red-letter day in the annals of the regiment. We, as Canadians, humbly hope and believe our visit will serve to strengthen those links which bind us [as] an Empire".[581] The king then presented medals: the Royal Victorian Order to Pellatt and Mason (third class), Rennie and Higginbottom (fourth class), and the silver medal of order to Colour-Sergt. M.D. MacDonald.[582] HM Queen Mary then met the officers.

Luncheon was served in the ballroom of the castle, and "Thereafter the company enjoyed a coach drive through the Royal policies, including the ancient pine forest of Ballochbuie, on to the picturesque Falls of Garrawalt—a favourite place with the late Queen Victoria—over part of the moorland skirting the base of the mountains, and winding at times by the banks of the River Dee."[583] After tea, the non-commissioned officers and the riflemen returned to the barracks to be entertained by the Royal Scots, while the officers dined "with the King . . . [overnighting] at the Castle until to-morrow morning, when the detachment returns to London, and will join the remainder of the regiment."[584]

Figure 36. The QOR being presented to the king at Balmoral, September 12.

While at Balmoral it's likely that several of the officers took this, the moment of a lifetime, to write letters home on the Balmoral Castle stationary, still black-edged in mourning for King Edward. One letter exists, sent by P. L. Mason to E.F. Gunther dated September 13. Mason writes, "Col. Pellatt, Rennie, Higginbottom and I have been honoured with an invitation by the King and have spent y'day [yesterday] and last night here. The place is a dream and the kindness of our hosts fulfils ones ideas of British hospitality. . . . Lord Kitchener is a fellow guest. He arrived last night. I tell you Gunther I would not like to be 'told off' by him. He is jolly, but 'that eye' of his."[585] Mason might have written several letters to family and other friends; the letter to Gunther was a bit of a brag since Gunther had been CO of the QOR and would most likely have been at the dinner if he had been on the trip.

Except for Scroggie, none of the press gang were present at the Balmoral review, so Toronto newspapers did not have articles describing the review, just captioned photographs, published some two weeks after the event. In Jim Scroggie's annotated comments on the photograph in his scrapbook of Queen Mary and Princess Mary he wryly observes, "Princess Mary gazing on my manly charms." Although the men were honoured to be invited to Balmoral, Scroggie was not the sort of man to let the pomp and circumstance cloud his satirical view of the event. The *News* published another bit of his doggerel, with a cartoon of him attired as an eighteenth-century colonial bowing to the king, titled, "An Historic Occasion," of which a selection is quoted here: "At Balmoral, / Our good old pal— / (Excuse us if our prosody is wrong), / Perhaps the accent strong / Should be upon the "mor."/ But don't get sore. / We always SAY / "BalMORal" any way. / But this is verse, / Or worse, / And so, / You know, / Some licence is allowed / To separate the poet from the crowd, / At Balmoral/ Our good old pal, / Jim Scroggie, stood, / As only Jimmie could, / The King came in, / Brave in a royal grin, / He wore no crown, / The thing was up in town, / Getting some slight repair."[586]

In contrast to the *News* account, the Toronto *Star* of September 29 announced that its *Toronto Star Weekly* edition for the following Sunday had wonderful photographs of the audience with the King and Queen at Balmoral:

> Foremost is the front page of Queen's Own pictures from England and Scotland. The Star Weekly has published in past weeks a number of photographs illustrating the regiment's famous trip, but this week surpasses all previous ones in interest, variety and color. One picture shows Queen Mary talking to Sir Henry Pellatt. . . . In another picture the pipers, who are escorting the squad to Balmoral Castle, are so lifelike that they seem to be walking out of the page. . . . There is a particular timeliness to these pictures, on account of the fact that the regiment will be home on Monday. No more appropriate souvenir of the spectacular trip has been published.[587]

The men from Balmoral returned to London on Tuesday evening, September 13. The other men from the QOR had arrived that afternoon, and the free time in London began. It's fair to observe that the next few days were probably the main reason that most of the men joined the QOR for the English trip.

CHAPTER
7

London

*The most memorable day of the Queen's Own trip to England
has passed, and not one member of the regiment will forget
the honor and praise heaped upon it by the great city
of London.*[588]

After leaving the Aldershot manoeuvres and surviving the long night's
march, the QOR men boarded the train at Alton Station, where most
quickly fell asleep for the ride to London. They arrived at the Nine
Elms station, fell in, and marched the two miles [3 km] to the Duke of
York's School at Chelsea where they were billeted. "The band of the
Irish Guards met the volunteer troops at the railway station and headed
the procession through the streets to the new headquarters. The route of
the march was lined with thousands of cheering people."[589] Along the
way the Irish Guard played "The Maple Leaf."[590] The *Evening Telegram*
wrote, "The crowds that lined the streets during the entire march didn't

see a lovely spectacle. The boys were tired out and they were untidy, clothes dusty, and some limped with sore feet."[591] George Argue wrote, "On the way our picture was taken for moving pictures, we arrived at the school at 4.30, we went to our quarters and put things away. We had supper at 5 o'clock after supper Colors gave a few of us tickets for the Empire, the Scouts and the Runts went together. It was a fine show. We saw the pictures of us, which were taken that afternoon. We left the theatre and took the tubes back to the school and we went to bed. We had marched 21 miles [34 km] and hadn't had any sleep for 41 hrs."

Photographs taken by local photographers were reproduced in British papers, as well as papers in Toronto. One photograph of the men arriving at Chelsea on September 13 was taken by the *Central News* of London and published in the *Globe* on October 1: "This photo shows the arrival of the regiment at the Duke of York's School where they remained while on their visit to London. They enjoyed the visit immensely".[592] That last sentence is probably an understatement. An article in the *Evening Telegram* was aptly titled "Now for the Good Times!"[593]

Figure 37. The QOR men arriving at the Chelsea school, September 13.

138

The centrally located Duke of York's School was an ideal place for the men to use as a base to explore London. "Most of the boys stayed at the barracks, a large, dull-looking, jail-like building for the training of regulars' children. Others were allowed to go to outside points for the week-end. Every day passes for the different theatres were given out, and of course everybody who had the opportunity went to some place of amusement. Every man staying at the barracks was ordered to be in at 1 a.m. Some complied with the order."[594] Shortly after arrival, the men received their promised compensation: "Non-coms received £3 10s and the privates £2 10s from the commander for thirty days' labor."[595] This was paid by Pellatt, not the Canadian government.

Each man had been given a couple of sheets of typed "Notes on London," a tourist guide of sorts. One point stated, "You can get a 'wash and brush up' for a penny or two at Stations and other places, also there are lots of Bath houses."[596] Since the men hadn't properly bathed in several days, "Some of us went to the Westminster Baths in the evening and parted with a week's accumulation of Hampshire dust."[597] Bathed, housed, and flush with money, the Canadians continued the exploration of London they had commenced while at Aldershot. There was only one commitment: they had to attend the luncheon at the Guildhall on Friday, September 16, but apart from that, the men were at liberty.

Other bits of tourist advice in the "Notes" were very useful: "Do not carry gold coins in the same pocket as other coins or mistakes will happen," and "Beware of pickpockets and poor neighborhoods, bunco men etc. are very expert," and most importantly, as every visitor to London can attest, "Great care should be taken to crossing streets as it takes time to get used to the different rules and the traffic moves much faster than we are used to."[598]

Pellatt and the officers were invited to several dinners through the week—one was a dinner at the Holborn restaurant, Wednesday, September 14. "Lieutenant-Colonel H. Fortescue and the officers and men of King Edward's Horse are entertaining Colonel Sir Henry Pellatt and the officers and men of the Queen's Own at a dinner at the King's Hall, Holborn Restaurant, tomorrow night. Lord Strathcona will be present."[599] A representative force of the QOR was invited: "The King

Edward's Horse, composed of colonial residents in Great Britain, have asked the officers and four non-commissioned officers and four men from each company."[600] Eaton seems to have attended and he wrote in the *Globe*, "This regiment entertained the officers and a number of non-commissioned officers and men at a magnificent banquet on Wednesday evening."[601]

The *Daily Sketch* announced, "Canadians to Have Free Run of the City" and "The Uniform to be a Passport to All Show Places."[602] The London notes gave suggestions of routes to take by the underground to tour the city and walks through parks and gardens. It also listed buildings to see when they were open and what it cost to enter them, for example, "Westminster Abbey open 9 till dusk, adm. To chapels, after 10.30, 6d., free Mon. & Tues."[603] (Pennies were called d after the Latin word denarius.)

Some clubs offered memberships to men, like the Union Jack Club: "This place is the soldiers' home in the kingdom's big city, and good use is made of it. . . . The Queen's Own boys have been made honorary members and rest there when tired, or eat substantial meals while in the metropolis sight-seeing."[604] The journalists "who are accompanying the regiment have been made honorary members of the London Press Club, which has as members more famous newspapermen and artists than any other organization in the world," and they were put up at the Yorick Club.[605] The reporters had also been made honorary members of the Institute of Journalists, which was holding its annual meeting in London.[606] They had been invited to a lunch at the House of Lords on Saturday, September 10, which they could not attend, since they were on manoeuvres. Then on Tuesday evening, there was the annual conference dinner at the Hotel Cecil, the Strand, which they were invited to, as well as a conversazione (a reception) at the Guildhall on Thursday evening.[607] There is no way to know if the men of the press gang attended any of these events, but it is possible. It is very likely that the photographer Arthur Gleason attended these events, as he understood the value of networking with Canadian press barons and by the next year, he was the official photographer of the Institute of Journalists, Canadian Division.[608]

The diaries of Argue and Henshaw show contrasting types of visits to London. Argue timed his visits of the city around mealtimes at the school, going out in the morning, coming back for lunch, going out in the afternoon, and then coming back for supper. Whereas Henshaw had lunch when he was out, when he visited the zoo he had lunch there, and he had dinner out several evenings. Another difference is that Argue went to movie theatres, whereas Henshaw saw plays: *Henry VIII, The Dollar Princess*, and *The Chocolate Soldier.* Both Argue and Henshaw, and other QOR, visited the exceptionally popular 1909–1910 Japan-Britain exhibition in the area of London known as the "White City."[609] As well, men went shopping in the stores on the Strand. Argue went to Harrod's, buying gloves and ties, gifts which were easy to carry.

Most of the men visited the best-known sites: the Tower of London, St. Paul's Cathedral, Piccadilly Circus, the wax works, the National Gallery, the Tate Gallery, the British Museum, and the zoo. Henshaw wrote, "I do not intend going into details of all the interesting things I saw in London, as that would fill a large sized encyclopedia." The *Evening Telegram* reported, "As the time in London is short, visits are rushed. Homesickness is not contagious among the boys. There is too much excitement for that sort of thing. . . . At nights theatres are visited, and orchestras please all with 'The Maple Leaf.'"[610] Tickets to music-halls were given freely, and they spent many evenings at the Coliseum, the Alhambra, the Palace, the Tivoli, and the Empire. The music hall environments would have been raucous and wild, truly an eye-popping experience for the young men from Toronto.[611]

When Henshaw was in London on the weekend off from Aldershot, September 4, he and others had dinner at Simpson's on the Strand, and a man at the next table "asked if we were the Canadians?" They struck up a conversation, and he invited them to his home, where he showed them some objects from his military career. On this visit to London, the officer, Captain Grewing, "took us to see the Royal Mint and the dungeons and other places in the Tower which the general public is not allowed to see."

The British Press was fascinated with the QOR men. The *Daily News* interviewed a dozen strapping Canadian lads who gave their impressions of London "with the frankness and engaging charm of youth."[612] One said, "I've been in New York and Chicago . . . but London is a lot finer. I should like to live in London and work in Toronto, where most of us come from, at the same time. You see, it's much more exciting here, but wages are better at home. Most of us are clerks, and we easily make £3 or £4 a week in your money."[613] The conservative nature of the young QOR men was also lauded: "We went into a bar and found women serving drinks. That is not allowed in Canada. There seems to be saloons everywhere in London, now in Toronto, with 400,000 inhabitants, there are only 110 bars, and they are not allowed unless they are attached to proper hotels. Then we saw women drinking in saloons." And he spoke with utter disgust: "That is not allowed in Canada. Our rule is no women in saloons. We aren't allowed to go until we are twenty-one, and we can't buy cigarettes until we are eighteen."[614] The reporter added the comment, based on his conversations with the lads: "One fact about the Queen's Own Rifles is worth stating. A good half of the lads now in London are teetotalers. . . . Quite half, probably three-quarters of the people in Canada don't touch liquor."[615] Although this latter claim seems fantastical, it was clear that Toronto, known as "Toronto the Good," was most certainly not as liberal or sophisticated as London or other large American cities, therefore, to the inexperienced QOR boys it would have been quite a revaltory experience.[616] Due to their youth, many were still students, and it is likely that they were not used to drinking, although, for sophisticates like the journalists Ned Sheppard, Scroggie, and their friends this was not the case. Though Brown and MacLaren, known to be abstemious later in life, probably did not over-indulge.

The *London Evening News* published an interview with six men in the QOR titled "Canada's Sons in the City." The article began by noting that "Many are clerks, workers in skilled trades, business men, journalists and University students, who have been released from their studies by the summer vacation."[617]Photographs of the young men were also included. One was R. Murray Smythe. "Out of the whole regiment of 630 men he is number 13" and was therefore known as "Lucky." Smythe (twenty) had gained nine lbs. [4kg] on the trip. He was a clerk at T. Eaton Co. in the dry goods department. He commented that "London is the finest city he has struck. . . . He had not seen a stylish dressed lady till he came to London, 'If London is stylish then Toronto is not—that's all I've got to say.'"[618] John Henry Wilson was a shipping clerk who had been in the QOR for two years: "We certainly have changed our opinion about the English Regulars during the maneuvers. . . . We had the impression that they were a rough lot. . . . It is my opinion that you could not meet a finer set of men anywhere."[619] Wilson had gained eight lbs. [3.6 kg] on the trip. Edgar R. Verrall (twenty-eight) was a clerk and had been in the QOR for eight years.[620] He was one of the best baseball players in the regiment and said, "I don't find the climate here very different from Canada except in the amount of rain you get. . . . It amuses me to see how many people go about prepared for rain on a fine day, carrying an umbrella and mackintosh."[621] The fourth Toronto man was Earl R. Suddaby (twenty). He was a commercial traveller. He told the reporter that he had gained fifteen lbs. [6.8 kg]. He had been a member of the QOR before the trip, "His views on England he found it very difficult to express. He is full of appreciation for everything he sees in London and England. . . . What astonishes me most . . . is the traffic. I wonder that there are not hundreds killed every day. I think the way the motor-omnibuses rush in and out and down the streets is something wonderful."[622] Suddaby added, "The most remarkable feature of London [is] the excellence of its theatres and music halls, of which you can never have enough."[623]

Walter J. Charlebois was described by the paper as "The Frenchman" because he was a French-Canadian who spoke English and French fluently. He was a machinist by trade, and he was an entertainer, singing songs for the regiment.[624] "On the voyage across he gave entertainments every night, and whenever an opportunity occurs at home or abroad he is ready to amuse the regiment with song or imitation."[625] Because of his photograph in this article it is possible to identify Charlie in the photographs of the QOR's Disturbance Committee.

Finally, John A. Newsome (twenty-one) was described as having "a strong body, a sound heart, and a clear head . . . the qualifications he brings to regimental duties."[626] In Toronto he was a law stationer and a newly married man who had forgone a honeymoon with his wife to join this trip. He had been in the QOR for four years and had gained eight lbs. [3.6 kg] thus far, a testament to the plentiful food provided to the men.[627] Newsome's father sent one of his letters to the *World,* which was published on October 3 under the heading "What one saw in Lunnon."[628] Newsome wrote, "We have astonished everyone here, ourselves included, at our endurance on heavy marches, etc., and when one comes to think of it, it is not remarkable that a lot of green boys from offices, stores, factories, etc., plunged into conditions that try even the strongest men, should hold their own, as to endurance at all events, with the regulars at Aldershot, which is the model of a military instructive depot?"[629]

It's interesting that the men gained so much weight; it would almost make one think that they did not eat well in Toronto. Perhaps the real reason for the adding of the kilos was the regularity of three hearty meals, mostly meat and potatoes, which were probably not the men's usual diet at home. They appreciated the hustle and bustle of London, a world-class city, and the opportunity to visit so many historic, cultural and theatrical venues, which were easily accessible due to excellent public transit. Visiting London was an unforgettable experience for them, and as much as they loved Toronto, it paled in comparison.

On Thursday, there was the opportunity to "visit the Thames Shipbuilding Yard, where a super-Dreadnought is in the course of construction."[630] Non-commissioned officers and some of the men "will be taken to Greenwich by motor car, and will be shown over the engineering and motor works and the Naval Museum. After luncheon they will be conducted through the Thames Tunnel to Canning Town, where they will see the new super-Dreadnought which is being built there."[631]

By far, the major event in London was the lunch at the Guildhall at the invitation of the lord mayor and City Corporation of London, on Friday, September 16. The *Daily Sketch* wrote, "On Friday the City Corporation will entertain the regiment to dejeuner in the historic Guildhall, to which they will march through gaily-decorated street lined [as they are sure to be] by thousands of people."[632]The men had been in their khaki field uniforms while on manoeuvres, so on Wednesday, Henshaw wrote, "This morning we were occupied in drawing dress uniforms and busbys from store." This was the most ceremonial and prestigious event of the English trip and was well covered by English newspapers and their photographers. The QOR were in full dress uniform, wearing their busbies (hats) with distinctive red plumes.

On Friday morning, the men assembled on the grounds of the Duke of York's School, where they were first inspected by Lord Roberts, after which "The men of the regiment then removed their headdresses and gave three cheers of Lord Roberts with great enthusiasm." [633] Jaffray Eaton described it: "Then, at the word of Sir Henry Pellatt, the men removed their busbies and gave three real Canadian cheers for their Honorary Colonel, whole-hearted cheers, which must have been heard for a mile around, even through the din of London traffic." [634] Then the Honorable Mr. Haldane arrived and inspected them, made remarks and "Three more equally ardent cheers were given for the War Minister and the regiment started on its long march to the Guildhall." [635]

Figure 38. Three cheers for Lord Roberts at the Duke of York School, Chelsea, September 16.

The QOR left the Duke of York's to parade to the Guildhall at 11:00 a.m. The *Mail and Empire* reported, "The Queen's Own is the fourth regiment ever accorded the honor of marching through the City of London. The Royal Marines, the Royal Fusiliers and the Buffs are the only other regiments given such a privilege."[636] One article in the *Star* asked, "Can anybody who has not been to London realize what it means to hold up London traffic along most thoroughfares for an hour or so as the Queen's Own did on Friday?"[637] In the days before, large proclamations had been posted along the route to alert people to imminent road closures. "For an hour before the commencement of the parade the world-renowned London police force had directed all vehicular traffic off the streets of the route, so that the regiment had a clear course all the way. . . . Thousands of policemen lined the roads, finding great difficulty in keeping the crowds from shoving right into the parade."[638]

The crowds were enormous. "It is estimated that not less than one million people turned out to see the Canadians. On every street of the march the crowds were so dense that traffic was stopped for hours. And the greeting the multitude extended to the regiment will never be forgotten; it was magnificent".[639] Roy Riggs wrote, "Through nearly seven miles [11 km] of crowded, cheering streets, the 600 passed. It was a proud occasion to hear praises being shouted from every side. The streets were decorated with flags and banners. 'Bravo, Canadians!' 'Well done, Sir Henry!' were the cries as the laborer and the lord took off their hats to honor the regiment. . . . And little groups from Canada gathered together to make themselves known, and one knot of well-known Toronto girls almost made the ranks waver as they waved big flags at their friends."[640] An iconic photograph of the men marching across the Holborn Viaduct, published in the *Canadian Courier*, captures the magnitude of the event.

Apparently, "The sale of souvenir booklets about the doings of the Queen's Own whiled away the time of the waiting crowd."[641] The *Canadian Gazette* noted that "The cheering was general and lusty, intermingled with cries of 'Good old Canadians!' . . . Some enthusiasts threw cigars and packets of cigarettes at the men, with the request to 'smoke their health.'"[642]

QUEEN'S OWN RIFLES IN LONDON

Not since the Troops came home from the South African War, has there been such cheering in London Streets, as when the Queen's Own Rifles marched twelve miles through the Metropolis of the Empire. Our photograph shows the Canadian Regiment passing along Holborn Viaduct.

Figure 39. The march to the Guildhall through the streets of London.

147

The parade was led by the band of the Coldstream Guards and then the QOR band. When they arrived at the Guildhall "a guard of honor was formed up of the London Rifle Brigade [Territorials], under Major King, who presented arms as the Canadians passed by. There was also a small troop of girl scouts, standing rigidly at attention, who were anxious to show too that they were Imperialists."[643] Upon arrival "the men stacked their arms in the hallways."[644] The officers and distinguished guests were received in the Guildhall art gallery: "The Assembly Hall, where the regiment and other guests sat down to luncheon, was filled in its utmost capacity, nearly a thousand being present."[645]

As for the toasts, the lord mayor addressed the men, and Sir Henry Pellatt responded. "It fell to the lot of Hon. Rodolphe Lemieux and Sir James Whitney to propose the health of the Lord Mayor and the great Corporation. The two, although on opposite sides of politics at home were in perfect accord here."[646] Other Canadian guests included Mr. F. William Taylor (with Mrs. and Miss Taylor) of the Bank of Montreal.[647]

Jack MacLaren wrote, "The men were taken to their places and waded into turtle soup as a preliminary. Ancient hall was lavishly decorated with flags, a perfect canopy of Union Jacks and British emblems. The tables were adorned with beautiful flowers and laden with countless delicacies. . . . There is little use mentioning the food. It was indescribable. Not soldiers were the Canadians—they were kings. It was a gorgeous function undoubtedly."[648] John Newsome wrote home to his father saying, "Talk about banquets, there were more dishes, liquid and solid, than I have ever seen before, big bottles labeled 'Mums' Extra Dry, 'Port,' 'Sherry,' and many others too numerous to mention."[649]

In Ontario, some took issue with the fact that the meal was a déjeuner and the menu was in French. There was a sarcastic article in the *Ottawa Free Press,* which was republished in the *Star:* "There has been another 'insult' to the English language. Just think of it! At the luncheon given by the Corporation of the City of London in Guildhall on Friday, in honor of the Queen's Own, not only was the meal described as 'dejeuner,' but the whole bill of fare was IN FRENCH. In order that there can be no doubt as to the truth of this matter, we have gone to enormous expense (one penny) and great labor (namely, reading The London Daily

Telegraph) to procure for readers actual proof of this plot on the part of some unknown miscreant to put the French language in the place of honor, and we are, therefore in a position to give the Canadian public the text of this bill of fare (no, we beg pardon, menu)."[650] The article concludes with "What are we going to do about it? How is it that cables have not brought us sizzling protests from Sir James Whitney against this additional proof that the British Empire is going to the domination bow-wows as rapidly as it can get there?"[651]

Newsome wrote, "They do their utmost to make us feel at home individually and collectively, and their best is good; why, the London City Council voted £1200, or about $7000 for the dinner."[652] The meal was a "remarkable feast which . . . consisted of seven courses and seven kinds of wine—the same for all ranks."[653] It certainly was fine dining in the French style, starting with *Tortu Claire* (turtle soup), *Mousse de Homard* (lobster mousse), *Chapon Farci aux Langues de Rennes* (capons stuffed with reindeer tongues), lamb, beef, British Cumberland ham, and for dessert, Charlotte Russe, amongst other selections.

One Toronto pundit opined, "There is no higher pinnacle. The men of the Queen's Own have supped turtle soup in the Guildhall in presence of Gog and Magog. Crowned heads feel honored when such an invitation comes to them."[654] Gog and Magog were two ancient medieval deities that protected the City of London and in 1910 their statues stood guard in the Guildhall; these had been carved some 200 years earlier.[655] Indeed, an invitation to dine at the Guildhall was an invitation of a lifetime. So even if Premier Whitney did not get to visit the king, he did indeed dine like a king!

The men were given an elaborate copy of the menu as a souvenir. Jaffray Eaton observed in an article sent by cable to Toronto and published quickly in the *Globe* on September 17, "It was interesting and significant to note before the regiment marched away the keen interest displayed by Generals and other military officers of high rank in the Canadians. As a matter of fact rank, as such, was non-existent, private soldiers and Generals fraternized in a spirit of good-fellowship, and the latter quite readily responded to all the demand for their autographs."[656] Newsome's letter to his father in the *World* added more:

Figure 40. Cover of the souvenir of the Guildhall luncheon.

150

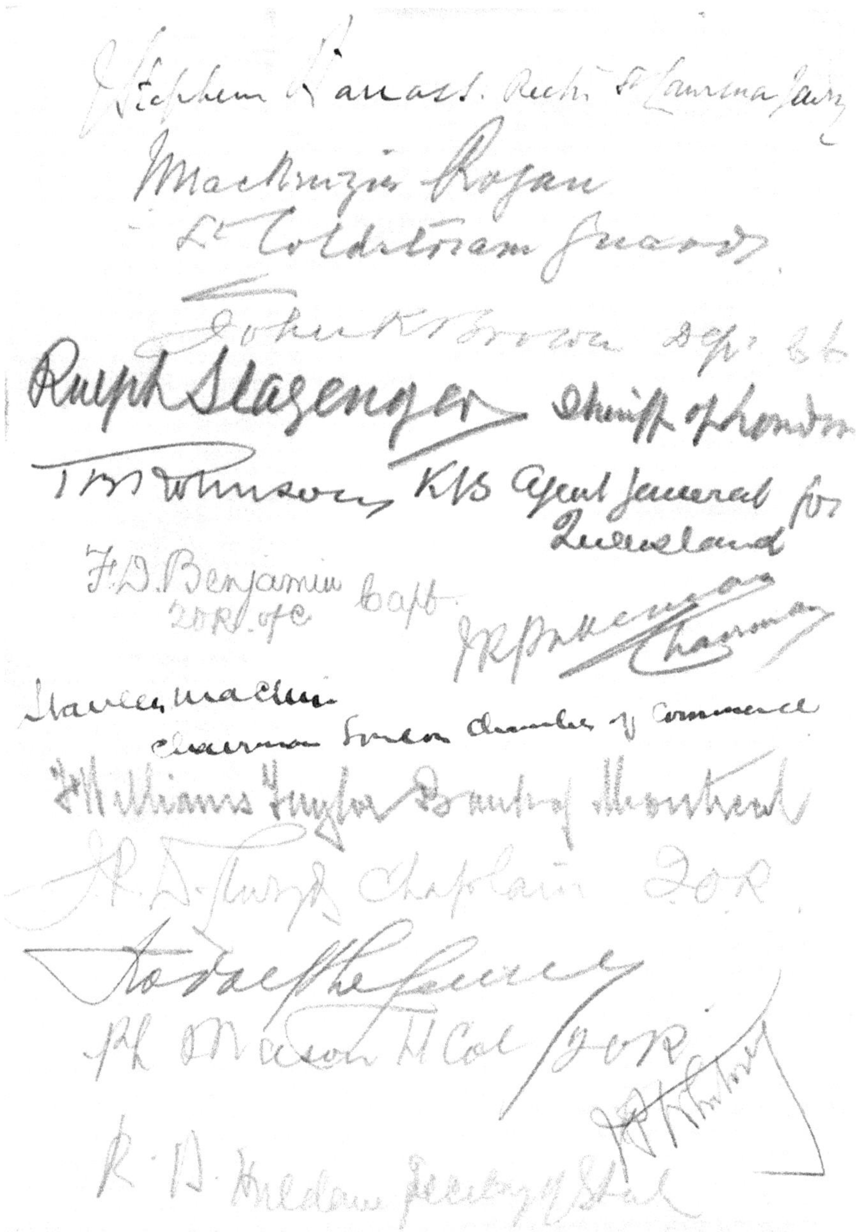

Figure 41. Inside cover of a souvenir menu featuring autographs.

I am sending you my menu with some fairly distinguished names on the covers, as I asked several for their autographs; among others you will see Premier Whitney's, who got a wonderful reception and made a great speech and Lord Strathcona, with whom I had the pleasure of talking. I told him if all the signatures he wrote out (as he was writing autographs for several of us) represented cheques, he would soon be bankrupt; he replied 'Yes, my boy, if the cheques were for large amounts.' He was kind enough to laugh at my little joke; a fine old chap he is. I also talked with Hon. Rodolphe Lemieux (our postmaster-general). He made a fine speech. Take care of the menu. It will be invaluable in the years to come, as it contains autographs of men like Gen. Mackenzie Heniker, the Lord Mayor, and others. I talked with every man whose signature is appended.[657]

Today, although the menus are quite rare, they are not invaluable.

Ontario's premier, Sir James Whitney, told the *Globe,* "The function at Guildhall was one never to be forgotten by those who participated in it, and the warm and generous hospitality of the Lord Mayor and Corporation of the city of London was most marked. Indeed, one finds it very difficult—unless one is a professional journalist—to give a satisfactory description of a function like the one in question."[658]

After lunch, the men marched back to the Duke of York's school by a different parade route. Argue wrote in his diary, "We arrived there at 1. We sat down to the big dinner at 1.30. it was over at 3.30. we left the Hall at 4 and paraded back to the school, No. 8 leading. We went 6 mile this time. We arrived back at 6." It's interesting to note that the press gang's, H Company, No. 8, was in the lead on the return march.

Considering the amount of wine served at lunch, and knowing that many of the QOR were not drinkers, at the reunion of the trip in 1939, Major Lindsey commented, "It is to be noted that there was not a single casualty on the way home."[659] In Newsome's letter he wrote, "I was at the Palace Theatre . . . and saw moving pictures of ourselves being inspected by Lord Roberts when marching into the Guildhall, and these were taken only four or five hours previous to seeing them on the screen. I tell you London can teach us many things that we never dream of in speed in all directions."[660]

None of the reporters wrote in detail about the experience of the march through London, but it must have been exhilarating. In the Toronto *News* the account of the march from the armouries to Union Station on the departure evening of August 13 provides a description, which is in some ways comparable, although not of the same magnitude:

> Hand-clapping was followed by cheering; then suddenly came a roar of applause, from outside as the 25,000 within sight of the Armories caught a glimpse of the head of the khaki-clad men coming through the doors. The men were stepping out, and swinging along at the trail in great style this time. It was a fine sight. . . . Then the band, 100 strong, under Bandmaster Waldron of the 10th Royal Grenadiers, blared forth with the Queen's Own Regimental March, the men began to smile. It sounded good. . . . Seldom has such a crowd of pushing, puffing, perspiring people pushed, puffed and perspired their way down town to see a regiment march to the station. . . . Street cars were blocked, carriages, autos, bicycles and motor-cycles held up, and jammed in between the neck-craning thousands who seemed to have no fear of being tramped on or run over. Cheering and handclapping accompanied the regiment from the Armories to the time their train rolled out. They 'swung their way through the admiring thousands' who crowded onto the street car tracks, regardless of consequences. It was one triumphal march, all right.[661]

The QOR men in their dress uniforms made quite an impression on Londoners, a Canadian resident wrote to the *Star*:

Another instance of how completely "the Canadians" have caught the popular fancy of Londoners was brought to my notice in the King's road, Chelsea, on Saturday. I was a long way from the Duke of York's school where the regiment is quartered and was hurrying along, scarcely conscious of a sidewalk display so familiar as to have long since ceased to attract my notice. I refer to the work of that curious tribe that seem to abound in London, the pavement artist. This man had the usual number of 2-foot square [.6 m] pictures—landscapes, seascapes, figures, and what not—drawn in colored crayons with more or less cleverness. I was almost past when I saw a life-sized portrait, head and shoulders, of a Queen's Own corporal as he appeared the day before on the way to the Guildhall. The detail of the uniform as far as I could see was quite correct and underneath was written "One of our Canadian visitors."[662]

One other official event that week included Pellatt distributing the colours to the 4th Ealing Troop of Boy Scouts on Saturday, at Gunnersbury Park.[663] Jaffray Eaton, in a cable despatch, wrote that Pellatt "delivered a short address to the boys, telling them something of the way in which the Scout movement was advancing in Canada."[664] A few officers attended this event with Pellatt. The QOR men continued their explorations of London. Diarist Henshaw took the opportunity to visit his uncle at Grafham Grange, Guildford, returning to the barracks on Sunday evening.

Pellatt and the QOR Officers emphasized repeatedly that the behaviour of the men must always be exemplary, and since no negative incidents made it into newspapers, it's assumed that there were none. But over 600 young and mostly naïve men let loose in the megalopolis of London no doubt led to various interactions of a personal nature, those which could not be written about in Toronto newspapers, nor described in letters and postcards sent home. On the return to Toronto, one member of the QOR remarked that the men had "acted as gentlemen," alluding to the likelihood that while on visits to dance and music halls, the young men partook of more than just music and dancing.[665] Furthermore, considering the number of men on the trip, it's more than likely that both heterosexual and homosexual encounters occurred, even though the latter were illegal at the time. London was a large, exciting city and appetites of all sorts could be explored with anonymity and probably were.

On Tuesday, September 20, the QOR men "ended their week's holiday in London. . . . At half-past 12 they left their quarters at the Duke of York's School, Chelsea, where a large crowd gave them a hearty 'send-off'. . . they marched over Chelsea Bridge and arrived at Nine Elms Station. . . . Within ten minutes they were 'all aboard' and away, the Scots Guard band playing the 'Maple Leaf' and the Canadians cheering their thanks out of every compartment."[666] Argue wrote in his diary that they packed their clothes and handed them in, and then they "fell in at 11.20 and at 12.30 we started off. The Scotch Guards played us to the station . . . 3.30 we had arrived in Whitechurch, we fell in on the platform and marched 5 miles to where we were to camp." The Queen's Own band remained in London until the sailing date of Saturday, September 24.

When interviewed by the *Times* about London, one QOR rifleman expressed, "Not one of us will go back with any of the prejudice against Englishmen that we had got in Canada from some of the rapscallions we sometimes meet over there. From the Lord Mayor and his turtle soup downwards, we have had such hospitality as we should never experience in our own country."[667] The rush of the experience of being in London was overwhelming, and MacLaren wrote, "There is only one regret, and that is that the army manoeuvres are on [and] after the good time in London. The Torontonians would rather go home."[668] After five weeks away from Toronto, the men were nonetheless "keen to do their best . . . [over] the next three or four days."[669]

CHAPTER

8

Salisbury Plain, The SS Canada and Home

*Well done, Queen's Own! This was the thought that found
expression in the magnificent demonstration of welcome
which marked the homecoming of the gallant regiment yesterday.*[670]

As the men entered their sixth week away from Toronto there must have
been feelings of homesickness, or at the least, an element of traveller's
fatigue. As MacLaren had written, many wished they could go home after
London. Departing the afternoon of Tuesday, September 20, the QOR
headed to the British Army manoeuvres on the Salisbury Plain, arriving
at Whitchurch Station where they detrained and marched 8 km to their
camp. For this portion of the trip, the QOR's final involvement in the
1910 war games, there are only brief accounts published by the soldiers
of the press gang. Most information comes from Jaffray Eaton, who as
an observer was able to record the events as they transpired.

Up until now it can be said that the QOR were the "darlings" of the media and the British people, while in these manoeuvres they were just cogs in the great wheel of the army. To be fair, the QOR men knew this, and some looked forward to these "battles" as the highlight of the trip. Since this was an official military operation, there are no photographs of the QOR, and there are few photos of the event in local papers.

The general situation of the "war" was described in the *Globe* with a simple map of the theatre of operations.[671] For these manoeuvres the British Army was divided into two forces: the Blue Army, under the command of Lieut.-General Sir Charles Douglas, which was located generally to the west of the town of Salisbury; and the Red Army, commanded by Lieut.-General Sir H. Smith-Dorrien, which was located to the east of Salisbury. The QOR were assigned to the Red Army and beginning from a camp near the town of Whitchurch, northeast of Salisbury, they had to march southwest towards the Blue Army.

With 50,000 members of the British Army, regulars, and territorials (British militia volunteers) engaged, what was the role of the QOR? Ned Sheppard wrote, "England's whole pack of war dogs had been unleashed for the occasion, but although the strength of the army was 50,000 men, there was but little for the Canadians. . . . Their part in the manoeuvres consisted of marching for three days in fairly easy stages."[672] MacLaren wrote, "The last manoeuvres were a cinch as far as we were concerned. The Queen's Own were on the reserve force and about 40 miles [64 km] of marching were covered in three days which is considered pretty easy. To be candid, in all their military experience in England the Q.O.R. privates at least did very little of anything but route marching."[673] Eaton wrote that the Red and Blue forces were in position for a big battle on Friday, the 23rd, and that the QOR had marched for fifteen miles [24 km] along the River Avon and were in "fine condition" and "eager for blood."[674] Excerpts from George Argue's diary plotted the route: September 21, they marched fourteen miles [22.5 km] through Salisbury to Quarley Hill, "where there was an old Roman trench"; Thursday, September 22 they marched sixteen miles [25.7 km], "Near where we camped there was an old Roman amphitheatre built years ago;" and finally, on Friday, September 23, they were up at 1:30 a.m., and they marched fifteen miles [24 km] to Chislebury Hill.

Argue's description of what happened next was quite concise: "We were put into action. We attacked the hill. We were taken out of action at 5.30." Henshaw's eyewitness account was similarly brief but dramatic: "[We] heard the booming of guns in front and to our right. . . . Soon we heard the crackle of rifles and the 'put-put' of the machine guns and knew that we were in for a busy time. Soon we emerged from a wood and I had a glance at the scene of mimic fighting. . . . [The enemy was on a steep hill, 200 feet [60.9 m] high, the] . . . din of rifle fire was now tremendous and as we neared the top by rushes . . . when we were put out of action by the umpire."

It was Jaffray Eaton's article, where Eaton, ever the keen observer, presents an account of the panorama of events as they unfolded, named the names of all the significant military and political leaders and observers and recounted the dramatic role of the QOR in the taking of Chislebury Hill: "It was an old Roman camp called Chislebury Ring, the top of this ridge, which overlooked the entire surrounding country."[675] Eaton described the scene:

> More like a huge picnic or a day at the Exhibition in Toronto was the ground on top of the ridge at Chislebury Ring than a battlefield. People from all the country round were gathered on this point of vantage to see the fun. At noon parties opened picnic baskets and had lunch somewhat cruelly, in sight of the soldiers who had eaten nothing since last night. The onlookers were a real obstacle to the proper conduct of the battle at that point, but nothing could be done. They all had manoeuvres passes. There were many great men among them. Under a Union Jack indication the director of operations, General Sir John French, talked with Hon. Winston Churchill, dressed in the uniform of a major of Oxford Yeomanry. Farther off, on a point by himself, watching the operations in civilian clothing stood Field Marshal Lord Kitchener, the 'man out of a job,' and

the man who many say ought to be in Mr. Haldane's position. Lord Roberts with his daughter, was there in an automobile, still in his old age vitally interested in all the work of the British army. John Burns was there with a bicycle, on which he followed the manoeuvres, all through . . . chatting all the while with the men. [676]

Of these well-known figures of nineteenth- and twentieth-century British history, the one who might be least known today is John Burns. At the time, Burns was well known as the first working-class man to become a cabinet minister in British parliament; he was also known for riding his bicycle.[677] His conversations with the working men of the army, and possibly the QOR, are unknown, but talking with them aligned with his roots in the working class.

New to the armed forces, "The army airship 'Beta,' a small-sized dirigible balloon, hovered throughout over the scene of operations, and during each day covered the whole area where troops were engaged. She was, however, quite neutral. . . . Colonel Clapper rode the balloon and "dropped reports at points marked by a large white cross on the ground."[678] So unusual was the deployment of the *Beta* that photographs of it were common in the newspapers. For the first time, two airplanes were also employed, however, due to bad weather, including fog and wind, they were not used successfully. In fact, one pilot was captured after he landed, and the umpires ruled him out.

But at Chislebury, the Blue Army held the ridge, and it was the QOR of the Red Army who were tasked with taking it:

It was a long, hard climb, and there was very little cover, and the hail of imaginary bullets around and among them was continuous, but still they kept on, and the last fifty yards [45.7 m] of the ascent was gained with one rush and cheers. . . . The Queen's Own captured it from the Blues. But sad to tell, when the umpires had a short discussion, it was decided that the gallant 600 Canadians must return to the bottom of the hill again.

In making the ascent, the loss of life among them would have been too great. Nothing daunted by their reverse and their sadly reduced ranks, "all that was left of them" were preparing to make another even more determined assault on the heights, when they were suddenly attacked in force on their right flank and in rear. It might have fared ill indeed with the Queen's Own then, but just at this juncture General Sir John French ordered the "stand fast" to be sounded, and the annual manoeuvres of the British army for 1910 were over.[679]

Ned Sheppard concluded, "It was a considerable hill. Built on very much the same style of architecture as Scarboro Bluffs, it was hard charging. . . . The army manoeuvres turned out to be the original cinch. . . . Logically, legally, and metaphorically, they were all left lying cold in death on the battlefield, but actually they were in the best of health."[680] It's not surprising that Sheppard compared the Chislebury Hill to the Scarboro Bluffs—both were white, but while the bluffs were sand, the hill was chalk. [681]

In summary Eaton wrote:

> The army manoeuvres were then, it must be owned, a bit disappointing to most of the Queen's Own, as these had, to a great extent, been looked forward to as a sort of grand climax to their period of training in England."[682] The last night in England was uncomfortable, the men had to bivouac and as the luggage was 14 miles [22.5 km] away, they slept on the ground, or in haystacks, wagons and sheep pens, and lay around fires. Around one in the morning singing of "Has Anybody Seen Sir Henry?" . . . [announced] the arrival of the Queen's Own transport that was thus heralded . . . [and] blankets were speedily issued to those who were not already too comfortable to bestir themselves."[683]

A British Pathé film clip of the great autumn manoeuvres of 1910 survives. [684] In this, Sir Winston Churchill is seen on his horse, Lord Roberts is being driven in an open car to observe the operations, there is an airplane flying about in the fog, and finally, there is a dramatic charge of the horsemen of the cavalry, which shows the immense scale of the exercises.

In a detailed analysis of the manoeuvres, Sir John French, inspector-general of the forces, praised "the worthy representatives of Canada." Sir John thought that they had done extremely well.[685] A dinner at the Ritz in London was held for the foreign officers and Pellatt and the other officers were invited. An article in the *Times* wrote that "with the exception of Dr. Llwyd, the chaplain, [other QOR officers] were unable to be present owing to the return of the regiment."[686] However, Llwyd seems to have been on the SS *Canada* for the trip home, so the account in the *Times* was mistaken.

Argue wrote, somewhat dryly, about the last morning in England on Saturday, September 24: "We handed our blankets in and had breakfast and at 8.30 we marched to Dinton station, the Buffs played us down. We left Dinton at 10.30 dinner was handed out to us on the train. We arrived in London at 1.30." Ned Sheppard described it as "A Great Send-Off by all the Regulars," and the "Leicester's fife and drum band marched them to the station, two miles away [3 km], playing before and after the Canadians' bugle band. Cheers, then more cheers, were going throughout the march."[687] The Duke of Connaught was at Dinton station with a farewell message from the king wishing the QOR, "God-speed and a safe return to Canada."[688] The *Times* wrote, "There was a great exchange of fraternal greetings and tokens between the Canadians and the Buffs, to which regiment the Queen's Own is now unofficially affiliated, and when the trains for Liverpool had gone scarcely a cap of shoulder badge remained to the members of the East Kent battalion—who had accompanied the Canadians to the station—nearly all had been given as souvenirs to their comrades of a month."[689]

In London, the QOR band and luggage were collected, and the train continued to Liverpool, arriving at 5:30. The QOR band led them to the ship, the SS *Canada*, it "sailed at 6.50. we got our rooms and at 9 we had supper then . . . went to bed. There was a big crowd to see us off."[690] The sail-away was quite dramatic: "As the vessel cast off the band played the National Anthem, while the riflemen cheered lustily and waved hats and handkerchiefs, and the steamers on the river sounded their sirens or whistles until the Canada was some distance down the Mersey."[691]

The lord mayor of Liverpool was present at the train station to wish the QOR farewell, and his wife, the lady mayoress, gave Lady Pellatt "a bouquet of pink carnations."[692] However, Lady Pellatt did not board the ship. After she saw the men off, she returned south to see to the care of those left behind due to typhus, one of whom was her son, Reg. Only one of the sick men, a frail George Riddell, returned with the QOR on the *Canada*; the others in various degrees of ill-health stayed behind to recover.[693] However, it is possible that the Pellatts were already aware of the sad news at the time of the ship's departure, that Lieut. Roy Gzowski had died that morning in the hospital at Aldershot.[694] The week previous, the Gzowski family had been notified that young Roy had taken a turn for the worse. One of his brothers, Norman Gzowski, was mid-Atlantic on his way to Roy's bedside when the news broke.[695] The men were informed of his death on Friday, September 30. Jaffray Eaton wrote, "Their sorrow was intensified to deepest gloom on Friday morning when the news of the death of Lieut. Roy M. Gzowski was conveyed to them by marconigram to Sir Henry Pellatt."[696]

Lieut. Roy Morris Gzowski was given a full military funeral at Aldershot on September 30. "The Buffs furnished a firing party, and the pipers of the Cameron Highlanders played the lament, 'The Flowers of the Forest.'"[697] Tragically, Gzowski's death was the second of a young rifleman during the QOR's 1910 semi-centennial events.

Unfortunately, it quickly became apparent that the westward transit was not equal to that of the eastward. The SS *Canada*, although of the same line as the *Megantic,* the White-Star Dominion, was not nearly as accommodating. There was no first class, the officers were in second, and all the men were in third class, with six men to a cabin.[698] Jack MacLaren described it as being in steerage and complained that the portholes could not be opened, so there was no fresh air.[699] Ned Sheppard was particularly annoyed with the lack of bathing facilities onboard. The men had not bathed since London and had been looking forward to doing so while at sea, which did not happen. Sheppard declared, "The Queen's Own was not a very clean regiment when it marched from the train to the ship at Liverpool." And it was also not very clean when they arrived in Toronto where they were all looking forward to "Toronto, the city of hot baths and civilian clothes."[700]

The meals were declared inedible. "The first breakfast resulted in a small riot . . . [there was] hurling of plates of bacon and eggs in front of the steerage steward and asked if that were the sort of food to give human beings. After that things brightened considerably."[701] George Argue seems to have made friends with the cook and wrote, "After supper we had a feed in our state room of fish and onions and ice-cream . . . [and the next night] After supper gander [another QOR Pte.] and I went to the cook and got the grub for our supper in our room we got everything ready for the supper and then went on deck till 9 o'clock. We then went to the room and . . . We made a racket for awhile and went to bed." To add to the misery of the trip, the weather was awful. "The only place worthwhile was on the deck and during three days of the voyage rain fell and there were rough storms."[702]

Then the men were affronted when they were issued immigration cards. "When a day out they were all handed neatly printed cards, to be shown to Government officials whenever required."[703] Sheppard explained, "It was a sad blow to Canadians born, and although there was a certain amount of bad feeling because they had been treated so differently in the mother country . . . [regardless] they came into Canada immigrants."[704] MacLaren reported that on the immigration card, "written on the back in twelve different languages is a paragraph to the effect that it should be kept for three years and ready to be looked at by Canadian immigration officials whenever required."[705] He then added that most likely these cards would be put into a gilt frame. Scroggie pasted his into his scrapbook, and Henshaw affixed his to his diary with the added note "Specimen of immigration cards issued to the first immigrants who were ever lunched at the Guildhall."

Arriving at Québec City, the SS *Canada* had two passenger lists: the first was the Passenger Manifest, the second was the Outgoing British

Passengers List.[706] On the manifest, Eaton is listed as a journalist, MacLaren is listed as a correspondent, and the other members of the press gang are listed as clerks. But on the Outgoing British list, it seems the lads had a bit of fun identifying their professions: Brown was a packer, Riggs a bookkeeper, Scroggie a trader, Sheppard a carpenter, and MacLaren a designer. Eaton, in second class, was a tourist.

One important event on board was when Lieutenant-Colonel Mason "on behalf of the officers and men, [presented] a silver cup to Lady and Colonel Pellatt. Colonel Mason made a short speech in which he told the commanding officer that the cup was bought by subscription amongst all ranks, and meant to show a little of their appreciation for the worries and expenses he had incurred."[707] Pellatt "expressed the opinion that the regiment, in all its ranks, had done everything possible to uphold the honor of the city and country it came from."[708]

A concert was also planned in the third-class dining hall on the last night of the sailing. However, there was some controversy when the men arrived in the hall: "Not so pleasant was a certain amount of ill-feeling arising last night over the inclusion of the Stars and Stripes in the decorations of the dining saloon on the occasion of the concert. The officers of the regiment refused in a body to attend the concert unless the flag was taken down. The flag stayed up, and the concert was held."[709] The QOR band did perform but not in uniform.[710]

The *Canada* arrived at 10:00 a.m. on Sunday, October 2, and the ship docked "under the shadow of the citadel . . . [where] They saw the purple and green and gold of the maple trees, the blue haze of the Laurentian hills and the bright sun of an early fall day, and these things all spoke of home."[711] With the ship's docking, the Toronto *Star* dispatched another reporter, E.J. Archibald, to record their arrival. There was no military presence at the dock, but there were hundreds of local citizens waving hats and handkerchiefs. "When the first shore line was thrown and made fast, a cheer went up. . . . Then the band broke loose . . . played 'O' Canada, and that started them cheering again."[712] Songs were sung, some "were choice. . . . Some of them don't look well in print."[713] What was most noticeable were the perfect English accents: "Let's all go down to the Strawnd, An' have a banawa."[714] While the men were still on board, the local telegraph company sent messengers "with sheafs of blanks in their hands, and man after man spent a quarter on his first message home . . . [and importantly the messengers brought letters from home]. Letters came off in bundles, too, and many a man dropped into a sunny corner of the deck to read the home news."[715]

Figure 42. The review at the docks, Québec, October 2.

After lunch was served, the men heard that Governor-General Lord Earl Grey was to review the troops on the Dufferin Terrace, and that would require a long climb up the hill to the Chateau Frontenac. "A howl of dismay went up. 'Got to tramp up that hill and listen to another speech, eh? We've listened to 'bout forty-seven speeches now,' growled the Queen's Own."[716] It was decided that the QOR officers would meet Lord Grey on the terrace, and then he would review the men on the dock. After the inspection, Lord Grey made a few remarks: "He was proud of them, and all of Canada should be proud of them too."[717] Eaton, in the *Globe* wrote Grey's comments, "Colonel Sir Henry Pellatt, I congratulate you on the example you have given and the service you have rendered to Canada and the Crown. . . . I may say that these uniforms have been worn for the past two months by day and often by night, sometimes lying in the dust of the road, and their appearances here to-day reflects great credit both on the men and their tailor."[718] That Lord Grey commented on the durability of the uniforms was an acknowledgement that the government had paid for them!

Archibald, the *Star's* Québec correspondent, praised the men on the dock: "All national egotism aside, the Q.O.R. looked like a real regiment drawn up there in the sunlight. They had the look of a regiment which had really done a little hard service. The uniforms were used a little, the rolled overcoats just a little worn, and the gun stocks slightly scratched. They were a more effective-looking regiment than the one that marched away seven weeks and one day before; they looked as though they could give an account of themselves if it were necessary."[719]

Once on the train, the men were given lunch boxes. The *News* wrote, "It took but a few minutes to entrain and get away to Montreal. It had been arranged that sandwiches and coffee were to have been handed around on the train, and a hush fell upon the songsters when it was announced that they had gone bad and had to be thrown away. Never was a Colonel of a regiment more beloved than when a dining car was attached and the men led in small squads to a real meal."[720] MacLaren wrote, "After travelling four hours on the train, half-starved and suffering the pangs of hunger, they were marched into the dining car and given the grandest meal tasted in some time . . . a big, fat, juicy steak and salmon relieved the soreness on the train and the troops actually fed in the dining car between Quebec and Montreal like real citizens and not like soldiers out of mess tins."[721]

They arrived in Montréal around 9:00 p.m., had three hours of free time, then boarded the train for Toronto at midnight. Henshaw and his fellow travelling companion, Horsey, both lived in Montréal and left the regiment at that time. The trip to Toronto was long, but not arduous. As Argue wrote in his diary, "We were 20 miles [32 km] outside of Montreal all night and at 5.30 we pulled out, it was a very slow trip up. Breakfast 10 . . . Peterboro we arrived at 1.50, the City had us sent lunches down to us. We stayed there till 2.30." They then continued on to the Leaside Station where the two trains were joined into a single train, twenty-one coaches pulled by two engines, which arrived in North Toronto at 5:00 p.m. where they detrained and walked to the armouries.[722]

At the North Toronto station "The whistle of a locomotive and the cheering of the crowd, which now filled every point of vantage, windows, on roofs and on the tops of box cars, announced that the special train was pulling into the station. It arrived with bronzed young soldiers leaning out of every window and the band playing merrily."[723] The *News* wrote, "When that big black mogul with 15 cars attached nosed into sight of North Toronto station yesterday afternoon at 5 o'clock, 5,000 pairs of straining eyes thought it the finest, bravest, prettiest locomotive that ever sailed along a pair of tracks."[724] The point was made that "Admiration of the Queen's Own Rifles has been mounting up for many weeks, fanned by the accounts sent from the Old Country."[725]

There were, on arrival, welcoming remarks, but as Sheppard wrote, "To be quite frank they are rather dreading an official reception in Toronto. They have had a plethora of receptions and reviews, and want to get home as quickly as possible. However, they are quite prepared to obey orders and march as far as necessary. They will look like soldiers who have seen active service, there is no doubt of that."[726] Mayor Geary spoke, "Welcome home, and on behalf of the people of the loyal city of Toronto, [I] express the fervent hope that the future career of the Queen's Own Rifles may be as brilliant and glorious as its past has been, and trust that health, happiness and prosperity may ever be vouchsafed to its members."[727] Sir Henry responded and then "Taking off his silk hat and waving it in the air Mayor Geary led the cheers for Sir Henry and the Queen's Own Rifles."[728]

The *Telegram* reported an overheard conversation between two women: "'What an awful job it must have been for one man to take all them fellows over,' said a sympathetic lady with a sigh. This so pleased her neighbour, she turned and said with mock solemnity, 'Yes it was. He had to wash and dress them every morning.'"[729]

The parade route to the armouries was lined with thousands of people. "They were greeted at the station . . . with as much enthusiasm as if they had returned victors from a conflict, and their progress through the city streets was a veritable triumphal procession."[730]

When dismissed "Such handshaking and hugging and kissing and backslapping when the words 'Queen's Own Dismiss' rang out in the flag bedecked armories. . . . When a fond mother and sister had got through hugging their young soldier, the Telegram heard the girl ask her brother if London was all it was said to be. The reply she got was remarkable 'It is more than it has ever been said to be. The contrasts impressed me most. In one short hour we moved amid a riot of opulence and a sink of inequity and filthy squalor. It made us thoughtful and thankful,' he added, with a meaning glance at his mother."[731]

Jack MacLaren wrote:

> After each company had carried their accoutrements into the store rooms they returned to the main floor, and received a few parting words from their captain. The men in the company closed in on the cap. In a bunch that resembled a Rugby scrum, and when the last word was in they sent up three wild cheers and a tiger—all but K company did this. K company be it known, is the regiment's choir, and have a printed hymn book all their own. They call it "Hymns Ancient and Modern." It is precisely what it is called. So when they saw their captain's mouth shut for the last time, they broke into the most delightful harmony, rendering their "Doxology" in a manner unlike anything to be heard in either St. Paul's Cathedral or Westminster Abbey.[732]

Clearly the men's affection and respect for their company officers had strengthened and solidified during the trip, as had, no doubt, their friendships with their fellow QOR.

Of course Scroggie wrote a poem for the *News*: "Let's cheer / they're here / that was a noble sight / last night / Sir Hen / ry and his merry men . . . . / And then / we saw Sir Hen / likewise the men / the buglers blew / the bandsmen too / the drummers did their best / banging like all possessed / the slide trombones / blatted in joyous tones / said Scroggie:

What a dickens / of a fuss / for us! / And Scroggie said: What rot / we've only been to / Haldershot!"[733]

One change, noticed by many mothers in the reception crowd at the armouries, was the presence of moustaches on their sons' upper lips, with "new grown moustaches, [showing] advanced years and enlarged experience."[734] The *Telegram* even had a small cartoon drawn, captioned "My, Hasn't it Grown."[735] The issue of moustaches had been the topic of an article in the *Star* earlier in the summer: "The Moustached QOR" which began with "Canadians have been somewhat puzzled by the report that Sir Henry Pellatt's troops have been asked to let their moustaches grow, preparatory to visiting England."[736] While in Québec it appears that some men took the opportunity to begin cultivating lip hair, Jaffray Eaton commented on August 17, "The sun has shone brightly each day . . . which . . . had had the usual effect on the faces of all. It has also had the effect of showing up the young moustaches much better, especially the fair ones."[737] A poetic ode to moustaches appeared in the *Star* after the return, penned by an unknown correspondent under the title "Their Moustachlets" it went thus, "We would not mock the Q.O.R. / Nor at their whiskers scoff / We'll spread the glad news near and far / When'er they shave 'em off."[738]

The men were anxious to get home. "The arrival and the parade and the final 'fall out' in the Armories were done with in little more than an hour and the crowds went home. . . . The six hundred men who have been gone seven weeks from home, slipped back again into their places. . . . At six the streets were jammed. . . . At seven they were empty. . . . The city had swallowed her sons as again as a parched garden drinks a little rain."[739] After going home, George Argue wrote in his diary, "Had bath and changed clothes. Supper 8. After supper daddy and I went to see uncle John. Home 12." Except for Jack MacLaren, all the reporters still lived with their families in Toronto, and all probably did the same when they arrived home: baths, dinner, and then telling stories.

With the trip over, and the men back at work or at their university studies, it was time for some reflection. The editor of the *Mail and Empire*, H.H. Wiltshire, who wrote opinion pieces in the Saturday paper under the pseudonym "The Flaneur" praised the trip, writing:

It is no exaggeration to say that everybody in Canada has followed with a vivid, almost a personal interest, the visit to England of the Queen's Own Rifles of Toronto. We have naturally been proud of the efficiency displayed by the corps when on duty, and more than pleased at the hearty reception accorded our men on their arrival, the handsome way in which they have been treated throughout the visit, the kindly feeling displayed everywhere, and the splendidly enthusiastic farewell at Liverpool as the corps embarked on its home trip. It has been a journey of which every one of the six hundred will have an acute and grateful recollection for the remainder of his life; it has been a physical benefit, a course of education in several ways, and an added bond of imperial unity. Sir Henry Pellatt has initiated a movement which will become general and periodical throughout the whole British Empire. The financial cost to him had, of course, been heavy, but it would be difficult to show how one hundred thousand dollars could have been more beneficially expended. It is satisfactory to record that from the start everything has gone without a hitch, every detail has been carried through with military precision and discipline. It is now our duty to see that such a welcome is given our returning fellow-citizens as they will show fitting appreciation of the magnificent record they have made.[740]

This praise for Pellatt and his marvellously generous gesture was almost universal.

On the editorial page of the *World,* remarks were glowing, but with a caveat of the pain and suffering of the service of privates:

It is one thing to march down the home streets with the crowds applauding and the friends and relatives smiling welcome and the old town all alight with the sweetness that belongs nowhere but home. And it is another thing altogether to have marched those weary miles, with blistered feet, with aching bones, with muscles stretched to the limit of fatigue, and with the plodding grimness of a tired unflinching soul. Read Zola's 'Downfall' if you want to understand all that misery. You can't be too good to the boys who did it. It was done for Canada, done for Toronto, done for the old flag. All honor to Sir Henry, who made it possible. The boys will tell you they would not do it again, not for ten thousand dollars. Of course they wouldn't, not for the sake of going to England, but if the Empire asked it, if Canada needed it, if the King called for them, do you think the boys would hang back? That is the eternal wonder of patriotism and loyalty and sacrifice, and our Canadian boys have blazed the path.[741]

The comment about not wanting to do the trip again likely came from Brown; who knows what put him off the trip, the rigorous training? the stress of London? the military life?

A final poetic verse from Scroggie bemoaned the fact of going back to work, titled "The Morning After." It went "A strange electric atmosphere possessed the local room; / The able City Editor had quite forgot his gloom. . . . The Special Writer leaned him back / and fixed his lovely tie. / He looked about the office with a / glad and merry eye. . . .Twas Scroggie telling of his trip / to dear old London town. / Describing how the turtle soup / went gaily gurgling down. / Or how he and his messmates slept / in soft and slippy clay / or how they felt when they were / told to rise and march away / Or what the King remarked to them / or what Smith-Dorrien said, / Or how it felt to march twelve miles / on half an ounce of bread. / Just then the Cit. [city editor?] bestirred him / self and raised a lusty shout / 'How do you lobster think we'll / get the bally paper out?'"[742] Scroggie, and the others of the QOR, probably told, and retold, stories of the trip for many years to come.

On return to Toronto, Sir James Whitney, Ontario's premier, pro-nounced the QOR trip a great success: "Too much praise and appreciation

172

can hardly be devoted to this subject [the trip] and Sir Henry Pellatt deserves every word of commendation heard."[743] Whitney experienced the quiet pride of seeing the QOR men in London and at Aldershot, saw a dramatic London parade, and relished the thrill of dining at the Guildhall. It is no surprise that he praised Pellatt and the QOR.

It was announced on October 6 that there would be no fall training for the QOR, the English trip being sufficient. This meant that for those members of the regiment who did not go overseas, there would be no fall manoeuvres.[744] At this time, Sir Henry was planning to return to England to offer support to those officers who were still recovering in hospitals. Only one recovered member had returned with the QOR, Sir Henry's private secretary, George Riddell. Vincent Massey's parents and brother, Raymond, went to England to be with him. He eventually returned to Canada in January of 1911, and because of his illness he was absent from all the QOR training in England.[745]

When a recovering Dr. Winnett, one of the QOR's doctors on the trip and an associate coroner for Toronto, returned home on November 11, his comments to the *Star* were very specific concerning the illness. Harking back to the comments made by the 8th Royal Rifles of Québec, when they stated that no oysters were served at the Garrison dinner and that there might have been something about the trip on the *Megantic*, Winnett attributed "The epidemic of typhoid which attacked a number of the regiment's officers, and was responsible for the death of Lieut. Gzowski, to some clams eaten aboard ship on the voyage over. 'Those who took those suffered afterwards, while those who refrained were all right,' said Dr. Winnett."[746] Eating contaminated clams and oysters was a common cause of typhoid fever.[747] However, it was not the eating of clams on the *Megantic* that had caused the outbreak.

At the conclusion of the trip, the Militia Department in Ottawa convened a board of medical officers to meet to investigate the cause of the outbreak, which they correctly identified as an epidemic. They met November 28 and Dr. Winnett and other officers of the QOR gave evidence. The board determined that the food served by the caterer hired for the officers at Lévis was the source of contamination, as two waiters, who had also eaten the Officers' Mess food, contracted typhoid fever at approximately the same time the QOR officers did.[748] The milk at Lévis was considered a possible source of infection but ruled out when it was determined that the milk provided for the men and the officers was from the same supplier. Ultimately, no specific source for the infection was identified. Ned Sheppard, who criticized the food served to the riflemen, probably considered himself lucky to not have eaten the "better" food served in the Officers' Mess! Truly, if 600 men had been struck ill with typhus it would have been an epidemic of disastrous proportions. As it was, it was still a tragedy that weighed heavily on the men of the QOR.

In the end, the success of the trip depended on three sources of funding: Pellatt, the Canadian military, and the British military. The Canadian military department covered the expenses of the uniforms, the Lévis camp, the guns, and the drill sergeants. The British military covered the expenses of Aldershot, the Duke of York's School residency, ammunition, and the autumn manoeuvres. Other costs of the trip were all up to Pellatt "as his own expense": transportation costs and salaries, altogether estimated at $40,000, not an inconsiderable amount at the time. Possibly as much as 1.3 million Canadian dollars in 2024.

There was much discussion about Pellatt's support of the QOR celebrations during the year. Was it for the greater good or was it for his ego? With the passage of time and the change in Pellatt's fortunes, public opinion ascribed the trip to his vanity. In 1910 civic philanthropic endeavors of this scale were uncommon in Toronto. The Massey family's founding of the Fred Victor Mission for homeless men in 1894 was a significant early social endeavour. It was after 1910 that wealthy families began to support the formation and construction of the Art Gallery of Toronto, the Toronto General Hospital, the Toronto Housing Corporation, and the Royal Ontario Museum. Philanthropy was a means of supporting the public good, and for some of Toronto's newly wealthy families had the added benefit of providing an entrance into high society.[749] Some philanthropic gifts were intended for the well-being of a specific community, for example, the Massey family's donation of the student centre at the University of Toronto, Hart House, which was planned beginning in 1910.[750] Similarly, Pellatt's support of the Queen's

Own Rifles, was specific to the QOR, although Pellatt did support other Toronto civic philanthropic projects, such as the Royal Ontario Museum.

Pellatt seems to have been a soft touch if someone with a request for assistance came asking. At his funeral, one mourner told the story that when he approached Pellatt, in his position as an elder of a church asking for a donation for the building fund, Sir Henry asked what amount was needed, and then "promptly wrote him a cheque for the full amount."[751] The church in question was not identified, apparently it was a church for a Black congregation.

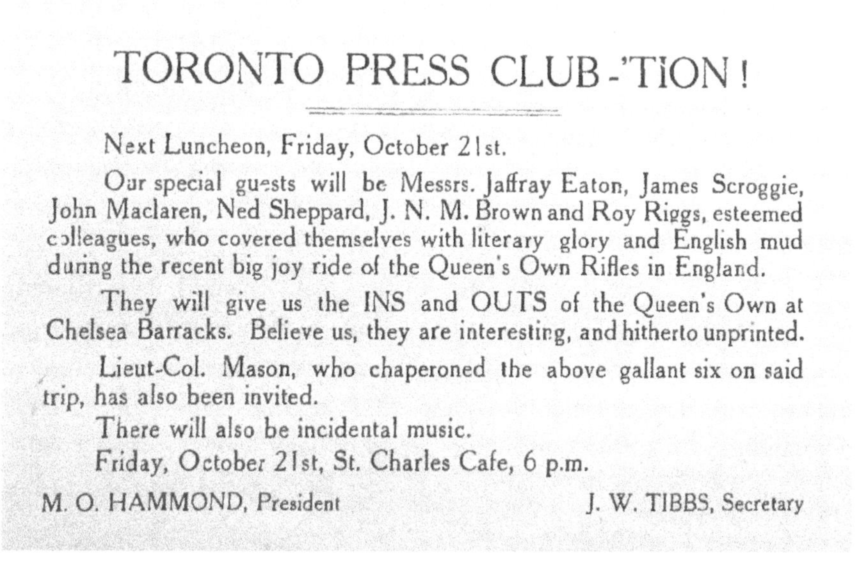

TORONTO PRESS CLUB -'TION !

Next Luncheon, Friday, October 21st.

Our special guests will be Messrs. Jaffray Eaton, James Scroggie, John Maclaren, Ned Sheppard, J. N. M. Brown and Roy Riggs, esteemed colleagues, who covered themselves with literary glory and English mud during the recent big joy ride of the Queen's Own Rifles in England.

They will give us the INS and OUTS of the Queen's Own at Chelsea Barracks. Believe us, they are interesting, and hitherto unprinted.

Lieut-Col. Mason, who chaperoned the above gallant six on said trip, has also been invited.

There will also be incidental music.

Friday, October 21st, St. Charles Cafe, 6 p.m.

M. O. HAMMOND, President   J. W. TIBBS, Secretary

Figure 43. The invitation to the Toronto Press Club reception for the press gang.

On arrival back in Toronto, the members of the press gang resumed their journalistic careers, but one more event waited for them. They were feted by the Toronto Press Club on Friday, October 21, when they were invited to a "Toronto Press Club-'tion!" to be held, beginning at 6:00 p.m. at the St. Charles Café.[752] It was announced that "Our special guests will be Messrs. Jaffray Eaton, James Scroggie, John Maclaren, Ned Sheppard, J.N.M. Brown and Roy Riggs, esteemed colleagues, who covered themselves with literary glory and English mud during the recent

175

big joy ride of the Queen's Own Rifles in England. . . . They will give us the INS and OUTS of the Queen's Own at Chelsea Barracks. Believe us, they are interesting, and hitherto unprinted."[753] For these young men, as long as they stayed in journalism, the Toronto Press Club continued to play a role in their career development and social lives.

As the QOR's eventful year continued to its close, the newspapers of Toronto continued to cover local and international news. City news included the ongoing debate about the best location for the viaduct across the Don River, either along Bloor St. as recommended by the city, or Howard Avenue, which was advocated by others. International news was dominated by the revolution and overthrow of the monarchy in Portugal. Then there was the trial of Dr. Crippen and Miss LeNeve. Crippen's trial began on October 18, and he was quickly found guilty on October 22. After an appeal was rejected, he was hanged on November 23. Miss LeNeve was acquitted and released on October 25.[754] The second Grey Cup football championship was held in Hamilton in November at the Hamilton Cricket Club, where the Hamilton Tigers were defeated by Toronto's Varsity team. Thousands of fans from Toronto, mostly young collegians, took special trains to Hamilton for the game, overwhelming the community after the win with parades downtown, both in Hamilton and Toronto. The comment was made that the chaos came from "having a metropolitan affair conducted at the village level."[755] The rivalry between Toronto and Hamilton has very deep roots! And with that, the eventful year of 1910, ended.

CHAPTER
9

The Great War, The Reunion and The Passings

It is said that 1910 was a year to be alive if you were a young man and lived in Toronto and belonged to the Queen's Own Rifles. [756]

The conclusion of this story will be told in this chapter in three parts; first up to WWI; second, after the war to the 1939 reunion; and then the final stories of the members of the press gang and a few other notables of the trip. For some of the men of the press gang membership in the QOR lapsed after the trip. [757] Some men of the gang were friends going into the trip, and although the trip may have tested those friendships, they remained friends afterwards. These young men were colleagues before England through the nature of their work and their memberships in the Toronto Press Club. [758] In 1912, Jack MacLaren, then of the *Mail and Empire*, ran for secretary, and Jaffray Eaton, of the *Globe*, ran for auditor—only Eaton won. [759]

As the years passed. some reporters remained in newsprint journalism, while others did not. Then the Great War happened, and it changed their lives; three died in WWI, while three others lived their lives with various successes and challenges. Roy Riggs was not identified as a reporter for the *Mail and Empire* before the trip; he was a stenographer. After the trip he was employed as a secretary to Mr. John Westren, the general manager of the Dunlop Tire Company.[760] When war was declared, Riggs went to England and enlisted in the Royal Flying Corps.[761] His first flying assignment was two months in Cairo, Egypt, then he was transferred to France early in 1917. He piloted planes "at the speed of 135 miles [217 km] an hour when it was in full flight, and it was the fastest machine in the squadron." While overseas he had written his family a card: "Wish you were here to enjoy the fun."[762] He had been flying photographic missions over occupied German territories when he crashed over France on July 22, 1917.[763] The article announcing his death read, "Another of Toronto's young Kings of the air has been killed."[764] The last paragraph of the obituary spoke such profoundly sad words: "He was a young man with a bright future, of a quiet, retiring disposition. The knowledge of his marked success in flying came through his friends in France. He will be deeply missed by a wide circle of friends as one of those clean-living, clear-visioned honest lads who gave his life for his country."[765] He clearly loved flying and I wonder, was he the young reporter standing beside Jim Brown at Toronto's first aviation meet in 1910? Riggs is commemorated at the Jarvis Collegiate Institute War Memorial.[766] He was the first member of the press gang to die.

Jaffray Eaton continued as a reporter at the *Globe*, still living with his grandfather, the Hon. Robert Jaffray, the president of Globe publishing company.[767] Like other young journalists Eaton's reporting did not appear under his name. In 1912 he was given an assignment to examine social issues on Ontario farms. This resulted in a series of articles, which appeared in the *Globe* from July 10 to July 23, taking him from Windsor in the west to Prince Edward County in eastern Ontario.[768] A summary article was published on January 2, 1913, where he concluded, "The Ontario farmer of to-day is a modern man. He is no longer shut off from the world. He has a telephone in his house. His mail is delivered at his home every day. Already in a few favored localities he has electric light in his buildings. The day is in plain sight when electricity will do much of the farm work. . . . The year 1912 has done much to make the farmer's life more attractive. The next few years will do more."[769]

To keep up his rifle skills Eaton became a founder of the Toronto Newspaper Rifle Association.[770] He was on track to follow in the Jaffray family footsteps into the management of the *Globe*. However, family tragedy intervened when his father, Christopher Eaton, died suddenly in February of 1914, and Jaffray returned to Owen Sound to close his father's family business, the Eaton Brewing and Malting Company.[771] During this time, Eaton continued his commitment to the 147th (Grey) Battalion, Owen Sound, becoming a major, and then the Great War was declared in July of 1914.[772] The responsibility of dealing with his father's estate meant that he could not go overseas until matters were settled, but eventually he did and when in England he wrote his uncle William Jaffray about going "to France [to do] his bit."[773]He was killed in action at Passchendaele, October 26, 1917, "in his first engagement at the fighting front."[774]

The story of his death was recounted by Lieut. Tom Rutherford, an Owen Sound friend, in a statement written some ten years later: "[It was 5 a.m.] we [Jaffray and Rutherford] shook hands and each with our little sections of four men, went his separate way. . . . A flash of light in the semi-darkness behind us told us that our shells were coming, so we laid low in shell-holes lest any fall short. The first rounds came in almost a straight line right in front of us, but the second rounds were not so good and many fell short as the guns had very little platform in the mud a mile behind. I think it probably was one of these that got Jaffray Eaton as I found his bones when I visited Passchendaele 16 months later before we left Belgium to come home to Canada. Someone had apparently covered him up with earth where he fell and put up a little picket cross about a foot high, but the rains had washed his skull clean and while I could find no identity disk I knew it was Jaffray by his teeth which were quite distinctive."[775] It might seem that Rutherford's comments about finding Eaton's remains are unfeeling, but consider the horror and shock of death that he had become accustomed to over his time at the front. It is a testament to his respect for Eaton that he returned to search for his remains to give himself and Eaton's mother some closure. Ultimately, the location of Eaton's grave is not known and he is commemorated at the Menin Gate, Ypres, Belgium.[776] Twenty years later, when Norman Lambert retired as an editor of the *Globe,* he spoke about "that gallant grandson [of Sir Robert Jaffray], Major Jaffray Eaton, who joined the Globe reportorial staff about the same time as I did, and later fell in the Great War, will ever stand out in one's mind as one of the finest gentlemen in this whole world."[777] Jaffray Eaton was the second member of the press gang to die. He is remembered at the Grey Roots Museum & Archives, Owen Sound.[778]

Ned Sheppard worked for the *Star* into 1911, after which he travelled to New York where he worked for the *New York Sun*, then by February of 1912 he was in Vancouver as city editor of the *Vancouver Sun*.[779] The editor of the *Sun*, John P. McConnell, had worked with Ned's father in Toronto on *Saturday Night*.[780] By 1916 Ned was managing editor of the *Vancouver Sun Weekly*.[781] Then he enlisted in the Royal Flying Corps, leaving his wife, May, and infant son, Ned, in Vancouver.[782] While in service in France, he contracted tuberculosis and was sent home medically unfit in 1918, spending the next years of his life in sanitoria across Canada, mostly in BC, at the Tranquille and Balfour sanitoria.[783]

In typical Ned Sheppard fashion, his love of newspapers led him to publish a paper while at Balfour, the *Balfour Bugle*, with the motto "Wherein We Blow Our Own Horn" with a Latin dedication "AVE ATQUE VALE:" translation, "Hail and Farewell."[784] The first issue was printed October 1, 1919 and consisted of four pages, with the usual Ned humour the pages numbered 1, 6, 13 and 18, because he promised a paper of eighteen pages! Its intentions, proclaimed on the front page, "The Balfour Bugle is the result of the desire of the patients . . . to give [amongst other things] some concrete sense of the honor conferred on the Sanitorium by the visit of His Royal Highness the Prince of Wales."[785] The *Bugle*, written entirely by Ned, conveys some of the realities of being seriously ill, but with a sense of morbid humour; there is an article titled "What to Wear" informing those men who are bedridden, "Silk hats will not be the order of the day . . . [imagine] his Highness entering a bedroom confronted by an apparition languidly reclining, tastefully arrayed in pink pyjamas surmounted by a topper."[786] Only later, in another comment, is it poignantly apparent that Ned, talking about the editor as "the bed-ridden autocrat," is writing about himself.[787] He adds "The Bugle may blow again and it may not. Much depends on the vagaries of a well known member of the bacillus family. . . . In the meantime we hope that the Bugle does not blow too brazenly. We are modest people, wishing to give no offence [at least not often] and hoping that our first issue will be taken in the spirit that it was written."[788]

One person who reminisced about Sheppard was E.A. Corbett, his roommate at Balfour.[789] (This Corbett was no relation to the A.V. Corbett of the 1910 QOR.) Ned "occupied a big double room facing the lake." Corbett was taken up to the room he was to share and a knock on the door elicited the response "Friend or enema?" Ned told Corbett, "I [have] a hole in my left lung as big as a beer mug. I've been trying to keep it filled. . . . [then] He lifted his emaciated six-foot-two frame, staggered to a dresser and produced a bottle of Johnny Walker."[790] Corbett wrote, "This was my brilliant and fascinating roommate for nearly a year. He was a dying man . . . but his cheerfulness and courage made our room a rendezvous" for staff and patients alike.[791] "He occupied himself with the publication of a weekly newspaper called The Balfour Bugle, which he typed out himself and had published in the city of Nelson. It contained . . . one brilliantly written major article, news notes and ribald jokes. The 175 patients waited eagerly each week for its appearance."[792] Corbett left Balfour in the fall of 1920.[793]

In a rare moment, Ned describes himself when he wrote, "The above space [a blank box] was reserved for one of those brilliant flashes of Rabelaisian humor on which the Editor prides himself."[794] The writing in the *Balfour Bugle* harks back to Ned's 1910 columns in the *Star*, however, unlike the unbridled enthusiasm for life in those columns, in these there is a wistful tone, a pragmatic introspection, the perspective of a man facing death. The Balfour sanitarium "operated between April 1917 and closed December 1920, when the remaining 25 patients were transferred to Tranquille, near Kamloops."[795] At the time of the June 1921 Canada census, Sheppard was at a sanitorium in Gravenhurst,

Muskoka, Ontario, while his wife and son were in Vancouver.[796] He returned to BC where he died on October 18, 1921.[797] Ned was the third member of the press gang to die. Until the end of his life, he continued to "riff" on the theme of pyjamas, silk or otherwise. There must be an inside joke here, one which we will never know about.

Next, the lives of the three remaining journalists and Pellatt will be reviewed from 1910 up to the time of the reunion dinner held in Toronto in 1939.

Jim Brown continued working at the Toronto *World*, then in 1913 he moved to Calgary where he began working at the Calgary *News Telegram*. While in Calgary he made (or renewed) the acquaintance of Kate Wiltshire, a journalist for the *News Telegram*. Kate was the daughter of H.H. Wiltshire, the editor of the *Mail and Empire*.[798] Soon, a daughter was born to the couple. Adding to the family was his adoption of two sons from Kate's previous marriage. In 1916 they moved to Vancouver, both working as journalists for the *Sun*. In 1918 he became managing editor of the *Vancouver Sun*. Although there is no direct evidence that Brown moved to Vancouver because of Ned Sheppard, it certainly seems more than a coincidence that he would go to the *Sun* just when Sheppard was leaving. Brown also worked at the *Vancouver Star*, the *Vancouver Daily World*, and the *Vancouver News-Herald*.[799] Brown did not enlist in WWI; his only military experience was his time with the QOR on the English trip, however, his younger brother, W. E. Alway Brown, did join the QOR and was killed in action near Arras, France, September 4, 1918.[800]

One of Brown's stepsons recounted a story about when he was an editor of a Vancouver paper: "The owners asked . . . Dad to write an article of some mines that were going under. It appeared the paper owners were loaded with poor stocks that they wanted Dad to write a false editorial on and laid a Thousand dollar bribe on his desk. I can still see the hurt on his face as he came home that day with the news that he had resigned." [801] As a result of this resignation in March of 1932, Brown started a local weekly Vancouver newspaper, *West End Topics*. The review in the *Vancouver Sun* wrote, "If succeeding issues of West End Topics maintain the standard of the first, I imagine that

Mr. Brown will have little cause to worry. His lead editorial, in which he pokes fun at our local economic theorists, is refreshingly sensible. Most of these little community weeklies fall into the error of believing that to get along one must toss bouquets in all directions. Mr. Brown wisely includes the occasional ripe tomato." [802] This paper seems to have been short-lived, possibly as few as five issues, not for lack of news, but lack of advertisers.[803]

Figure 44. Jim Brown, Vancouver.

Brown continued working in Vancouver newspapers as well as writing feature articles for *Liberty*, the *Toronto Star Weekly*, *Canadian Business,* and the *Canadian Mining Magazine*. One article written for *MacLean's* in 1937 addressed an innovative labour situation at the Consolidated Mining and Smelting Company in Trail, B.C.[804] The content of the article is not a matter for discussion here, but what is worth examining is the style of writing in comparison to how he wrote in 1910. Brown gathered the facts, interviewed people, asked questions about the issues at the plant, and wrote a detailed analysis of the unique labour and management relationship. The article, like those he wrote in 1910, had a "folksy approach," the attempt to get the view of the common man: "During the last evening in Trail, I stood in a hotel lobby and watched the faces of the men and women who passed. Upon none did I see the big city tenseness, civilization sourness, life's bitterness."[805] This does echo his writing style twenty-seven years earlier. He and his wife returned to Toronto in December 1938, in time for the 1910 reunion dinner planned for 1939.[806]

At the time of the trip, Jim Scroggie had been a reporter for the *News* since 1909. He was a son of George E. Scroggie, who for twenty-two years was the advertising manager of the *Mail and Empire*, a man who, when he retired in 1929, established his own advertising agency.[807] The Scroggie family had newspapers and advertising in their blood. Jim worked at the *News* until 1911. The next year he worked at Gagnier Advertising and starting in 1913 he began as an advertising agent at the *Evening Telegram*, a post he held with increasing responsibility for the next forty years.[808] He did not serve in WWI, but his younger brother, George T. Scroggie, did. George was seen in one of the photographs of the men in Toronto in Scroggie's scrapbook.

After the trip, Jack MacLaren left the *Telegram* for the *Mail and Empire*, but by March of 1912 he was with Brown, at the *World*.[809] MacLaren, while at the night desk, broke the story of the sinking of the *Titanic* in April of 1912: "Remaining late at the office long after the editorial room was deserted and the paper had been 'put to bed,' he received the first bulletin over the telegraph wire telling that the S.S. Titanic, the world's greatest liner, was sinking in mid-Atlantic on her maiden voyage. Using telephones, messengers, automobiles and horse-drawn cabs, Mr. MacLaren managed to round up sufficient printers, stereotypers and press-room men to rush an 'extra' on to the street with the biggest disaster story of the generation."[810] The "EXTRA" had an article about Major Peuchen of Toronto's QOR, who was a passenger on the ship. This was likely written by Brown and MacLaren, who through their stint with the QOR were familiar with him. "Major Peuchen has never seen active service. But on account of his long experience, is considered one of the most efficient military men in Canada. When the Queen's Own went to England for the army manoeuvres in 1910 he took a distinctive part in the regiment. The Victorian Order of the third degree was conferred upon him by King George at Balmoral Castle. . . . He is an officer of striking appearance, rather stout, and wears a neatly-cut, pointed beard, slightly streaked with grey."[811] (However, he was not a member of the Balmoral contingent.) His family and friends had called the *World* for any news. It was known that Peuchen was a member of the Royal Canadian Yacht Club and was an avid yachtsman. This was mentioned in the article, and would seem to have been a desperate comment, since being on an ocean liner in the middle of the Atlantic is not comparable to sailing on Lake Ontario. Ironically, it was this that saved his life, as he was allowed into a *Titanic* lifeboat specifically because he had nautical experience.[812] Peuchen died in December 1929 after the stock market crash.[813] Amazingly, in 1987 his wallet was recovered from the *Titanic* wreck debris field and included his Toronto streetcar tickets![814]

After the "extra" hit the streets, that same day, MacLaren received a personal letter from the managing director of the *World*, H. Maclean: "Both W.F. and I thoroly [sic] appreciate the good work you did in helping to get out the Extra this morning. It was real journalism in the best sense of the word and gave our opposition a good beating. Nelson tells me that much of the credit of this is due to your prompt action."[815]

Jack's career after his time at the *World* included working at papers in Calgary and Vancouver, cities chosen perhaps not coincidentally, but because of his friends Brown and Sheppard.[816] It is known that he worked at Gagnier Advertising Services in Toronto, where Scroggie had worked, when he left in 1916 to work as a war correspondent for the *Telegram* for nearly a year, and then as an editor of *Saturday Night Magazine*.[817] In his attestation papers at his conscription in 1918, he lists his occupation as a journalist.[818] He stated his previous military service as six months with the QOR, showing he joined the QOR specifically for the trip. His wartime service was as a wireless operator in Niagara-on-the-Lake.[819] After the war he moved into the advertising business, eventually establishing his own firm, MacLaren Advertising in January of 1935. As well as owning the broadcast rights of *Hockey Night in Canada*, his company's clients included significant companies: Imperial Oil Ltd., Canadian General Electric, and General Motors of

Canada.[820] The connections between Jack MacLaren and Jim Scroggie were intergenerational and long-lasting. Scroggie's brother, George T. became a barrister around 1921 and acted as the in-house lawyer for MacLaren's Advertising Agency and as the "agency's company secretary for more than forty years."[821] In 1938–1939 MacLaren and Scroggie worked together as the organizers for H Company at the QOR reunion banquet.

Figure 45. John (Jack) A. MacLaren, July 1930, Toronto.

After the trip Art Gleason moved his photography studio from Montreal to Toronto, and from 1911 until 1914 he was a "photographer to Canadian Northern Railway . . . and for three years covered the line from Quebec to Vancouver Island. Construction was in progress in the west and had to be photographed. . . . Travel . . . in an official party of three was mostly by packhorse. The party had 12 packhorses, to be led or enticed over logs flung across rivers and streams."[822] In 1917 he established a commercial photography studio in London, Ontario, although "his greatest satisfaction was from news pictures."[823] One of his early commercial jobs was aerial photography of the London region. He remembered "steadying a 15-pound Graflex camera in the cockpit of a World War I biplane one spring day in 1919 [while he] nervously focused on western Ontario wobbling below and snapped the shutter."[824]

After the trip the 600 men went their different ways, and only a few threads are followed here: F.R. Henshaw continued in his military career, and George Argue became an accountant in Toronto.[825] The three men who shared the Lévis press tent went their different ways: M. R. Helliwell served in the WWI Canadian Army Medical Corps and became a family doctor in Kincardine, Ontario; R.B. Johnston remained in the QOR and served in WWI, after which he became a lawyer practicing in St. Catharines, Ontario; and C.E. Molland served in the UK armed services in WWI and returned to China to work in the Chinese Postal Service in Shanghai.[826]

The two well-known men of the entertaining Disturbance Committee, Walter Charlebois and Joseph Salvaneschi, continued in the QOR. Charlebois was a machinist, and he also entertained at concerts in hospitals with the QOR orchestra.[827] He was involved in Toronto's Bow Wow Minstrels (BWM), which were formed in 1910 by forty employees of the T. Eaton Company. This was a blackface performance group.[828] The BWMs had "learned the art of minstrelsy and [sang] for the pleasure and profit of benevolent societies and social clubs," including Toronto's Dale Presbyterian Church Choir.[829] Their concert in February of 1911, their second annual, had "a chorus of forty singers, six end men, and half a dozen ballad singers . . ."[830] and included bone and tambourine playing, and "buck and wing dancing, step-dancing and banjo playing."[831] These minstrel performances were offensive to Toronto's Black community, who had requested, unsuccessfully, that City Hall have them stopped.[832] Charlebois died unexpectedly after an operation at St. Michael's Hospital, in Toronto, March 13, 1912. He was thirty-one years old. In his obituary, he was remembered as a "valued member of the entertaining staff of the Queen's Own Rifles." Flowers and wreaths were sent by Sir Henry and other friends, interment was in Penetanguishene.[833] The Bow Wow Minstrels entertained at QOR smokers up to March of 1914 and ceased to exist after the onset of WWI.[834]

Joseph C. Salvaneschi was a chef at the Prince George Hotel. In 1914 he was guest at a QOR smoker on March 11, and at this "successful" evening he presented the QOR with "a handsome cup to be shot for by members of the company."[835] Salvaneschi served with other men from the QOR in the 3rd Battalion overseas. He arrived back in Canada, November 1915, "suffering nervous disability, the result of a concussion at Givenchy."[836] Then he went back overseas, serving as a sergeant cook and later as a superintendent of cooking and an inspector of field kitchens.[837]

The complaints about the Ross rifles made by the men of the QOR in 1910 were only magnified during the war. In one article, returning men were interviewed and the comments about the Ross rifles were shocking: "I have seen men crying in the trenches because they only had Ross rifles and felt they were no protection . . . at first, when the men began to throw their Ross rifles away and grab Lee-Enfields, the officers objected but soon they got over that."[838] Ross rifles were eventually replaced in 1916 by the British-made Lee-Enfields, but not before there were losses of Canadian lives.[839]

Although not a member of the 1910 trip, but likely known by some of the QOR men, a brief mention deserves to be made of Dr. C.S. Wright, Toronto's young man on the Scott's Antarctic expedition. It is well-known that Scott perished along with other crew members on his return from the south pole. Wright, who was nicknamed Silas by the crew of the *Terra Nova,* was a member of the retrieval party sent to find Scott and confirm his death. On a visit to Toronto, in June of 1913, he recounted discovering Scott's tent on November 12, 1912: "I saw a white mound in the distance which I thought was a cairn.... As we drew nearer we saw that it was the top half of a tent. We hurried up to it, and dug down through the drifts, we found Captain Scott, Dr. Wilson and Lieut. Bowers."[840] When asked by a reporter what they looked like, with emotion he said "They seemed asleep; rather worn looking of course, but quite calm and peaceful," and the decision was made to leave them "in the place where he [Scott] did his life work."[841]Wright was feted in Toronto but returned to England where he continued his career as a physicist and glaciologist.

In Toronto, Sir Henry is best known for the construction of his elaborate home on the hill, Casa Loma, which he and his wife lived in briefly from 1914 to 1923. The mid-1920s were challenging years for him, and as a result his circumstances had dramatically altered. Through mismanagement and bad business decisions, he was destitute. Then his wife Mary died (1924). But he still owned their beloved summer home on Mary Lake, in King Township, north of Toronto.[842] The Mary Lake farm was the location of a celebration to honour Sir Henry's fiftieth year in the QOR in June of 1926.

A photograph of eight men of the Queen's Own Rifles Association, who were planning these celebrations, was published in the *Globe*.[843] Another planning committee was chaired by QOR Regimental Sergeant-Major E.A. Butler, who had been on the English trip.[844] An invitation was extended to the Buffs to attend and "nine ambassadors from their comrade English regiment, the Buffs, the oldest military organization in the British Empire" attended. "The expenses of the visit are being met by the Colonel of the Buffs and certain retired officers."[845] There was a reception at the armouries on Tuesday, June 22, where the QOR "arranged themselves into a hollow square. Into the centre of this most dramatically marched the nine distinguished visitors and with them Sir Henry Pellatt."[846] Sir Henry spoke: "It is more than a pleasure for me to meet you here this evening to meet representatives of our old comrades, the Buffs, whom we crossed the sea to visit in 1910 and who now have returned that visit."[847] Col. Reginald Pellatt, now CO of the QOR also spoke: "Those of us . . . who were fortunate enough to be in England in 1910 will never forget your courtesy."[848] After the reception, the

QOR marched to the cenotaph in front of City Hall where there was a welcoming ceremony and a wreath was laid.

On Wednesday, the non-commissioned officers were entertained at the Sergeants' Mess, while the officers dined at Reginald Pellatt's home. At the mess, the QOR's R.S.M. Butler "proposed the toast to the King. Then, welcoming the representatives of the historic regiment, he called for a toast to The Buffs. He made reference to the visit of the Queen's Own in England in 1910, emphasizing that The Buffs had assisted the unit in every way possible. He instanced the courtesy extended by remarking that the Queen's Own Band had been absent of a route march, and the Buffs sent out their own band to escort the regiment in."[849] The reporters had written about that experience and how thrilling it was for the QOR.

The most important celebration happened at Mary Lake on Saturday, June 26. "Sir Henry Pellatt's jubilee of militia service was commemorated on Saturday afternoon at Lake Marie by unique ceremonies in a unique amphitheatre. Like a miniature Lake Louise as serpentine of turquoise in the emerald setting of miniature mountain, this jewel carved by glaciers lies several miles to the west of the motor-polished highway north of Yonge Street."[850] Two thousand people attended, arriving in cars and buses, which were parked in fields around the property, which was a "picturesque farm . . . the barns were larger than the house."[851] A marquee tent was pitched on the lawn beside the house, and a stage was set up for the ceremonies. Sir Henry "was in the blue and gold uniform of a brigadier-general with scarlet and white cock feathers in his plumed hat. . . . He dominated the fete with generous proportions which vouch for a generous disposition. In his portly smiling presence one did not need to be told that he had been the regiment's guide, comforter and friend."[852] He was presented with a ceremonial sword. "'Sir Henry Pellatt,' said the Lieutenant-governor [the Hon. Harry Cockshutt], facing the broadcasting disc, 'your services in the last fifty years have been very commendable and outstanding and I congratulate you. I hope all will devote themselves to their country as you have done.'"[853] A panorama photograph was taken as the sword was given to Pellatt and was published in the *Star*, June 28. This view shows the house behind the receiving stands and the barns to the left. The lake is to the back of the participants, with the drop to the lake naturally creating an "amphitheatre." The Duke of Connaught sent a congratulatory telegram on the occasion.[854] The *Globe* reported there were "three aeroplanes from Camp Borden" conducting manoeuvres in the sky, while the reporter from the *Star* waxed poetic: "And as all of the visitors and well wishers rolled homeward they saw in the dusk aeroplanes gamboling like bats and swooping with swallows in a daring vespertinal salute to the genial lord of the manor and hero of the fete." The last event of Pellatt's jubilee was a dinner, July 1, at the Royal Canadian Yacht Club, hosted by the QOR Association.[855]

By the mid-1930s the daily newspapers of Toronto had changed—the *News* ceased publishing in 1919, and the *World* closed in 1921.[856] The *Globe* was purchased by the flamboyant George McCullagh in 1936, shortly to be followed by his purchase of the *Mail and Empire*. These two papers were combined into the *Globe and Mail*, and in a display of vanity his initials GM would forever be the acronym of the paper.[857] The *Telegram* and the *Star* continued as strong and popular as ever.

At the festivities of 1926 the current members of the QOR were celebrating Pellatt's fifty years in the regiment. The next major QOR event was the celebration of Pellatt's eightieth birthday in 1939. This was seen as an opportunity to host the first reunion of the young men who went on the English Trip in 1910, nearly thirty years before. For this dinner a committee was struck, led by Colonel Kirkpatrick, and a smart-looking brochure was printed and distributed. It listed memories of 1910 including, "Dr. Crippen! . . . Guildhall (wow!) . . . The Buffs?"[858] "Well, just in case you may have forgotten, the Old Gang is again going to 'Fall In' and the occasion is the eightieth birthday of Sir Henry."[859] Although it is not known who designed this brochure, it certainly has the polish of an advertising agency, possibly MacLaren's, as he, along with Jim Scroggie, was an organizer for H Company. The planning began in 1938, and the Royal York was booked for the event on January 6, 1939, the exact day of Sir Henry's eightieth birthday.

This was a different operation than the usual QOR event, since most of the men they were hoping would attend were not currently in the QOR and neither were all the organizers. Furthermore, only those who had been on the trip in 1910 were invited, so that politicians and senior military men who wished to attend were denied permission unless they were 1910ers. The blurb on the registration form stated that this reunion was long overdue, due to WWI intervening, and now it was time to "show Sir Henry something of our appreciation of his wonderful kindness to us individually."[860] Not stated, but well known by the organizers, was the fact that Sir Henry's health was in decline, and the reunion had to happen soon so that Sir Henry would be present. At the time of the dinner, Pellatt had been reduced to living in a room in his chauffeur's home in Mimico.[861] His financial situation meant that the men would have to pay their part; a two-dollar bill sent with registration information guaranteed a ticket.

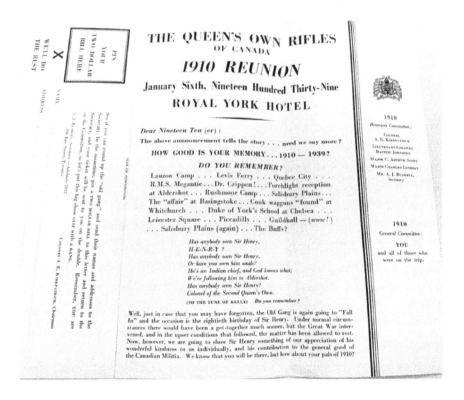

Figure 46. Inside details of reunion brochure.

The day before the dinner, the *Star* had a short article about the event: "They're going to turn the tables on Sir Henry. In 1910 Sir Henry Pellatt played host to 640 men and officers of the Queen's Own Rifles on a six-weeks trip to England. . . . Tomorrow night, on Sir Henry's 80th birthday, more than 300 of those '1910' originals will be host to their former commander officer at a reunion dinner in the Royal York Hotel."[862] The *Globe and Mail* wrote, "Strictly speaking it is Sir Henry Pellatt's birthday party; yet as this reporter understands it, it is much more that a birthday party. It is a salute, across a gulf far wider than years, to 1910."[863] There would be toasts, there would be songs, the band and the bugle band would play, "and once again they will sing the theme song of that mighty voyage of 1910, 'Has Anybody Seen Sir Henry.'"[864]

The *Star* reporter added, "Views of the trip will be shown."[865] Glass slides of photographs of the trip were prepared. The slides included images of the pageant, the training at Lévis, the fun on the *Megantic*, marching in Liverpool, training in Aldershot, the Duke of York's School in Chelsea, entering the Guildhall and Lieut. Roy Gzowski's cenotaph. Some of the images were from the Gale & Polden postcards, others were the photos that Art Gleason took.[866] The *Globe and Mail* reported, "A highlight of the evening was the showing of lantern-slide photographs of the trip, accompanied by running comment, some instructive, some ribald."[867] Showing them would have brought back memories and resulted in much commentary, laughter, and solemnity, knowing that some of the young 1910ers in the photographs did not come home from the trip nor WWI.

A souvenir reunion menu was printed with a timeline of Sir Henry's career with the QOR, with a brief history of the 1910 trip written by Major C.B. Lindsay, and a few photographs.[868] The menu itself included sketch drawings of significant events of the year from the garden party to the Guildhall luncheon.

A reception was held in an antechamber before entering the ballroom for dinner, where there was some hilarity over the name "Slim." Apparently, during the trip, the young men had been regularly called slim as a nickname, indicative of their height and build; at the reception it was obvious that these portly gentlemen were no longer slim. "Gosh,

Figure 47. The toasts for the reunion banquet with sketches of 1910 events.

where did you get that? . . . patting 'Slim' on the belt! . . . [and] a few of the originals attempted to wear their original QOR tunics but lack of slimness spoiled the original effect."[869] Before dinner the men "stood in little groups, thumbing through old albums, exchanging well-thumbed snapshots. There was one of Sir Henry himself, for example, stretched out on English grass in the early hours of dawn on a morning in 1910, his cap pulled down over his eyes, a coat bundled under his head. 'He was tired that morning' remarked the photographer with an affectionate smile as he squinted at the snapshot. 'We caught him taking a little nap.'"[870]

Congratulatory telegrams were read from "Massey," the Hon. Vincent Massey, the Canadian high commissioner in London, who had been Lieutenant Massey on the trip; L.M. Cosgrove, Canadian trade commissioner in Sydney, Australia, who had been a private on the trip, one of the RMC men; Ontario's Lieutenant-Governor Albert Matthews; and Prime Minister William Lyon Mackenzie King. With great excitement, a cable was read from Buckingham Palace, from HRM Queen Mary, who in 1928 was appointed colonel-in-chief of the regiment: "Your Colonel-in-Chief has great pleasure in sending you warmest congratulations on the occasion of your 80th birthday" signed Mary R., Queen Mary.[871]

Throughout the evening "Cheers broke out on almost the least excuse, but when 'the good old band' paraded in and played the Queen's Own March, the cheers were deafening. 'Thirty-five members went over,' said Col. Johnston, 'look at them now—there's only ten left.'"[872] But "everybody enjoyed it and cheered for more. It was that kind of evening . . . and Sir Henry sat back and enjoyed every bit of it. It was his 'night.'"[873] The band, what was left of it, "a scant dozen men. . . . Stepped, heads erect, brisk . . . [into the ballroom] . . . With a zip and a zing that brought every man in the ballroom to his feet with napkin waving in the air, the band of 1910 circled the banquet tables in single file, playing the regimental march. Somebody started to sing: 'The Queen's Own Rifles they came this way, and broke things up in an awful way: You can bet your life there'll be hell to pay, when the Queen's Own Rifles come back this way.'"[874]A toast was made to Sir Henry: "To the far corners of the ballroom it was obvious that tears dimmed Sir Henry's eyes".[875]

In a photo essay published in the *Globe and Mail* after the reunion, Art Gleason was described as "the official photographer of the Queen's Own Rifles of Canada."[876] The reunion dinner was a success and the 225 attendees, enriched by reliving the experiences of their youth, returned to their lives.[877]

Figure 48. The reunion dinner in the Royal York, January 6, 1939.

Figure 49. Sir Henry and Colonel A.E. Kirkpatrick at the reunion banquet.

Two months later, on March 8, Sir Henry Pellatt died. His obituary in the *New York Times* focused on the fact that "to the average Toronto citizen he was known as the man who built Casa Loma."[878] His death notice in the London *Times* listed his Queen's Own Rifles credentials, observing "at his own expense [he] took a contingent of his regiment over to England for the manoeuvres of 1910."[879] Even over twenty-nine years later, the trip to England was remembered and acknowledged.

The Toronto newspapers were full of his story, his business successes and failures, his home, "Casa Loma [which] was probably the most romantic thing that ever happened to Toronto, certainly its most glamorous building."[880] Always mentioned was his love for the QOR and the 1910 trip to England, "This was the climax of Sir Henry's long association with the Queen's Own Rifles. In the long and honorable history of this crack Canadian regiment no one played a more important part than Maj.-Gen. Sir Henry Pellatt."[881] The QOR honoured him with a funeral service with full military honours, worthy of their beloved honorary colonel.

The service was at St. James Cathedral on King Street. "Sprinkled abundantly through the mourners who jammed the cathedral long before the service begun were the men who a few short weeks ago stood in the great banquet hall of the Royal York Hotel and charged their glasses while he stood proudly erect with eyes dimmed by emotion. They were the men who told Sir Henry while he lived how much they appreciated his kindly interest and generosity by honoring him on his eightieth birthday."[882] Although the newspapers were filled with the names of the who's who of Toronto society who paid their respects, there were also stories of other regular citizens who had experienced Sir Henry's kindness and generosity over the years. One man, William Jackson, paid his respects saying that "He comforted me greatly in my sorrow, and helped me financially when my wife was ill. . . . [Jackson] was batman to Sir Henry on several trips, the last of which was to New York about 30 years ago."[883]

The procession, on leaving the church after the service, walked west towards Richmond Street where the sidewalks were filled with mourners who removed their hats in respect. "As the flag-draped gun-carriage bearing the body of the old commander of the Queen's Own Rifles rolled through the corridor of King Street, a cold March wind swirled snow over the scene of impressive dignity and plucked at the white and scarlet feathers of Sir Henry's cocked hat lying upon his sword of ivory and gold atop the casket."[884] At Richmond St. the casket was transferred to a hearse for the ride north to the Forest Lawn cemetery and the Pellatt family crypt. At the mausoleum, "The buglers of the old band of 1910, the same band that marched gaily around the room during Sir Henry's happy birthday party a few weeks ago, blew 'Last Post' and 'Reveille.' Thus was said farewell to the laird of Casa Loma."[885] The journalist for the *Star* wrote, "That was the end of the afternoon's ceremonies, end of 80 years, end of a life, end of a character, end of a period. There will never be his like again. People live in a different mood from that which gave him his individuality and his fame. Away before the last war, when the world was young."[886]

Figure 50. Sir Henry Pellatt's funeral procession.

The three remaining reporters of the press gang continued to live in Toronto. Jack MacLaren, of the very successful MacLaren Advertising Co. Ltd., died on vacation in Miami, Florida, on June 11, 1955.[887] He was remembered as a newspaper journalist, an honourable and principled man, a giant in the advertising business.[888] "There was no place, in his own company's dealings, for the false, the garish, or the sensational. . . . The good health and good repute of the profession today are a tribute to his untiring work in that regard."[889] He was the fourth man of the press gang to die.

After the reunion Jim Brown and his wife moved permanently to Toronto from Vancouver. In 1943 his wife, Kate Wiltshire Brown, died.[890] Brown continued his newspaper career in the editorial departments of the *Star* and the *Globe and Mail*.[891] In 1944 Jim married Susan Grant and had a second family.[892] After he retired, he had a small company, Jim Brown Printing, which operated from the basement of his home. There he had a printing press, numerous wooden drawers filled with type, and a darkroom to develop photographs. After over fifty years of being in the newspaper business, presses and printing were in his blood. In March of 1958 he took me, then eight years old, to see the test flight of the Avro Arrow jet airplane at Malton airport north of Toronto. Today, as I reflect on that day, I wonder what he was thinking. Was he contemplating the changes he had seen since reporting on Toronto's first airshow, was he also remembering the other events of 1910? Brown died March 9, 1964, and was described by the *Globe and Mail* as "a veteran newspaperman." At the time of his death, he was a member of the Toronto Press Club and was the longest practising journalist of the press gang.[893] He was the fifth member of the gang to die.

Art Gleason died May 27, 1964, after a successful career in newspaper and commercial photography.[894] Before his death he continued to work in semi-retirement. In 1956 "he shot aerials of 102 communities for the *London Free Press*. In 30 hours' flying he covered 3,000 miles and shot hundreds of negatives."[895] Museum London mounted an exhibition of twenty-five of his aerial photographs, July 2, 2022, to April 23, 2023, leading with a quote from Art that "aerials give me a thrill."[896]

Jim Scroggie worked in the advertising department of the *Telegram* until 1955 and the advertising business until 1957. He retired in 1963 and died on July 27, 1967.[897] His son James Scroggie Jr. also worked in advertising, working at MacLaren's around 1955 and then several other agencies.[898] There is probably more to Jim Scroggie's story, but what is known is that at some point in time his family donated his scrapbook of the English trip to the Queen's Own Rifles Museum and Archives.[899]It was this donation that allowed a look into this clever, comical man and provided an irreverent and personal look at the other reporters on the 1910 trip as well. Jim Scroggie, who famously did get to meet the king, was the last member of the press gang to die.

With the writings of the reporters of the press gang, there is a feel for the boyish enthusiasm and the optimistic excitement about their present and future, embodied in the lives of these 600-plus men from Toronto in 1910. At the trip's conclusion, QOR men were interviewed when they arrived back in Canada. What did the trip mean to them? "Some say that they enjoyed every minute of the trip, others that they're glad now that it's all over; that they went along for the experiences they have had. . . . When it comes to the luncheons, and 'spreads' and, above all the banquet at Guild Hall—well just watch them smile as they tell about what happened. Some of them, perhaps, won't tell all that happened, that glorious day, that is not to the folks at home. But whatever they did, it is conceded that they always acted as gentlemen should do under the circumstances."[900]

Over the course of the trip, Sir Henry gave countless speeches and toasts for which he developed a rote script: the QOR were enthusiastic, upstanding young men from the colonies ready to train, ready to fight, ready to support the Mother Country. To him these were the most significant aspects of the trip.

What did Sir Henry think of the trip on a more personal level? In June of 1926, at the celebratory event at Mary Lake, Pellatt spoke of the impact of the trip:

> There was a great cheer when Sir Henry Pellatt arose to acknowledge all these honors. "This unique and extraordinary gathering . . . makes this the most embarrassing moment of my life." But as he looked back over his life, which was like a chain with many links of happy moments, the occasions of happiest memory were connected with the QOR, "it seems to me that I have grown up in the regiment. . . . One thing that stands out is its trip to England in 1910. I shall never forget the amazing welcome we received, particularly from the Buffs. . . .

We went through the army manoeuvres . . . and, well, we all came out alive anyway."[901]

In his remarks at the 1939 reunion banquet, his feelings towards the men of 1910 were apparent: "He replied to a toast, 'I am at a loss for words. . . . Far too much tribute has been said about that 1910 trip already. . . . I'm so glad to see so many of the boys of the old brigade here. . . . Old boys, did I say . . . why damn it all . . . you all look like a fine bunch of men to me right now.'"[902]

He never spoke of the burden of responsibility he felt for the men on the trip. However, after his death, his friend, fellow 1910er and QOR colleague, Dr. P. G. Goldsmith, spoke with reporters saying, "During the entire trip he was more concerned about the health and comfort of the 600 odd men who were with him than he was about the success of any of the proceedings or ceremonial parades."[903] No doubt the deaths of John Reginald Thorn and Lieutenant Roy Gzowski and the illness of the men with typhus weighed heavily on him.

In terms of the lives of the 600-plus 1910 QOR men the impact of the trip cannot be underestimated; it had the potential to change their lives, and it probably did. The reunion dinner showed their love and respect for Pellatt, and his words to them showed that the feelings were reciprocal.

During the 1960s and 1970s the men of the English trip passed away. Their children and grandchildren knew less and less of the trip and then it was forgotten. Over the years since, it has been the subject of little research; it was considered of so little import that it is not mentioned in Pellatt's Dictionary of Canadian Biography entry.[904] From a scholarly point of view, it is true that the English trip is not relevant when trying to untangle Pellatt's complicated financial and political machinations. From a Canadian military-history perspective, the trip was seen at the time as a successful endeavour, but today it is seen as a self-serving publicity event.

The Queen's Own Rifles remember the trip. Their museum, fittingly located in Casa Loma, has a display about 1910. The QOR Museum and Archives website has photographs and documents from the trip, as well, it has the Nominal Roll, which lists the names of the men who went to England.

In the broader context, with the end of the Edwardian Era and the encroachment of unrest in Europe leading to World War I, the men of 1910 were the last youths of a naïve time, one which was the beginning of the end of the period of white Anglo-Saxon Protestant prevalence in Toronto. Although the stories of the press gang, Sir Henry Mill Pellatt, the QOR's semi-centennial celebrations of 1910, and the English trip are incredible, it must be acknowledged that these were complicated times socially and politically, and the issues that faced many of the citizens of Toronto such as poverty, racism, homophobia, and suffrage, were ever present. This trip did not address those issues, nor did it resolve any of the world's looming political crises. The English trip did not change Sir Henry Pellatt's life, but it did change the lives of the young men who took advantage of his generosity.

In retrospect, what was the experience of the QOR men? Doubtless there were 600-plus different recollections, but they all shared seven weeks where these young men, many not previously in the militia, were one; they drilled, camped, and bunked together, paraded before dignitaries, marched for hours both day and night, slept in open fields, scrambled up hills with rifles blazing, dined at the Guildhall as guests of the City of London, and some even met the king! Through it all, they were united in a single, most important objective, they were members of the Queen's Own Rifles of Canada, and as riflemen of this honorable regiment they represented Toronto and Canada with pride.

What an experience the youthful reporters of Toronto's newspapers had. What an unparalleled adventure the young men of Toronto's QOR were given by Sir Henry Pellatt. His fantastic vision of sending a regiment to England was actualized, to the benefit of hundreds of Toronto's youths who otherwise would never have had the opportunity of such a generous adventure. Pellatt's dream became their dream. A reporter for the *Globe and Mail*, in an article to celebrate Pellatt's birthday in 1939, wrote somewhat wistfully, "It's a long way back to 1910, but it is said that 1910 was a year to be alive if you were a young man and lived in Toronto and belonged to the Queen's Own Rifles."[905]

ACKNOWLEDGEMENTS

As you can see, the writing of this book required a lot of research in various archives in Toronto. At those archives I was assisted by many wonderful people, and I hope that I have thanked everyone. The first archive I visited was the Queen's Own Rifles Museum and Archive, located in Casa Loma, Toronto. This is staffed by dedicated volunteers who were very helpful in making documents, files, and photographs available for my research. I would like to thank CWO Shaun Kelly, CD (Ret'd) Curator, and Major John M. Stephens, CD (Ret'd), Director and Archivist, and Briahna Bernard, MMst, Collections Manager. I would also like to thank LCol Chris Boileau, CD, Commanding Officer of the Queen's Own Rifles of Canada for the thoughtful foreword.

Finding historic newspapers was a challenge. The Toronto Public Library online resources have the Toronto *Star*, the *Globe,* and the *Globe and Mail*. The Toronto *Evening Telegram* was available in the *Toronto Star* Newspaper Room of the library. Beau Levitt and the staff of the Baldwin Room of the Toronto Public Library were very helpful. The Scarborough Historical Society Museum and Archives was the source of the *Mail and Empire*. Rick Schofield made this available for research. He also helped find obscure issues of the Toronto *Sunday World*. The *World* was available through Canadiana online. Julia McIntosh of the Library and Archives of Canada directed me to the Mills Library at McMaster University, which has the Toronto *News* on microfilm.

In seeking access to the Vincent Massey archives for 1910, Tys Klumpenhower and Aerin Leavitt of the University of Toronto Archives and Principal Nathalie Des Rosiers, Kathryn Middleton, Alexia Clarke of Massey College were helpful.

I would like to acknowledge the assistance of Alannah Metherel, Legislative Assembly of Ontario; Paul Sharkey and the reference team, City of Toronto Archives; Gina Dewaele, Elgin County Archives; Norah Janvick, Toronto Camera Club; Renée Le Maire, London Public Library; Amber Lloydlangston, London Museum, and Marnee Gamble, University of Toronto Archives; and Karin Noble of the Grey Roots Museum and Archives, Owen Sound.

I would like to thank Edward Enright who provided me with information about his grandfather, Jack MacLaren.

Throughout this project I have been assisted by family and friends without whose support this would never have been completed. I would like to thank Lilias Brown-Little, Marta Bradbury, Jim Kapches, Eric Sabourin, Ko Kapches, Alice Kapches, Carole Stimmell, Robert W.C. Burgar, Veronica Maidman, Jean-Luc Pilon, Christine Caroppo Clarence, Linda Pomerleau-Treboute, and Jerry and Jane Garbutt.

When I first visited the QOR's museum and archives I had hoped to find a book that told the story of the English Trip of 1910. Soon I discovered there was none, and I realized that it fell to me to fill the gap. I know that there are more stories to be told, ones in long forgotten diaries and photographs hidden away in Toronto's dusty attics. This is one account of Toronto in 1910, the Queen's Own Rifles, Sir Henry Pellatt, and the English adventure of over 600 young men of Toronto, including six reporters in the press gang, one of whom, coincidentally, happened to be my father.

ENDNOTES

1 In 1910 the "English" style of spelling was not yet adopted in Ontario, so armories was not spelled armouries as they are today. For quotations the spelling used is that of the day.

2 Carlie Oreskovich, *Sir Henry Pellatt: The King of Casa Loma*, McGraw-Hill Ryerson Press, Toronto, 1982. David Roberts, "PELLATT, Sir HENRY MILL," in ***Dictionary of Canadian Biography***, vol. 16, University of Toronto/Université Laval, 2003–, accessed June 30, 2023, http://www.biographi.ca/en/bio/pellatt_henry_mill_16E.html.

3 In the newspaper articles for 1910 there are no accents added to French names or words, so when quoted the articles will be as they were written with no accents.

4 The *Globe*, September 10, 1910:1.

5 https://www.hmdb.org/m.asp?m=220653

6 The *Globe*, January 27, 1910:4.

7 The *Globe*, January 27, 1910:4.

8 https://www.merriam-webster.com/dictionary/roorback

9 The *Globe*, January 14, 1910:14.

10 The *Globe*, January 22, 1910:28.

11 The *Globe*, January 27, 1910:4.

12 The *Globe*, January 27, 1909:

13 The *Globe*, January 28, 1910:14.

14 The *Star,* January 28, 1910:9.

15 David Roberts, "PELLATT, Sir HENRY MILL," in *Dictionary of Canadian Biography*, vol. 16, University of Toronto/Université Laval, 2003–, accessed November 14, 2022, http://www.biographi.ca/en/bio/pellatt_henry_mill_16E.html. Carlie Oreskovich, *Sir Henry Pellatt: The King of Casa Loma*, McGraw-Hill Ryerson Press, Toronto, 1982. The Queen's Own Rifles are referred to as the Q.O.R. or the QOR. For this paper QOR will be used, Q.O.R. is often used in quotes. Additionally, the Archives of the QOR will be references as the AQOR.

16 The *Globe*, August 11, 1910:1.

17 Paul Rutherford, 1982. *A Victorian Authority: The Daily Press in Late Nineteenth-Century Canada*, University of Toronto Press, Toronto :53-59.

18 https://qormuseum.org/history/timeline-1900-1924/1910-nominal-roll-on-leaving-toronto-for-aldershot/ Oreskovich mentions six reporters, but does not name them, nor discuss them (1996, xiii, 102). The *Star* archives are available through the Toronto Public Library, online newspapers, and ProQuest Historical Newspapers. The *World* is accessible on-line, https://www.canadiana.ca. The *News* clippings are in James Scroggie's Scrapbook, The Queen's Own Rifles of Canada Regimental Museum and Archives, Toronto, 1 Austin Terrace, Toronto. 1910 News Clipping Scrapbooks, #02232, hereafter AQOR.S. The *News* is also available on microfilm at the Mills Library, McMaster University, Hamilton, Ontario. The *Telegram* archives are on microfilm in the Toronto Star Newspaper Room of the Toronto Public Reference Library. The *Mail and Empire*

(M&E) newspapers are held in the Scarborough Historical Society Archives, 6282 Kingston Rd., Scarborough.

19 The *Globe* archives are available through the Toronto Public Library, online newspapers, ProQuest Historical Newspapers.

20 The articles from the UK are in scrapbooks at the City of Toronto Archives (CTA) and the Queen's Own Rifles Archives (AQOR).

21 He is identified as a reporter on the *Megantic* immigration document. UK-Ireland Incoming Passenger List, SS *Megantic*, arriving in Liverpool, August 17, 1910.

22 https://central.bac-lac.gc.ca/.item/?op=pdf&app=CEF&id=B2813-S041 Attestation Paper.

23 Jaffray Eaton Dies in Action. *Globe*, Nov. 2, 1917:9. Dean Beeby, "JAFFRAY, ROBERT," in *Dictionary of Canadian Biography*, vol. 14, University of Toronto/Université Laval, 2003–, accessed October 31, 2022, http://www.biographi.ca/en/bio/jaffray_robert_14E.html.

24 *Might's City of Toronto Directories.*

25 Letter to the Editor, The *Globe*, Dec. 19, 1896:7.

26 He is listed as a member of the Toronto Press Club and as an employee of the *Globe* in the program for the annual theatre nights, 1909. Toronto Press Club, Fifth Annual Theatre Nights, Royal Alexandra Theatre, June 18, 19, 1909. No additional publication information. Brown Family collection. (Hereafter TPC:FATN)

27 On the cruise portion of the QOR trip to England, Eaton identified himself in the immigration documents as a reporter; he travelled in first class, unlike the rest of the regiment who were in second and third class. UK-Ireland Incoming Passenger List, SS *Megantic*, arriving in Liverpool, August 17, 1910.

28 The *Globe*, September 22, 1910:6.

29 The *Globe*, August 20, 1910:1.

30 Mima Brown Kapches family information.

31 *Might's City of Toronto Directories.* The *World* is accessible on-line, https://www.canadiana.ca. TPC:FATN, pps.31-32.

32 This number is inexact because some issues of the *Sunday World* are missing, and these had articles about the trip.

33 Letter to Nicholas Carter Brown, August 3, 1980, in N. C. Brown Fonds, Elgin County Archives, Diaries 1896–1902. *Might's City of Toronto Directory 1908.* He is listed as an employee of the *Globe* in the TPC:FATN.

34 Edward Enright, email, February 12, 2023. Enright, May 17, 2023, letter. Enright is MacLaren's grandson.

35 The *Evening Telegram* archives are available on microfilm in the Toronto Star Newspaper Room of the Toronto Public Reference Library. *Might's City of Toronto Directory, 1910.* AQOR:S.

36 Flight-Lieut. Riggs Killed. Toronto *Star*, July 31, 1917. Riggs is memorialized on the WWI plaque at Jarvis Collegiate Institute. Diane Ledo, Jarvis Collegiate Institute, October 23, 2023.

37 AQOR:S. On the *Megantic*'s passenger list he is described as a clerk. Flight-Lieut. Riggs Killed. Toronto *Star*, July 31, 1917. He is in the photograph of H Company in *Souvenir of the Visit of the 2nd regiment "Queen's Own Rifles of Canada" to the Aldershot Command, August-September, 1910.* Gale and Polden Ltd., Aldershot, 1910, AQOR.

38 Canada Nominal Rolls and Paylist for Volunteer Militia, 1857-1922, 1909-1910, 2nd Battalion, Queen's Own Rifles, Ancestry.ca.

39 Ancestry.ca

40 George E. Scroggie, in "Advertising for 22 Years," The *Globe and Mail*, December 3, 1943.

41 *Mail and Empire*, August 20, 1910. SHSA

42 TPC:FATN.

43 A home in a neighbourhood, which was demolished in the 1950s for the expansion of Lakeshore Blvd. http://spacing.ca/toronto/2017/03/04/lost-streets-south-parkdale/ https://www.boulevardclub.com/About/History.aspx accessed January 5, 2023. George E. Scroggie, In Advertising for 22 Years, The *Globe and Mail*, December 3, 1943.

44 The *News*, August 13, 1910:1. AQOR.S:34.

45 Canada Nominal Rolls and Paylist for Volunteer Militia, 1857-1922, 1909-1910, 2nd Battalion, Queen's Own Rifles, Ancestry.ca.

46 AQOR.S:9.

47 The *Varsity*, University of Toronto, October 5, 1909.

48 Ramsay Cook, "SHEPPARD, EDMUND ERNEST," in *Dictionary of Canadian Biography*, vol. 15, University of Toronto/Université Laval, 2003–, accessed October 31, 2022. Rutherford, Paul, 1982, A Victorian Authority. *The Daily Press in the Late Nineteenth Century Canada.* University of Toronto Press, Toronto.

49 https://www.thestar.com/about/history-of-the-toronto-star.html?utm_source=share-bar&utm_medium=user&utm_campaign=user-share accessed October 31, 2022

50 Sheppard identified himself as a reporter on the *Megantic* passenger list and filed over twenty articles on the trip. UK-Ireland Incoming Passenger List, SS *Megantic*, arriving in Liverpool, August 17, 1910. The *Star* archives are available through the Toronto Public Library, online newspapers, ProQuest Historical Newspapers. AQOR.S:11.

51 Brown Family Collection.

52 The *Star,* August 13, 1910:1.

53 The *Globe*, September 24, 1910:A5.

54 A few A.A. Gleason photographs are in the London Public Library, London, Ontario, but none are of the trip. (London Public Library email 11 September 2023). He was born in Québec in 1877 and died in London, Ontario, in 1964.

55 The Institute of Journalists Canadian Division, Montreal, 1911:52.

56 The *Globe*, June 27, 1908:A6. The *Globe*, August 1, 1908:A1, A2, A6, The *Globe*, July 30, 1908:1. The *Globe*, June 20, 1908:A6.

57 *London Free Press*, October 11, 1958. "These Oldtimers Have Shot the Works." By Lenore Crawford.

58 *Canadian Courier*, Vol. VIII (No. 12) August 20, 1910; *Canadian Courier*, Vol. VIII (No.13) August 27, 1910; *Canadian Courier*, Vol. VIII (No. 16) September 17, 1910; *Canadian Courier* Vol. VIII (No. 18) October 1, 1910; *Canadian Courier* Vol. VIII (No.19), October 8,1910.

59 F.R. Henshaw, AQOR.02240, George W. Argue, AQOR.02047.

60 *Might's City of Toronto Directory 1910.* I did not search all Might's for the employment records of the over 600 names on the roll, just H company.

61 *Might's City of Toronto Directories.*

62 Canada Nominal Rolls and Paylist for Volunteer Militia, 1857–1922, 1909–1910, 2nd Battalion, Queen's Own Rifles, Ancestry.ca.

63 The QOR Nominal Roll names him A.V. Corbett, the passenger lists for the *Megantic* and the *Canada* name him E.V. Corbett.

64 TPC:FATN. Ned Sheppard is listed as a reporter for the *Star* in *Might's City of Toronto Directory* from 1908, but he is not named as a member of the Toronto Press Club in the 1909 programme. However, in the University of Toronto's *Varsity* it is written that he left his studies to become a journalist at the *Star* in the fall of 1909, so perhaps before then he was working sporadically at the paper. The *Varsity*, Vol. XXIX, October 5, 1909. Riggs is not in the Press Club programme from 1909.

65 The Toronto *Star*, April 15, 1910.

66 David Flint, *Henry Pellatt*, (The Canadians), 1978, Fitzhenry & Whitesie, Don Mills, ON. Carlie Oreskovich, *Sir Henry Pellatt: The King of Casa Loma*, McGraw-Hill Ryerson Press, Toronto, 1982.

67 *The Queen's Own Rifles of Canada, 1860-1960*. Lieutenant-Colonel W.T. Barnard, The Ontario Publishing Company, Don Mills, Ontario, 1960. https://qormuseum.files.wordpress.com/2012/09/wt-barnard-history.pdf;

68 Carlie Oreskovich, *Sir Henry Pellatt: The King of Casa Loma*, McGraw-Hill Ryerson Press, Toronto, 1982. David Roberts, "PELLATT, Sir HENRY MILL," in *Dictionary of Canadian Biography*, vol. 16, University of Toronto/Université Laval, 2003–, accessed June 30, 2023, http://www.biographi.ca/en/bio/pellatt_henry_mill_16E.html.

69 Mike O'Brien, "Manhood and the Militia Myth: Masculinity, Class and Militarism in Ontario, 1902–1914" Labour/Le Travail, 42 (Fall 1998), 115-41. *James Wood, Militia Myths: Ideas of the Canadian Citizen Soldier 1896–1921*. UBC Press, Vancouver, 2010.

70 Chris Sharpe "Enlistment in the Canadian Expeditionary Force 1914—1918." *Canadian Military History* 24, 1 (2015).

71 Ken Bell and Desmond Morton, Royal Canadian Military Institute, 100 Years, 1890-1990, RCMI, Toronto. https://archive.org/details/royalcanadianmil00bell/mode/2up?view=theater Accessed February 5, 2023.

72 Mike O'Brien, "Manhood and the Militia Myth: Masculinity, Class and Militarism in Ontario, 1902-1914". *Labour/Le Travail*, 42 (Fall 1998), 115-41

73 https://www.ancestry.ca/search/collections/1935/

74 Garry J. Burke, 1966, "Good for the Boy and the Nation: Military Drill and the Cadet Movement in Ontario Public Schools 1865—1911," PhEd. Dissertation, Institute of Education Studies of the University of Toronto. Page 29.

75 Workman was located at 180 Queen St. West, Might's 1910, uniform on display at QOR museum, viewed December 8, 2022; Pedro Mendes, Walter Beauchamp Tailors and the Queen's Own Rifles, https://qormuseum.org/tag/beauchamps/, Walter Beauchamp continues to tailor the QOR uniforms.

76 *The Queen's Own Rifles of Canada, 1860–1960*. Lieutenant-Colonel W.T. Barnard, The Ontario Publishing Company, Don Mills, Ontario, 1960: 68. https://qormuseum.files.wordpress.com/2012/09/wt-barnard-history.pdf

77 *The Queen's Own Rifles of Canada, 1860–1960*. Lieutenant-Colonel W.T. Barnard, The Ontario Publishing Company, Don Mills, Ontario, 1960:81. https://qormuseum.files.wordpress.com/2012/09/wt-barnard-history.pdf

78 *Star,* April 28, 1910:19, Star April 30,1906:2.

79 *Globe*, April 27, 1906:12, Star, April 30, 1906:2.

80 *Star*, April 30, 1906:2.

81 *Star* April 28, 1906:19.

82 Reid, Mark "The Quebec Tercentenary 1908: Canada's First National Military Pageant." *Canadian Military History,* 8, 2 (1999):53-58. https://scholars.wlu.ca/cgi/view-

content.cgi?referer=&httpsredir=1&article=1265&context=cmh accessed February 27, 2023.

83 Angela Bartie, Linda Flemming, Mark Freeman, Alexander Hutton and Paul Readman, Introduction, pp;1-29. In Angela Bartie, Linda Flemming, Mark Freeman, Alexander Hutton and Paul Readman, eds, *Restaging the Past, Historical Pageants, Culture and Society in Modern Britain.* UCL Press, 2020, London. H.V. Nelles, 1999, *The Art of Nation-Building: Pageantry and Spectacle at Quebec's Tercentenary.* U of T Press, Toronto.

84 H.V. Nelles, 1999, *The Art of Nation-Building: Pageantry and Spectacle at Quebec's Tercentenary.* U of T Press, Toronto: 146ff.

85 H.V. Nelles, 1999, *The Art of Nation-Building: Pageantry and Spectacle at Quebec's Tercentenary.* U of T Press, Toronto, fn 12, p. 348.

86 H.V. Nelles, 1999, The Art of Nation-Building: Pageantry and Spectacle at Quebec's Tercentenary. U of T Press, Toronto, p. 177.

87 Reid, Mark *The Quebec Tercentenary 1908: Canada's First National Military Pageant. Canadian Military History*, 8, 2 (1999):53-58. https://scholars.wlu.ca/cgi/viewcontent.cgi?referer=&httpsredir=1&article=1265&context=cmh accessed February 27, 2023.

88 *Globe* July 21, 1908:3

89 Reid, Mark "The Quebec Tercentenary 1908: Canada's First National Military Pageant." *Canadian Military History*, 8, 2 (1999):53-58. https://scholars.wlu.ca/cgi/viewcontent.cgi?referer=&httpsredir=1&article=1265&context=cmh accessed June 24, 2023. The Grenadiers were the 10th Royal Grenadiers, now known as the Royal Regiment of Canada. Shaun Kelley, email June 24, 2023.

90 Walter James Brown, August 3 1908, letter to N.C. Brown, Dunboyne, Ontario. Nicholas Carter Brown Fonds, Elgin County Archives.

91 "Prince Reviews Sixteen Thousand Men on the Historic Plains of Abraham." The *Globe*, July 25, 1908, p.1. Barnard 1960:84-85.

92 Reid, Mark *The Quebec Tercentenary 1908: Canada's First National Military Pageant. Canadian Military History,* 8, 2 (1999):53-58. https://scholars.wlu.ca/cgi/viewcontent.cgi?referer=&httpsredir=1&article=1265&context=cmh accessed February 27, 2023.

93 Walter James Brown, August 3 1908, letter to N.C. Brown, Dunboyne, Ontario. Nicholas Carter Brown Fonds, Elgin County Archives.

94 The *Globe*, July 25, 1908:1.

95 The *Globe and Mail*, April 20, 1939:4.

96 John Stevens and Shaun Kelly, QOR Curators, email November 13, 2023.

97 The *Globe*, June 20, 1910:1.

98 The *Star*, March 29, 1910:13. The *World*, December 6, 1909:4.

99 The *Globe*, January 1, 1910:1.

100 The Toronto *Star*, January 11, 1910:8.

101 The Toronto *Star*, January 24, 1910:1.

102 The Toronto *Star*, April 2, 1910:1, May 16, 1910:1.

103 The Toronto *Star*, January 10, 1910:1.

104 The *Star*, March 19, 1910:1 Allannah Metherel, reference assistant, House Publications and Language Services Legislative Assembly of Ontario, informed me that there is no Hansard record for the Ontario Legislature before 1944, instead various newspapers reported and published on the legislature activities (email April 5, 2023).

105 The *Star*, March 19, 1910:1

106 The *Star*, March 21, 1910:1. "English Militancy and the Canadian Suffrage Movement," Deborah Gorham. *Atlantis: A Women's Studies Journal*, 1, no.1, Fall 1975, 83-112. The *Toronto World*, March 21, 1910:1. Miss Smith chained herself to the fence at 10 Downing Street in 1908.

107 "English Militancy and the Canadian Suffrage Movement," Deborah Gorham. *Atlantis: A Women's Studies Journal*, 1, no.1, Fall 1975, 83-112. The Toronto *World*, March 21, 1910:1.

108 The Toronto *Star*, April 19, 1910:1.

109 The Toronto *Star*, April 22, 1990:12.

110 The Toronto *Star*, May 5, 1910:1.

111 The Toronto *Star*, May 21, 1910:1.

112 Britannica, T. Editors of Encyclopaedia. "John French, 1st Earl of Ypres." Encyclopedia Britannica, December 13, 2022. https://www.britannica.com/biography/John-French-1st-Earl-of-Ypres

113 Ramsay Cook, "SMITH, GOLDWIN," in *Dictionary of Canadian Biography*, vol. 13, University of Toronto/Université Laval, 2003–, accessed April 15,2023, http://www.biographi.ca/en/bio/smith_goldwin_13E.html.

114 The Toronto *Star*, June 16, 1910:1.

115 In an article in the *Star* in 1913 he had returned to Toronto to rest and stay with his family and to visit old friends before returning to England. The Toronto *Star*, June 11, 1913:1, 17.

116 Toronto *Star* December 13 1909:2.

117 The *Globe*, July 2, 1890:1,8.

118 The *Globe*, July 2, 1890:1,8.

119 Toronto *Star* December 13 1909:2, Barnard 1960:87. The *Globe*, April 2 1910:13.

120 City of Toronto Minutes, Appendix A, Report No.1, p.98, January 21, 1910. The ball was actually held June 24th.

121 The *Globe*, June 18, 1910:9.

122 David Roberts, "PELLATT, Sir HENRY MILL," in *Dictionary of Canadian Biography*, vol. 16, University of Toronto/Université Laval, 2003–, accessed August 3, 2023, http://www.biographi.ca/en/bio/pellatt_henry_mill_16E.html.

123 The Toronto *Star*, Feb.25, 1910:1, March 15, 1910:1, March 26, 1910:1.

124 Queen's Own Rifles Semi-Centennial Reunion, week commencing June 18, 1910, 4pp. Toronto Public Library, Baldwin Canadian Collection, Toronto Public Library.

125 Shaun Kelly, personal communication, May 25, 2023.

126 The AQOR have the register of non-resident ex-members of the 1910 reunion, 00119.

127 Paul Readman, of the Historical British Pageants of England of King's College, London had no additional information on Henderson. Email communication May 31, 2023.

128 Queen's Own Rifles of Canada, Semi-Centennial Reunion and Historical Pageant, Official Souvenir Programme. 1910. Geo. I. Riddell, Secretary, 36 King Street East. Toronto Reference Library, Baldwin Room, Semi-Centennial Reunion. 1910, Series 340, sub-series 10, File 8. 42 pp. p.15. Although Henderson is not named in the programme, the text is that of Henderson's as seen in his script for the pageant. Henderson, John 1910, Queen's Own Toronto Pageant June 18, 1910, Baldwin Room, Toronto Reference Library, Toronto.

129 Queen's Own Rifles of Canada, Semi-Centennial Reunion and Historical Pageant, Official Souvenir Programme. 1910. Geo. I. Riddell, Secretary, 36 King Street East. Toronto Reference Library, Baldwin Room, Semi-Centennial Reunion. 1910, Series 340, sub-series 10, File 8. p.15.

130 Henderson, John 1910, Queen's Own Toronto Pageant June 18, 1910, Baldwin Room, Toronto Reference Library, Toronto. p.1.

131 The *Globe*, June 18, 1910:9

132 The *Star*, June 21, 1910:1.

133 The *Star* April 21, 1910:15

134 Henderson, John 1910, Queen's Own Toronto Pageant June 18, 1910, Baldwin Room, Toronto Reference Library, Toronto. p.9.

135 The *Star* May 6, 1910:11

136 The *Globe*, May 3, 1910: 8.

137 Henderson, John 1910, Queen's Own Toronto Pageant June 18, 1910, Baldwin Room, Toronto Reference Library, Toronto. p.9.

138 The *Globe*, June 21, 1910:5.

139 Queen's Own Rifles of Canada, Semi-Centennial Reunion and Historical Pageant, Official Souvenir Programme. 1910. Geo. I. Riddell, Secretary, 36 King Street East. Toronto Reference Library, Baldwin Room, Semi-Centennial Reunion. 1910, Series 340, sub-series 10, File 8. P.5.

140 Henderson, John 1910, Queen's Own Toronto Pageant June 18, 1910, Baldwin Room, Toronto Reference Library, Toronto. p.5. The *Globe*, June 18, 1910:9.

141 Henderson, John 1910, Queen's Own Toronto Pageant June 18, 1910, Baldwin Room, Toronto Reference Library, Toronto.

142 Queen's Own Rifles of Canada, Semi-Centennial Reunion and Historical Pageant, Official Souvenir Programme. 1910. Geo. I. Riddell, Secretary, 36 King Street East. Toronto Reference Library, Baldwin Room, Semi-Centennial Reunion. 1910, Series 340, sub-series 10, File 8. p.15.

143 The *Globe*, June 8, 1910: 8. The cost of the canvas included its shipment from London and the cost of erecting it and taking it down.

144 The *News*, June 21, 1910:2.

145 https://www.royalparks.org.uk/parks/st-jamess-park/things-to-see-and-do/monuments-fountains-and-statues/the-queen-victoria-memorial, accessed March 21, 2023.

146 The *Globe*, June 2, 1910: 8

147 https://androom.home.xs4all.nl/biography/p019813.htm, accessed March 21, 2023. Queen's Own Rifles of Canada, Semi-Centennial Reunion and Historical Pageant, Official Souvenir Programme. 1910. Geo. I. Riddell, Secretary, 36 King Street East. Toronto Reference Library, Baldwin Room, Semi-Centennial Reunion. 1910, Series 340, sub-series 10, File 8. p.5. The Star, June 21, 1910:1.

148 In a photograph in the official pageant programme, the Iroquois chief portraying Brant is wearing the identical hat and feather shawl given to Pellatt at the garden party in June. Queen's Own Rifles of Canada, Semi-Centennial Reunion and Historical Pageant, Official Souvenir Programme. 1910. Geo. I. Riddell, Secretary, 36 King Street East. Toronto Reference Library, Baldwin Room, Semi-Centennial Reunion. 1910, Series 340, sub-series 10, File 8. p.35.

149 The *Star*, June 16, 1910:6.

150 The *Star*, June 16, 1910:6.

151 The *Star*, June 17, 1910:3.

152 The *Star*, June 17, 1910:3.

153 The *World*, June 17, 1910:7.
154 The *World*, June 17, 1910:7.
155 The *World*, June 17, 1910:2.
156 The *Globe*, June 3, 1910:9.
157 The *Globe*, May 30, 1910:8.
158 The Toronto *World*, June 18, 1910:7.
159 The *News*, June 4, 1910:16.
160 The Toronto *Star*, June 18, 1910:1.
161 The *World*, June 20, 1910:1. The Gunther invitation is in City of Toronto Archives, Series 340, Sub-Series 10, File 8.
162 The *Globe*, June 20, 1910:5.
163 The *Star*, June 20, 1910:8.
164 The *Globe*, June 20, 1910:5.
165 The *Globe*, June 20, 1910:5.
166 The *Globe*, June 20, 1910:5, The *Star*, June 20, 1910:18.
167 The *News*, June 20, 1910:1.
168 The *News*, June 24, 1910:13, The *Star*, June 20, 1910:18. The name is also written as Tanauyuasara, Gunther Scarpbook, p.68. AQOR.
169 Gayle M. Comeau-Vasilopoulos, "ORONHYATEKHA," in *Dictionary of Canadian Biography*, vol. 13, University of Toronto/Université Laval, 2003–, accessed March 23, 2023, http://www.biographi.ca/en/bio/oronhyatekha_13E.html.
170 The *Star*, June 22, 1910:8.
171 The Toronto *World*, June 18, 1910:7, The Toronto *World*, June 20, 1910:1, The *Globe*, June 20, 1910:8.
172 The *Globe*, June 20, 1910:8.
173 The *Globe*, June 20, 1910:8.
174 The *Star*, June 16, 1910:1.
175 The *Globe*, June 20,1910:1,9.
176 The *Globe*, June 20, 1910:1,9.
177 The *Globe*, June 3, 1910:9. The photograph can be seen in the E.F. Gunther Scrapbook, AQOR.00290:66.
178 The *Star*, June 20, 1910:7.
179 The *Star*, June 20, 1910:7.
180 The Toronto *World*, June 18, 1910:7.
181 The *Star*, June 20, 1910:7. A copy of the programme for the Divine Service is in the E.F. Gunther Scrapbook, AQOR 00290.
182 The Toronto *Star*, June 20, 1910:3.
183 The Toronto *Star*, June 18, 1910:1.
184 The Toronto *Star*, June 20, 1910:3.
185 The Toronto *Sunday World*, June 26, 1910:1. No author given.
186 Pamphlet, Memorial Service at the University of Toronto, Monday, June 20th, 1910 at 3:30 o'clock p.m. City of Toronto Archives. Fonds 2, series 1099, item 533. See also, E.F. Gunther Scrapbook, AQOR 00290.
187 The three university students were, J.H. Mewburn, W.F. Tempest, and M. Mckenzie. Barnard, 1960:89.
188 The *Globe*, June 21, 1910:5.
189 The *Globe*, June 21, 1910:1,9.
190 The *Star*, June 21, 1910:6.
191 The *Star*, June 21, 1910:6.

192 https://qormuseum.org/soldiers-of-the-queens-own/9631-2/

193 The *Star*, June 21, 1910:3.

194 The *Star*, June 23, 1910:12. There is a photograph in the QOR archives of Thorn lying in his casket at home.

195 The *Star*, June 22, 1910:2.

196 The *Star*, June 21, 1910:3.

197 The *News*, June21, 1910:2.

198 The *News*, June 21, 1910:2.

199 The *Star*, June 21, 1910:1.

200 Henderson, John 1910, Queen's Own Toronto Pageant June 18, 1910, Baldwin Room, Toronto Reference Library, Toronto. p.10.

201 The *News*, June 21, 1910:2.

202 Barnard, 1960: 90.

203 The *News*, June 22, 1910:11.

204 The *Mail and Empire*, June 23, 1910:10.

205 The *News*, June 21, 1910:6.

206 The *News*, June 23, 1910:1, 13. Also found in City of Toronto Archives, *Casa Loma Scrapbook*, Fonds 471. Series 2225.

207 Mumby's Special Dining Room, CNE Grandstand, City of Toronto Archives, Fonds 200, Series 372, subseries 1, item 780. Photo taken March 21, 1928.

208 The *News*, June 23, 1910:1, 13. Also found in City of Toronto Archives, Casa Loma Scrapbook, Fonds 471. Series 2225.

209 The Toronto *Star*, June 25, 1910:22, the Globe, June 25, 1910:17.

210 The Toronto *World*, June 25, 1910:7.

211 The Toronto *World*, June 25, 1910:7.

212 The Toronto World, June 25, 1910:7.

213 The Toronto *World*, June 25, 1910:7.

214 City of Toronto, Minutes of Council, July 14, 1910, pp.227-228.

215 The *Globe*, July 29, 1910:9.

216 The *Globe*, July 29, 1910:9.

217 The *Star*, August 3, 1910:10.

218 The Toronto *Star*, June 25, 1910:1.

219 Toronto *World*, July 11, 1910:1, Toronto *Star*, July 11,1910:1, July 14, 1910:1.

220 I wonder if the man on the left is Roy Riggs? And if this meet stimulated his interest in flying, which he did when he enlisted in WWI.

221 Toronto *Star*, July 14, 1910:1, LeNeve is variously spelled Leneve.

222 The *Star*, July 14, 1910:1.

223 Toronto *Star*, July 26, 1910:1.

224 The *Globe*, October 1, 1853:1.

225 Toronto *Star*, December 13 1909:2.

226 Toronto *Star*, December 13 1909:2.

227 Toronto *Star*, December 11 1909:19.

228 Toronto *Star*, April 30, 1906:2.

229 Queen's Own Rifles of Canada, Semi-Centennial Reunion and Historical Pageant, Official Souvenir Programme. 1910. Geo. I. Riddell, Secretary, 36 King Street East. Toronto Reference Library, Baldwin Room, Semi-Centennial Reunion. 1910, Series 340, sub-series 10, File 8. p.39.

230 The *Times*, August 29, 1910:4.

231 https://qormuseum.org/history/timeline-uniforms/evolution-of-enlisted-uni-forms-of-the-qorofc/

232 The *Star*, December 13, 1910:2.

233 Queen's Own Rifles of Canada, Semi-Centennial Reunion and Historical Pageant, Official Souvenir Programme. 1910. Geo. I. Riddell, Secretary, 36 King Street East. Toronto Reference Library, Baldwin Room, Semi-Centennial Reunion. 1910, Series 340, sub-series 10, File 8. P. 39.

234 The Toronto *Star*, June 19, 1910:2.

235 *The Queen's Own Rifles of Canada, 1860–1960.* Lieutenant-Colonel W.T. Barnard, The Ontario Publishing Company, Don Mills, Ontario, 1960. https://qormuseum.files.wordpress.com/2012/09/wt-barnard-history.pdf;

Nicholas A.E. Mouriopoulos, A Serious Piece of Business.https://qormuseum.org/2014/09/15/a-serious-piece-of-business-part-i/

236 The *Star* April 14 1910:13

237 The *Star*, May 19, 1919:12. The Globe, Nay 24, 1910:8.

238 The *Globe*, July 5, 1910:8.

239 P.O. Force Increased by Twenty-Five Men. Toronto *Star*, September 28, 1910:1.

240 The *Canadian Gazette*, No. 1,432, Vol. LV, September 15, 1910:699-700.

241 The *Star* December 11 1909:19

242 F.R. Henshaw, Diary 1910, AQOR archival box 02240.

243 The *Star*, August 2, 1910:1.

244 Canada Nominal Rolls and Paylist for Volunteer Militia, 1857–1922, 1909–1910, 2nd Battalion, Queen's Own Rifles, Ancestry.ca. Scroggie and Brazill were in K company and Riggs was in M company. Nominal Roll 1904-1912, AQOR 00160.

245 Nominal Roll 1904–1912, AQOR 00160.

246 John A. MacLaren WWI record, https://central.bac-lac.gc.ca/.item/?op=pdf&app=CEF&id=B7017-S001 accessed Feb 6, 2023. Nominal Roll 1904–1912, AQOR 00160.

247 Barnard 1960, Mouriopoulos 2014, Oreskovich 1982. F.R. Henshaw, Diary 1910, AQOR; archival box 02240. AQOR:S.

248 https://www.acotoronto.ca/res_files/EdenSmithbk.pdf David Roberts, "MASSEY, WALTER EDWARD HART," in *Dictionary of Canadian Biography*, vol. 13, University of Toronto/Université Laval, 2003–, accessed September 19, 2023, http://www.biographi.ca/en/bio/massey_walter_edward_hart_13E.html. H. V. Nelles, "GZOWSKI, Sir CASIMIR STANISLAUS," in *Dictionary of Canadian Biography*, vol. 12, University of Toronto/Université Laval, 2003–, accessed September 19, 2023, http://www.biographi.ca/en/bio/gzowski_casimir_stanislaus_12E.html.

249 Mouriopoulos, Nikolas A.E., 2014, "A Serious Piece of Business": Sir Henry Pellatt, The Queen's Own Rifles of Canada, and the "English Trip" of 1910. https://qormuseum.files.wordpress.com/2014/09/qor48.pdf p. 20.

250 Queen's Own Rifles of Canada, Semi-Centennial Reunion and Historical Pageant, Official Souvenir Programme. 1910. Geo. I. Riddell, Secretary, 36 King Street East. Toronto Reference Library, Baldwin Room, Semi-Centennial Reunion. 1910, Series 340, sub-series 10, File 8. P. 39.

251 The Toronto *Star*, July 27, 1910:1.

252 The *Globe* July 14 1910:8.

253 John Shields and J. White, groomsmen, R.W. and T. Cussions, coachmen, W.V. Mills, valet and W.G. Pattie, chauffeur. The Cussions were from the Channel Islands,

and in the 1912 marriage licence of William he is living at Walmer Rd. Hill in the stables of Casa Loma, as of the 1921 census he was the manager of the stables.

254 None of the grooms or batmen are listed in the roll published in the *Globe*, August 13, 1910:9. The Nominal Roll is the list of those who went to England. https://qormuseum.org/history/timeline-1900-1924/1910-nominal-roll-on-leaving-toronto-for-aldershot/

255 K Company members in the 1910 H company included Capt. W.D. Allan, Lt. A.R. Lawrence, Col. Sgt. N.E. Murton, Sgt. L.R. Young, Sgt. G.N. Molesworth, Sgt. J.P.M. Sibbald, Cpl. J.P. Clarke, and privates, W.L. Bell, Brazill, J.R. Buller, G.I. Legate, A.G. Lester, A.S. Porter, H. Pratt, Scroggie and C.M. Young, some had been in the QOR since 1908. M Company members were R.B. Johnston, M.A. Helliwell and Riggs. Canada Nominal Rolls and Paylist for Volunteer Militia, 1857-1922, 1909-1910, 2nd Battalion, Queen's Own Rifles, Ancestry.ca. On his 1910 regimental enlistment papers Scroggie wrote K company, referencing his existing company affiliation in the QOR. Five other members of H Co. identified as K Co. in the Regimental Orders of June and July 1910; E.V. Corbett, G.W. Argue, H.G. Kerr, E.R. Andras and V.H.K. Moorehouse. This brings the total number of K Co. men, in H Co., on the English trip to 21. AQOR:S pp.52-53.

256 UK-Ireland Incoming Passenger List, SS Megantic, arriving in Liverpool, August 17, 1910.

257 Ancestry.ca

258 The *World*, August 4 1910:8.

259 AQOR:S page 47

260 *Evening Telegram*, August 13, 1910:15.

261 *Star*, August 9, 1910:2.

262 The *World*, August 11,1910:1,7

263 The *Mail and Empire*, August 11,1910:4

264 The *Times*, August 12, 1910:3.

265 The *Mail and Empire*, August 13,1910:4

266 The *Evening Telegram*, August 13, 1910:15

267 The *Globe*, August 13, 1910:9.

268 The *Mail and Empire*, August 15,1910:1

269 The *News*, August 15, 1910:3.

270 The *News*, August 15, 1910:1.

271 The *Globe*, August 15, 1910:6. A photograph of this can be found on the AQOR FLICKR 02069Z.

272 The *Evening Telegram* August 13, 1910:15.

273 The *Evening Telegram* August 13, 1910:15.

274 The *Star,* August 15, 1910:5.

275 The *Star*, August 15, 1910:5.

276 The *Star*, August 15, 1910:5.

277 The *Star*, August 15, 1910:5.

278 The *Star*, August 15, 1910:5.

279 The *Star*, August 15, 1910:5.

280 The *Globe*, August 15, 1910:1

281 The *Evening Telegram* August 15, 1910:1

282 The *News*, August 16, 1910:1. AQOR:S, p.38

283 *M&E* August 16 1910:1.

284 *Evening Telegram* August 15, 1910:1

285 The *World*, August 16, 1910:7.

286 *Evening Telegram*, August 15, 1910:1

287 *Evening Telegram*, August 15, 1910:1

288 The *World*, August 4, 1910.

289 The *World*, August 18, 1910:1

290 The *World*, August 18, 1910:1

291 The *Mail and Empire*, August 16, 1910:1.

292 The *World*, August 16, 1910:7.

293 The *World*, August 17, 1910:1.

294 The *Star*, August 16, 1910:9.

295 The *Star*, August 18, 1910:1,5.

296 The *Star*, August 17, 1910:7.

297 August 18, AQOR:S:38

298 The *Evening Telegram*, August 18, 1910:1.

299 The *News*, August 16, 1910:1. AQOR:S #02232:38.

300 Toronto *Star*, August16, 1910:9.

301 *M&E* August 16 1910:1

302 *Mail and Empire*, August 17, 1910:1.

303 The *World*, August 16, 1910:7.

304 The *News*, August 16, 1910:1. AQOR:S, page 38.

305 The *Star,* August 3, 1910:10.

306 *Evening Telegram*, August 18,1910:13

307 The *Star*, August 17, 1910:7.

308 The *Globe*, August 18,1910:1.

309 The *Star*, August 18, 1910:1,5.

310 *Evening Telegram*, August 18, 1910:18.

311 Bogaert, Kandace "Patient Experience and the Treatment of Venereal Disease in Toronto's Military Base Hospital during the First World War." *Canadian Military History* 26, 2 (2017).

312 The *News*, August 17, 1910:1, AQOR:S, p.38.

313 AQOR:S, *News*, August 17, 1910:1.

314 The *Star,* August 17, 1910:7.

315 *Mail and Empire*, August 17, 1910:1.

316 The *World*, August 20, 1910:2.

317 *Evening Telegram*, August 20, 1910:22

318 *Evening Telegram*, August 15,1910:1

319 The *Star*, August 18, 1910:1,5.

320 The *Star*, August 18, 1910:1,5.

321 The *Evening Telegram*, August 18, 1910:18.

322 The *Evening Telegram*, August 18, 1910:18.

323 The *Globe*, August 18, 1910:1.

324 The *Globe*, August 18, 1910:1.

325 The *Evening Telegram*, August 18, 1910:18.

326 The *Star*, August 19, 1910:2.

327 The *Star*, August 19, 1910:2.

328 AQOR.S #02232:39.

329 The *Globe*, August 19, 1910:1.

330 The *News*, AQOR:S, p. 40. Similarity of photo for Charlebois in "Canada's Sons in the City," *Evening News,* September 16, 1910. Sir Henry Pellatt and the Queen's Own

Rifles visit England. City of Toronto Archives, Toronto, Fonds 471, Series 2225, File 2. For Salvaneschi, The *Star*, November 15, 1910:2, photo of H. Salvaneschi, "Queen's Own man." And WWI enlistment record, describing him as "bald on top of head from forehead to occipital." LAC.

331 The *Globe*, September 5, 1910:8. On the *Megantic* passenger manifest Charlie is listed as a mechanic and Salvaneschi was employed as a chef in a Toronto hotel.

332 "Walter J. Charlebois Dies After Operation." The *Star*, March 16, 1912:12.

333 The *Globe*, June 20, 1910:8.

334 The *Star*, August 18, 1910:1,5.

335 The *Mail & Empire*, August 19, 1910:2.

336 Evening *Telegram*, August 18, 1910:18

337 The *News*, August 19, 1910:6.

338 The Evening *Telegram*, August 20, 1910:22.

339 The *Star*, August 20, 1910:9. Pickets are military guards or police.

340 The *Star*, August 20, 1910:9.

341 The *Globe*, August 20, 1910:1

342 The *Star*, August 20, 1910:9

343 The *Telegram*, September 3, 1910:6.

344 The Evening *Telegram*, August 13, 1910:15.

345 https://www.ancestry.ca/discoveryui-content/view/16793080:1518?_phsrc=FKd1386&_phstart=successSource&gsln=winnett&ml_rpos=3&queryId=a59adf132f3043d49d2732ae1b29c13d

346 Queen's Own Rifles of Canada, Semi-Centennial Reunion and Historical Pageant, Official Souvenir Programme. 1910. Geo. I. Riddell, Secretary, 36 King Street East. Toronto Reference Library, Baldwin Room, Semi-Centennial Reunion. 1910, Series 340, sub-series 10, File 8. p.39

347 The *Star*, September 3, 1910:12. With the reports from the *Megantic* the names of the press gang will associated with their articles.

348 The *World*, August 4, 1910:8.

349 The Evening *Telegram*, September 3, 1910:6.

350 UK and Ireland, Incoming Passengers Lists, 1876–1960. Liverpool England, August 1910. Megantic. Ancestry.com.

351 The *Star*, August 20, 1910:1. Alwyn Turner, 2024, *Little Englanders. Britain in the Edwardian Era.* Profile Books, London.

352 The *World*, September 4, 1910:5.

353 The Evening *Telegram*, September 3, 1910:6.

354 The *Star*, September 3, 1910:12.

355 The *Globe*, September 3, 1910:1.

356 The *Star*, September 3, 1910:12.

357 The *Star*, September 3, 1910:12.

358 The Evening *Telegram*, September 3, 1910:6.

359 The *Globe*, September 3, 1910:1

360 The *Globe*, September 3, 1910:1.

361 The *Globe,* September 3, 1910:1, The *Star*, September 26, 1910:5.

362 The Evening *Telegram*, September 3, 1910:6

363 The Evening *Telegram*, September 3, 1910:6

364 The Evening *Telegram*, September 3, 1910:6

365 The Evening *Telegram*, September 3, 1910:6

366 The Evening *Telegram*, September 3, 1910:6. This programme is in the Vincent Massey fonds, UTA, Massey Family Fonds, B1987-0082/129 (1):17.

367 The Evening *Telegram*, September 3, 1910:6.

368 The *Globe*, September 5, 1910:8.

369 The *Globe*, September 5, 1910:8.

370 Mary Jane Edwards, "DRUMMOND, WILLIAM HENRY," in **Dictionary of Canadian Biography**, vol. 13, University of Toronto/Université Laval, 2003–, accessed May 2, 2023, http://www.biographi.ca/en/bio/drummond_william_henry_13E.html.

371 Cheryl Thompson, "The Complicated History of Canadian Blackface," *Spacing*, October 29, 2018. http://spacing.ca/toronto/2018/10/29/the-complicated-history-of-canadian-blackface/ accessed June 28, 2023.

372 The *Star*, September 3, 1910:12. The Band was called variously Raz-ba-tay and Raz-ha-daz.

373 The *Globe*, September 5, 1910:8.

374 The Evening *Telegram*, September 3, 1910:6.

375 The *World*, September 4, 1910:5.

376 Non-protestant members included Roman Catholics W.J. Charlebois, Sgt. J. Salvaneschi, and Cpl. Lou Feldstein who was Jewish. There might be more who were not protestant.

377 The *Star*, September 3, 1910:12.

378 The *Star*, September 3, 1910:12.

379 The *Star*, September 3, 1910:12.

380 The Evening *Telegram*, September 3, 1910:6.

381 The *Globe*, September 3, 1910:1.

382 The *World*, September 4, 1910:5.

383 The *News*, September 3, 1910:1, AQOR.S, #02232:41.

384 The *World*, September 4, 1910:5.

385 The *World*, September 4, 1910:5.

386 The Evening *Telegram*, September 3, 1910:6.

387 The *Globe*, September 3, 1910:1.

388 The Evening *Telegram*, September 3, 1910:19.

389 The Evening *Telegram*, September 3, 1910:6, The Evening *Telegram*, September 2, 1910:19.

390 The *Star*, September 3, 1910:12.

391 The Evening *Telegram*, September 3, 1910:19.

392 The *News*, August 22, 1910:3. AQOR.S, #02232:41.

393 The *Star*, August 20, 1910:1.

394 The *Standard Empire*, AQOR Scrapbook, 02251.

395 No information was found about Hallam.

396 Nicholas Connell, 2013, *Doctor Crippen*, Amberly Publishing Co., UK. P.71. Bernard Grant, *To The Four Corners*, 1933, Hutchison & Co. London,

397 Percival Phillips, "Journalist, Dead." The *New York Times*, Jan. 30, 1937:17.

398 The *Times*, August 22, 1910:4.

399 Bernard Grant, *To The Four Corners*, 1933, Hutchison & Co. London. P. 45.

400 Bernard Grant, *To The Four Corners*, 1933, Hutchison & Co. London. P. 47.

401 *With The Royal Canadians*, Stanley McKeown Brown, Toronto, The Publishers' Syndicate, 1900.

402 The *Times*, August 29, 1910:4.

403 The *Times*, August 29, 1910:4.

404 Don Glassman, "Italian Liner to Defy the Waves," *Popular Mechanics Magazine*, April 1931, Vol. 55, No.4: 626-631.

405 The Evening *Telegram*, September 2, 1910:19.

406 The Evening *Telegram*, September 3, 1910:6.

407 The Evening *Telegram*, September 2, 1910:19.

408 The *Star*, September 24, 1910:1, 8.

409 *Daily News*, August 29 City of Toronto Archives #632442.

410 Joseph P. Clarke, The Toronto *Star*, February 9, 1910, pp.1, 14.

411 The Toronto *Star*, September 9, 1910:2,8.

412 The Evening *Telegram*, September 2, 1910:19.

413 The *Globe*, September 10, 1910:1.

414 The Evening *Telegram*, September 2, 1910:19, The *World*, August 23, 1910:1.

415 The Evening *Telegram*, September 2, 1910:19.

416 This is captured in a Gale & Polden photograph (No.1) in the Baldwin Collection of the Toronto Public Library, OHQ-Pictures-S-R-615.

417 The *Daily Standard* reported in the *Globe*, September 10, 1910:1.

418 The *Globe*, September 10, 1910:1.

419 The *World,* August 29, 1910:1.

420 The *Star*, September 9, 1910:2,8.

421 The *Star*, September 9, 1910:2,8.

422 The Evening *Telegram* September 2, 1910:19.

423 The *Globe*, September 10, 1910:1.

424 The Evening *Telegram*, September 2, 1910:19.

425 The *World*, August 29, 1910:1.

426 The *Globe*, August 29, 1910:1.

427 The *Globe*, September 12, 1910:4.

428 The Evening *Telegram*, September 2, 1910:19.

429 The *Globe*, September 12, 1910:4.

430 The *Globe*, September 12, 1910:4.

431 The *Canadian Gazette*, No. 1,430, Vol. LV, September 1, 1910:647.

432 The Evening *Telegram*, September 10, 1910:29.

433 The Evening *Telegram*, September 10, 1910:29.

434 The *Globe*, August 30, 1910:1.

435 The *Globe*, September 12, 1910:4.

436 The *Globe*, September 12, 1910:4.

437 The Evening *Telegram*, September 14, 1910:17.

438 The Evening *Telegram*, September 14, 1910:17.

439 The Evening *Telegram*, September 14, 1910:17.

440 The Evening *Telegram*, September 14, 1910:17.

441 The Evening *Telegram*, September 14, 1910:17.

442 The Evening *Telegram*, September 14, 1910:17.

443 The *Globe*, October 3, 1910:1,4.

444 The *Globe*, October 3, 1910:1,4.

445 The *Daily Mail*, August 31, 1910. City of Toronto Archives, Sir Henry Pellatt Scrapbook, 1990.7.4.

446 The *Star*, September 24, 1910:1.

447 The *Globe*, September 13, 1910:4.

448 *Daily Mail*, August 31 Scrapbook C of T. 1990.7.4

449 The *Star*, September 16, 1910:1.
450 The *Star,* September 16, 1910:1.
451 The *News*, September 4, 1910. AQOR #02232:44.
452 *Mail and Empire*, September 24, 1910.
453 *Mail and Empire*, September 26, 1910:3.
454 The *World*, September 13, 1910:6.
455 The *Star*, September 16, 1910:1.
456 The Evening *Telegram*, September 17, 1910:17.
457 The Evening *Telegram*, September 19, 1910:13.
458 The Evening *Telegram*, September 19, 1910:13.
459 The Evening *Telegram*, September 19, 1910:13.
460 The Evening *Telegram*, September 19, 1910:13.
461 The Evening *Telegram*, September 19, 1910:13.
462 The *Globe*, September 2, 1910:2.
463 The *Globe*, September 30, 1910:7.
464 The Evening *Telegram*, September 2, 1910:19.
465 Postcard, Chas. G. Winsor to Mrs. Rennie, 251 Huron St., Toronto. AQOR.
466 Postcard, Harry Wilcockson to Maude Wilcockson, Columbus Ontario. AQOR.
467 Postcard, from Courtney (no last name) to Miss C. Duke, 2 Montrose Ave., Toronto. AQOR.
468 Postcard from Willi Rossen to Mrs Rossen, 37 Moscow Ave., Toronto. QORA. Moscow Ave. was changed to Gough Ave. in 1924.
469 *Daily News*, September 2 Scrapbook C of T. 1990.7.4
470 *Canadian Gazette*, No. 1,433, Vol. LV, September 22, 1910:728.
471 The *Star*, September 12, 1910:3.
472 The *Canadian Gazette*, No. 1,431, Vol. LV, September 8, 1910:678.
473 The *Canadian Gazette*, No. 1,341, Vol. LV, September 8, 1910:678.
474 The Evening *Telegram*, September 10, 1910:29.
475 The *News*, AQOR.S p.43.
476 The *World*, August 4, 1910.
477 The Evening *Telegram*, September 2, 1910:19.
478 The *Star*, September 13, 1910:2.
479 The *Star*, September 13, 1910:2.
480 The *Star*, September 13, 1910:2.
481 The *Star*, September 13, 1910:2.
482 The *Star*, September 13, 1910:2.
483 The *Star*, September 13, 1910:2.
484 The Evening *Telegram*, September 2 1910:17.
485 The *World*, September 13, 1910:6.
486 The Evening *Telegram*, September 19, 1910.
487 *Daily News*, September 2, 1910, City of Toronto Archives Scrapbook 1990.7.4.
488 Edward Enright, MacLaren Family collections.
489 The *News*, September 15, 1910:3, AQOR.S, p. 44.
490 Visitors' Book, Aldershot 1910, Officers' Mess. AQOR, 00204.
491 The *Star*, September 12, 1910:3.
492 The *Star*, September 12, 1910:3.
493 The *Globe*, September 13, 1910:4.
494 The *Globe*, September 13, 1910:4.
495 The *Star,* September 9, 1910:2,8.

496 The *Globe*, September 15, 1910:1.

497 The *Globe*, September 15, 1910:1.

498 The *News*, September 17, 1910:11, AQOR.S #002232:45.

499 The *Star*, September 16, 1910:1.

500 The *Globe*, September 15, 1910:1.

501 The *Globe*, September 15, 1910:1.

502 The *News*, September 17, 1910:11. AQOR.S, p.45.

503 The Evening *Telegram*, September 17, 1910:17.

504 The *Globe*, September 17, 1910:3.

505 The *Star*, September 16, 1910:1.

506 Jack Cecillon, "PYNE, ROBERT ALLAN," in ***Dictionary of Canadian Biography,*** vol. 16, University of Toronto/Université Laval, 2003–, accessed June 19. 2023, http://www.biographi.ca/en/bio/pyne_robert_allan_16E.html. Toronto Star, September 6, 1910:7.

507 *Daily News*, August 31, City of Toronto Archives, Scrapbook 1990.7.4.

508 The *Globe*, September 17, 1910:3.

509 The *Globe*, September 17, 1910:3.

510 The *Star*, September 16, 1910:1.

511 Toronto *Star*, September 26, 1910:5.

512 University of Toronto Archives, Massey Family Fonds, B1987-0082/129 (05):57.

513 University of Toronto Archives, Massey Family Fonds, B1987-0082/129 (05):3.

514 The *Globe*, September 17, 1910:13.

515 The *Star,* September 16:1.

516 The *News*, September 17, 1910:11, AQOR.S #02232:45.

517 The *Globe*, September 17, 1910:3.

518 The *Globe*, September 17, 1910:3.

519 The *Globe*, September 17, 1910:3.

520 The *News*, September 17, 1910:11, AQOR.S, #02232:45.

521 The *News*, AQOR.S, #02232:45.

522 The *Globe*, September 17, 1910:3.

523 The *Globe*, September 17, 1910:3.

524 The *Globe*, September 17, 1910:3.

525 The *Mail and Empire*, September 24, 1910:15,25.

526 The *Globe*, September 17, 1910:3.

527 The *Star*, September 16, 1910:1.

528 The *Globe*, September 19, 1910:1.

529 The *Star,* September 24, 1910:1,8.

530 The *Globe*, September 19, 1910:1.

531 The *Globe*, September 19, 1910:1,3.

532 The *Globe*, September 19, 1910:1.

533 *Mail and Empire*, September 24, 1910:15, 25.

534 The *Evening Telegram*, September 26, 1910:16.

535 *Daily News*, September 9, 1910, City of Toronto Archives, Henry Pellatt Scrapbook, 1990.7.1

536 The *Star*, September 24, 1910:1,8.

537 The *World*, September 13, 1910:6.

538 *Daily News*, September 12, 1910, City of Toronto Archives, Sir Henry Pellatt Scrapbook 1990.7.1

539 The *Star*, September 24, 1910:1,8.

540 The *Star*, September 24, 1910:1,8.
541 The *Star*, September 24, 1910:1,8.
542 The *Star*, September 24, 1910:1,8.
543 The *News*, September 10, 1910:1. AQOR, #02232:45.
544 University of Toronto Archives, Massey Family Fonds, B1987-0082/129 (05):58.
545 University of Toronto Archives, Massey Family Fonds, B1987-0082/129 (05):53.
546 University of Toronto Archives, Massey Family Fonds, B1987-0082/129 (05):52.
547 University of Toronto Archives, Massey Family Fonds, B1987-0082/129 (05):50.
548 University of Toronto Archives, Massey Family Fonds, B1987-0082/129 (05):49.
549 The *Star*, September 10, 1910:1.
550 The *Globe*, September 23, 1910:8.
551 Toronto *Star*, September 10, 1910:1.
552 The Evening *Telegram*, September 12, 1910:8.
553 The *Globe*, September 26,1910:1.
554 The *Star*, September 13, 1910:13.
555 The *Star*, September 13, 1910:13.
556 The Evening *Telegram*, September 26, 1910:16.
557 The *Star*, September 24, 1910:1,8.
558 *Mail and Empire*, September 24, 1910:15, 25.
559 The Evening *Telegram*, September 26, 1910:16.
560 The Evening *Telegram*, September 26, 1910:16.
561 The Evening *Telegram*, September 26, 1910:16.
562 *Daily News*, September 13, 1910, City of Toronto Archives, Scrapbook #632442
563 *Mail and Empire*, September 26, 1910:3.
564 The Evening *Telegram*, October 1, 1910:21.
565 *Mail and Empire*, September 26, 1910:3
566 *Mail and Empire*, September 24, 1910:15,25.
567 The officers were Lieut.-Col. P.L. Mason, Major R. Rennie and Capt. G.M. Higinbotham; non-commissioned officers, Colour-sergeant M.B. MacDonald, Staff-sergeant H.E. Passmore, Corp. G.E. Freeman and Corp. H. New.
568 Dunn was a clerk, Standard Sanitary Mfg. Co.; Newton was a clerk at T. Eaton Co.; Hammond was a clerk; McRae a clerk; Muir was a clerk T. Eaton Co.; Stickney a clerk; Forsyth was a clerk at Manufacturers Life Insurance. *Might's City of Toronto Directory 1910* and the *Megantic* passenger list.
569 The *Evening Standard*, September 12, 1910. Actually the king had visited Canada in 1908
570 *Evening Standard*, September 12, 1910. City of Toronto Archives, Sir Henry Mill Pellatt Scrapbook, 1910.
571 *Evening Standard*, September 12, 1910. City of Toronto Archives, Sir Henry Mill Pellatt Scrapbook, 1910.
572 Newspaper clipping, (paper not named) AQOR.S:14.
573 Newspaper clipping, AQOR.S:18-20.
574 Newspaper clipping, AQOR.S:20.
575 *Might's City of Toronto Directory, 1910.*
576 Newspaper Clipping, AQOR.S:20.
577 Newspaper Clipping, AQOR.S:20.
578 Newspaper clipping, (paper not named) AQOR.S:14.
579 Newspaper Clipping, AQOR.S:20.

580 *Evening Standard*, September 12, 1910. City of Toronto Archives, Sir Henry Mill Pellatt Scrapbook, 1910.

581 The *Star*, September 13, 1910:7.

582 The *Canadian Gazette*, No. 1,432, Vol. LV, September 15, 1910:699-700.

583 Newspaper clipping, AQOR.S:16.

584 *Standard* September 12 City of Toronto Archives 1990.7.1.

585 E.F. Gunther Scrapbook, AQOR #00290.

586 The *News*, September 13, 1910:6. AQOR.S:37.

587 The *Star,* September 29, 1910:1.

588 The *Mail and Empire*, September 28, 910:10.

589 The *Mail and Empire*, September 14, 1910:1.

590 The *Mail and Empire*, September 26, 1910:3.

591 The Evening *Telegram*, October 1, 1910:21.

592 The *Globe*, October 1, 1910:A5.

593 The Evening *Telegram*, October 1, 1910:21.

594 The Evening *Telegram*, October 1, 1910:21.

595 The Evening *Telegram*, October 1, 1910:21.

596 AQOR.S, pp.58-59.

597 Henshaw Diary, AQOR,02240, pp.57-58.

598 AQOR.S, p. 58.

599 *Daily News*, September 13, 1910. City of Toronto Archives, Pellatt Scrapbook #632442.

600 The *Mail and Empire*, September 26, 1910:3.

601 The *Globe*, September 26, 1910:7.

602 *Daily Sketch*, September 14, 1910. City of Toronto Archives Henry Pellatt Scrapbook 1990.7.2

603 AQOR.S:59.

604 Evening *Telegram*, September 10, 1910:19.

605 The *World*, September 13, 1910:6.

606 The *World*, September 13, 1910:6.

607 AQOR.S, Jim Scroggie's various invitations and membership cards.

608 Canadian Division of the Institute of Journalists, Montreal 1911:24.

609 https://www.vam.ac.uk/articles/music-hall-and-variety-theatre#slideshow=15664669&slide=0 accessed June 5, 2023.

610 Evening *Telegram*, October 1, 1910:21.

611 https://www.vam.ac.uk/articles/music-hall-and-variety-theatre#slideshow=15664669&slide=0 accessed June 5, 2023. Alwyn Turner, 2024, *Little Englanders. Britain in the Edwardian Era*. Profile Books, London.

612 *Daily News*, September 15, 1910. City of Toronto Archives, Henry Pellatt Scrapbook #632442.

613 *Daily News*, September 15, 1910. City of Toronto Archives, Henry Pellatt Scrapbook #632442.

614 *Daily News*, September 15, 1910. City of Toronto Archives, Henry Pellatt Scrapbook #632442.

615 *Daily News*, September 15, 1910. City of Toronto Archives, Henry Pellatt Scrapbook #632442.

616 *Of Toronto the Good, a Social Study: The Queen City of Canada as it is.* C.S. Clark, The Toronto Publishing Company, Montreal, 1898.

617 "Canada's Sons in the City," *Evening News*, September 16, 1910. Sir Henry Pellatt and the Queen's Own Rifles visit England. City of Toronto Archives, Toronto, Fonds 471, Series 2225, File 2.

618 Robert Murray Smythe, 1880-1973.

619 John Henry Wilson.

620 Edgar Richard Verrall died October 22, 1922, pulmonary tuberculosis, veterans grave, Prospect Cemetery.

621 *Evening Times*, September 16, 1910.

622 Earl Rightman Suddaby, born August 8, 1890 died November 28, 1969, information from Canadian Military records.

623 *Evening Times*, September 16, 1910.

624 1911 Census of Canada, Walter Charlebois, age 30, machinist living 667 College St., Toronto, with widowed mother, Permilia Charlebois, (his mother was born in Penetanguishene, Ontario.)

625 *Evening Times*, September 16, 1910.

626 "Canada's Sons in the City," *Evening News*, September 16, 1910. Sir Henry Pellatt and the Queen's Own Rifles visit England. City of Toronto Archives, Toronto, Fonds 471, Series 2225, File 2.

627 John Alexander Newsome, lived in Toronto until 1921 when he moved to Los Angeles. Information from City of Toronto Might's Directory and Ancestry.com.

628 The *World*, October 3, 1910:9.

629 The *World*, October 3, 1910:9.

630 The *Canadian Gazette*, No. 1,432, Vol. LV. September 14, 1910:700.

631 *Standard*, September 12, 1910. Scrapbook 1990.7.1, City of Toronto Archives.

632 The *Daily Sketch*, September 14, 1910. Scrapbook 1990.7.1, City of Toronto Archives.

633 The *Times*, September 17, 1910:7.

634 The *Globe*, September 26, 1910:7.

635 The *Globe*, September 26, 1910:7.

636 *Mail and Empire*, September 26, 1910:3.

637 Toronto *Star*, October 1, 1910:21.

638 The *Globe*, September 26, 1910:7.

639 The *Globe*, September 17, 1910:1.

640 The *Mail and Empire*, September 28,1910:10.

641 The *Mail and Empire*, September 28, 1910:10.

642 The *Canadian Gazette*, No. 1,433, Vol. LV, September 22,1910:727.

643 The *Globe*, September 26, 1910:7.

644 *Mail and Empire*, September 17, 1910:1.

645 The *Globe*, September 26, 1910:7.

646 The *Globe*, September 26, 1910:7.

647 The *Canadian Gazette*, No. 1,433, Vol. LV, September 22,1910:728.

648 The Evening *Telegram*, October 1, 1910:21.

649 The *World,* October 3, 1910:9.

650 *Star,* September 22, 1910:8.

651 *Star*, September 22, 1910:8.

652 *World*, September 17, 1910:6.

653 "The English Trip." Major C.B. Lindsey, 1910 Reunion, January 6th, 1939. Royal York Hotel, Toronto. (no page numbers) AQOR, SC25, F24, 1910 Trip Reunion.

654 The *Globe*, September 17, 1910:6.

655 https://lordmayorsshow.london/history/gog-and-magog

656 The *Globe*, September 17, 1910:1.

657 *World*, October 3, 1910:9.

658 The *Globe*, October 5, 1910:8.

659 "The English Trip." Major C.B. Lindsey, 1910 Reunion, January 6th, 1939. Royal York Hotel, Toronto. (no page numbers). AQOR, SC25, F24, 1910 Trip Reunion.

660 *World*, October 3, 1910:9.

661 The *News*, August 15, 1910:3.

662 Toronto *Star*, October 1, 1910:21.

663 *Daily News*, Tuesday September 13, 1910. City of Toronto Archives, Sir Henry Pellatt Scrapbook. #63244

664 The *Globe*, September 19, 1910:1.

665 The *World*, October 4, 1910:7.

666 The *Times*, September 21, 1910:7.

667 The *Times*, September 21, 1910:7.

668 The *Evening Telegram*, October 1, 1910:21.

669 The *Times*, September 21, 1907:7.

670 The *Globe,* October 4, 1910:1.

671 The *Globe*, September 23, 1910:1.

672 The *Star*, October 1, 1910:3.

673 The Evening *Telegram*, October 3, 1910:

674 The *Globe*, September 23, 1910:1.

675 The *Globe*, October 6, 1910:7.

676 Britannica, T. Editors of Encyclopaedia. "John Elliot Burns." *Encyclopedia Britannica,* January 20, 2023. https://www.britannica.com/biography/John-Elliot-Burns. Accessed June 12, 2023.

677 https://www.theguardian.com/theguardian/2012/oct/02/john-burns-battersea-cycling-archive-1900

678 The *Globe*, October 6, 1910:7.

679 The *Globe*, October 6, 1910:7.

680 The *Star,* October 3, 1910:3.

681 The hill, near the town of Fovant was also the location of a training camp during the First World War, and men of the regiments training nearby carved their regimental badges into the hill. Now known as the Fovant Badges, the white chalk of the emblems are visible against the green of the hill and are a recognized as Scheduled English Heritage Monuments. https://historicengland.org.uk/services-skills/education/educational-images/the-fovant-badges-4491 . Accessed June 13, 2023.

682 The *Globe*, October 6, 1910:7.

683 The *Globe*, October 3, 1910:1,4.

684 https://www.youtube.com/watch?v=QnumhSQx204

685 The *Times*, September 26, 1910:7.

686 The *Times*, September 26,1910:7. However, Llwyd seems to have been on the SS Canada for the return voyage.

687 The *Star*, October 1, 1910:3.

688 The *Times*, September 26, 1910:7.

689 The *Times*, September 26, 1910:7.

690 Argue, Diary AQOR.

691 The *Times*, September 26, 1910:7.

692 The *Times*, September 26, 1910:7.

693 The *World,* October 4, 1910:1,7.
694 The *Star*, September 26, 1910:5.
695 The *Star*, September 26, 1910:5.
696 The *Globe*, October 3, 1910:1,4.
697 The *Globe*, October 11, 1910:11.
698 Henshaw Diary, AQOR.
699 The Evening *Telegram*, October 3, 1910:17.
700 The *Star,* October 3, 1910:3.
701 The Star, October 3, 1910:3.
702 The Evening *Telegram*, October 3, 1910:17.
703 The *Star*, October 3, 1910:3.
704 The *Star*, October 3, 1910:3.
705 The Evening *Telegram*, October 3,1910:17.
706 Outgoing British Passenger List SS Canada, SS Canada Passenger Manifest, Ancestry.ca.
707 The *Star*, October 3,1910:3.
708 The *Star*, October 3, 1910:3.
709 The *Globe*, October 3, 1910:1,4.
710 The *Star*, October 3, 1910:3.
711 The *Star*, October 3, 1910:1,4.
712 The *Star*, October 3, 1910:1.
713 The *Star*, October 3, 1910:1.
714 The *Star*, October 3, 1910:1.
715 The *Star*, October 3, 1910:3.
716 The *Star*, October 3, 1910:3.
717 The *Star*, October 3, 1910:3.
718 The *Globe*, October 3, 1910:1,4.
719 Toronto *Star*, October 3, 1910:3.
720 The *News*, October 3, 1910:3.
721 The Evening *Telegram*, October 3, 1910:17.
722 Argue, AQOR. The World, October 4, 1910:1.
723 *Mail and Empire*, October 4, 1910:1,3.
724 The *News*, October 4, 1910:2.
725 The *News*, October 4, 1910:2.
726 Toronto *Star*, October 3, 1910:1.
727 The *Globe*, October 4, 1910:1.
728 Evening *Telegram*, October 4,1910:9.
729 *Telegram*, October 4, 1910:9.
730 *Mail and Empire*, October 4, 1910:1,3.
731 The Evening *Telegram*, October 3, 1910:9.
732 The Evening *Telegram*, October 3, 1910:9.
733 The *News*, October 4, 1910:6.
734 The *Star*, October 4,1910:3.
735 The Evening *Telegram*, October 4, 1910:9.
736 The *Star*, July 11, 1910:6.
737 The *Globe*, August 18, 1910:1.
738 The *Star*, October 6,1910:8.
739 The *Star*, October 4,1910:1.
740 *Mail and Empire*, October 1, 1910.

741 The *World*, October 5, 1910:6.

742 The *News*, October 5, 1910:6.

743 The *Star*, October 5, 1910:7.

744 The *Globe*, October 6, 1910:9.

745 The *Globe*, September 24, 1910:5. *The Young Vincent Massey*, Claude Bissell, U of T Press, 1981, p.53. Incoming passenger list for the SS *Canada*. In his autobiography he makes no mention of the trip. *Vincent Massey, What's Past is Prologue*. 1963, Macmillan Co., Toronto.

746 The Toronto *Star*, March 17, 1906:1. The Toronto *Star*, November 11,1910:12. Toronto *Star*, September 13, 1910:13.

747 Rippey SR. Infectious diseases associated with molluscan shellfish consumption." Clin Microbiol Rev. 1994 Oct;7(4):419-25. doi: 10.1128/CMR.7.4.419. PMID: 7834599; PMCID: PMC358335. Accessed June 3, 2023.

748 The *Globe*, November 22, 1910:1, the *Globe*, November 19, 1910:8.

749 Adam, T. (2001). *Philanthropic Landmarks: The Toronto Trail from a Comparative Perspective, 1870s to the 1930s*. *Urban History Review / Revue d'histoire urbaine*, *30*(1), 3–21. https://doi.org/10.7202/1015939ar

750 *A Brief History of Philanthropy* at the University of Toronto, May 23, 2018, Martin L. Friedland, C.C., Q.C., LL.D., F.R.S.C., university professor and professor of law emeritus, University of Toronto. https://www.chancellorscircle.utoronto.ca/wp-content/uploads/Martin-Friedland-Talk-Philanthropy.pdf accessed August 3, 2023.

751 The *Star*, March 10, 1939:2.

752 AQOR.S:8.

753 AQOR.S:8.

754 Today there is some doubt cast upon Crippen's conviction. https://www.the-guardian.com/uk/2007/oct/17/ukcrime.science

755 The *Star*, November 28, 1910:12.

756 The *Globe and Mail*, January 6, 1939:13.

757 QOR Muster Roll Call 1904-1912, AQOR 00160.

758 Toronto Press Club, Fifth Annual Theatre Nights, Royal Alexandra Theatre, June 18, 19, 1909. No additional publication information. Brown Family collection. (TPC:FATN)

759 The *Globe*, January 12, 1912:8, The *Globe*, February 7, 1912:8.

760 Toronto *Star*, July 31, 1917:4.

761 Toronto *Star*, July 31, 1917:4.

762 Toronto *Star*, July 31, 1917:4.

763 Toronto *Star*, July 31, 1917:4.

764 Toronto *Star*, July 31, 1917:4.

765 Toronto *Star*, July 31, 1917:4.

766 Toronto *Star*, November 8, 1928:21.

767 Dean Beeby, "JAFFRAY, ROBERT," in ***Dictionary of Canadian Biography***, vol. 14, University of Toronto/Université Laval, 2003–, accessed June 19, 2023, http://www.biographi.ca/en/bio/jaffray_robert_14E.html.

768 The *Globe*, July 10, 1912:1; The *Globe*, July 13, 1912:21; The *Globe*, July 15, 1912:1; The *Globe*, July 23, 1912:7.

769 The *Globe*, January 2, 1913:13.

770 The *Globe*, February 17, 1912:8, The Globe, September 22, 1913:8.

771 The *Globe*, February 23, 1914:2.

772 The *Globe*, November 2, 1917:9.

773 The *Globe*, November 2, 1917:9.

774 The *Globe*, November 2, 1917:9.

775 Rutherford, Tom and Adair, Jason "The Battle of Passchendale: The Experiences of Lieutenant Tom Rutherford, 4th Battalion, Canadian Mounted Rifles." *Canadian Military History* 13, 4 (2004). < https://scholars.wlu.ca/cmh/vol13/iss4/6/>

776 https://www.veterans.gc.ca/eng/remembrance/memorials/canadian-virtual-war-memorial/detail/1591957

777 The *Globe*, March 28, 1934:10.

778 <https://greyroots.com/story/story-dedication-and-love-mrs-eaton-and-her-volunteers-canadian-greys-rooms>

779 *Might's City of Toronto Directory, 1911*, *Vancouver Sun*, February 12, 1912, *Vancouver Sun*, October 19, 1921:3.

780 D.A. McGregor, 1946, "Adventure of Vancouver Newspapers 1892–1926", *British Columbia Historical Quarterly* April; 89-142.

781 The *Advertising World*, London, February 5, 1916:17.

782 The *Star*, January 22,1916.

783 The *Vancouver Sun*, October 19, 1921:3.

784 https://www.kutnereader.com/post/the-balfour-bugle

785 https://www.kutnereader.com/post/the-balfour-bugle, The Prince of Wales visit to the Sanitorium is shown in a Pathe film, https://www.britishpathe.com/asset/101606/. The visit to Balfour is located at 15:26 to 16:14 minutes in the film.

786 https://www.kutnereader.com/post/the-balfour-bugle

787 <https://www.kutnereader.com/post/the-balfour-bugle>

788 https://www.kutnereader.com/post/the-balfour-bugle

789 E.A. Corbett, 1957, *We Have With us Tonight*. Ryerson Press, Toronto. No relation to the Corbett from Scroggie's scrapbook.

790 E.A. Corbett, 1957, *We Have With us Tonight*. Ryerson Press, Toronto. pp.6-7.

791 E.A. Corbett, 1957, *We Have With us Tonight*. Ryerson Press, Toronto. p.7.

792 E.A. Corbett, 1957, *We Have With us Tonight*. Ryerson Press, Toronto. p.7.

793 E.A. Corbett, 1957, *We Have With us Tonight*. Ryerson Press, Toronto. p. 22.

794 https://www.kutnereader.com/post/the-balfour-bugle

795 https://www.kutnereader.com/post/the-balfour-bugle, accessed June 25, 2023.

796 https://www.ancestry.ca/discoveryui-content/view/9106336:8991 https://www.ancestry.ca/discoveryui-content/view/3252974:8991?tid=&pid=&queryId=e3cea335e8eb8763faf473a303150db2&_phsrc=FKd1070&_phstart=successSource

797 *Vancouver Sun*, October 19, 1921:3. Ancestry.ca.

798 The *Globe*, February 15, 1911:1.

799 The *Globe and Mail*, March 11, 1964:51.

800 https://qormuseum.files.wordpress.com/2013/02/queens-own-rifles-book-of-remembrance-1866-1918.pdf
Most WWI volunteers enlisted through existing militias, the QOR commenced enlisting men in early August of 1914. *The Queen's Own Rifles of Canada, 1860-1960*. Lieutenant-Colonel W.T. Barnard, The Ontario Publishing Company, Don Mills, Ontario, 1960, p. 108. https://qormuseum.files.wordpress.com/2012/09/wt-barnard-history.pdf

801 Godfrey Brown, letter to Mima Brown Kapches, Feb. 29, 1985. Brown Family collection.

802 The *Vancouver Sun*, March 7, 1932 (page unknown), Brown family collection.

803 Brown family collections.

804 "Democracy in Industry." *Maclean's Magazine*, February 1, 1937, James McCredie Brown, pp.12-13, 32, 32, 34, 35.

805 "Democracy in Industry." *Maclean's Magazine*, February 1, 1937, James McCredie Brown, p 34.

806 The *Vancouver Sun*, December 15, 1938:10.

807 The *Globe and Mail*, December 3, 1943:7.

808 *Might's City of Toronto Directories, 1908–1955.*

809 *Might's City of Toronto Directories.* Press Club Treasurer, The *Globe*, March 21, 1912, p.8

810 "John A. MacLaren: Advertising Executive Started Career on Newspapers." *Globe and Mail*, June 13, 1955. John A. "MacLaren Dies Advertising Founder." Toronto *Star,* June 11, 1955. Biography of J.A. MacLaren, c.1955, Edward Enright, MacLaren Papers.

811 The *World*, April 16, 1910:2. Peuchen was not a member of the 1910 Balmoral officers, in the heat of the moment of writing the article it's not unexpected that such an error was made.

812 Alan Hustak, "PEUCHEN, ARTHUR GODFREY," in ***Dictionary of Canadian Biography***, vol. 15, University of Toronto/Université Laval, 2003–, accessed June 22, 2023, http://www.biographi.ca/en/bio/peuchen_arthur_godfrey_15E.html. https://qormuseum.org/soldiers-of-the-queens-own/peuchen-arthur-godfrey/

813 Alan Hustak, "PEUCHEN, ARTHUR GODFREY," in ***Dictionary of Canadian Biography***, vol. 15, University of Toronto/Université Laval, 2003–, accessed June 22, 2023, http://www.biographi.ca/en/bio/peuchen_arthur_godfrey_15E.html.

814 Toronto *Star*, January 4, 2008: A3.

815 Edward Enright, MacLaren family papers.

816 John Aitken MacLaren, Arts and Letters Club, Toronto, August 1955. Edward Enright, MacLaren papers.

817 *Might's City of Toronto Directory, 1916.* Biography for Canadian Who's Who, never published, Edward Enright, MacLaren papers.

818 https://central.bac-lac.gc.ca/.item/?op=pdf&app=CEF&id=B7017-S001

819 Edward Enright, email June 20, 2023.

820 Biography for Canadian Who's Who, never published, Edward Enright, MacLaren papers.

821 Edward Enright, email June 20, 2023. *Might's City of Toronto Directory 1920–1922.* James Scroggie Jr., James' son was the third generation in advertising and worked for MacLaren for as well.

822 *London Free Press*, October 11, 1958.

823 *London Free Press*, October 11, 1958.

824 The *London Free Press*, August 10, 1957:12, 14.

825 "George Argue Dies in his 62nd year." The *Toronto Star*, November 30, 1950:47. https://central.bac-lac.gc.ca/.item/?op=pdf&app=CEF&id=B4279-S018

826 Ancestry.ca

827 The *Star*, April 28, 1910:8.

828 The *Star*, December 5, 1910:5, The *Sunday World*, March 12, 1911:3.

829 The *Star*, December 5, 1910:5.

830 The Star, March 11, 1911:11, The *World*, February 13, 1911:2.

831 The *Star*, February 20, 1911:11.

832 For information about minstrels read Cheryl Thompson, *The Complicated History of Canadian Blackface*, Spacing, October 29, 2018. http://spacing.ca/

toronto/2018/10/29/the-complicated-history-of-canadian-blackface/ accessed June 28, 2023. Robin W. Winks, *The Blacks in Canada, A History*. 1997 2nd Edition, McGill-Queens University Press, Kingston, ON.

833 Toronto *Star*, March 16, 1912:12.

834 The *World*, March 12, 1914:7. Salvaneschi was at this smoker.

835 Toronto *World*, March 12, 1914:7. The Salvenschi Cup, QOR. 2018.23.001(1)-1913.

836 Toronto *Star*, November 15, 1919:1. In this article a photograph of Salvaneschi identifies him as H. Salvaneschi.

837 https://central.bac-lac.gc.ca/.item/?op=pdf&app=CEF&id=B8622-S002

838 Toronto *Star*, November 15, 1915:1.

839 https://www.thecanadianencyclopedia.ca/en/article/ross-rifle, Official History of the Canadian Army in the First World War, Canadian Expeditionary Force 1914-1919, Colonel G.W.L. Nicholson, C.D. 1962, Queen's Printer, Ottawa. P. 27, 156. https://publications.gc.ca/collections/collection_2009/forces/DA3-4462E.pdf

840 The *Star,* June 13, 1913:1

841 The *Star,* June 13, 1913:1

842 David Roberts, "PELLATT, Sir HENRY MILL," in *Dictionary of Canadian Biography*, vol. 16, University of Toronto/Université Laval, 2003–, accessed June 27, 2023, http://www.biographi.ca/en/bio/pellatt_henry_mill_16E.html.

843 The *Globe*, June 23, 1926:12.

844 The *Globe*, June 23, 1926:11, https://qormuseum.org/soldiers-of-the-queens-own/butler-e-a/ accessed June 28, 2023.

845 The *Globe* June 14, 1926:12, The *Star*, June 23, 1926:7.

846 The *Star*, June 23, 1926:7.

847 The *Star*, June 23, 1926:7

848 The *Star*, June 23, 1926:7.

849 Butler was a Cpl. In B Company in 1910. The *Globe*, June 24, 1926:11

850 The *Star*, June 28, 1926:4.

851 The *Star*, June 28, 1926:4. The *Globe*, June 28, 1926:11.

852 The *Star*, June 28, 1926:4.

853 The *Star*, June 28, 1926:4.

854 The *Star*, June 28, 1926:17.

855 The *Globe*, July 2, 1926:9.

856 James Bradburn, "Toronto Newspaper Histories: The World of William Findlay Maclean." *Historicist* March 17, 2012.

857 Mark Bourrie, *Big Men Fear Me*. Biblioasis, Windsor, 2022:87-105.

858 1910 Reunion Program, AQOR 04746

859 1910 Reunion Program, AQOR 04746

860 1910 Reunion Program, AQOR 04746

861 David Roberts, "PELLATT, Sir HENRY MILL," in *Dictionary of Canadian Biography*, vol. 16, University of Toronto/Université Laval, 2003–, accessed July 1, 2023, http://www.biographi.ca/en/bio/pellatt_henry_mill_16E.html.

862 The *Star*, January 5, 1939:26.

863 The *Globe and Mail*, January 6,1939:13.

864 The *Star*, January 5, 1939:26.

865 The *Star*, January 5, 1939:26.

866 In1938 there were two companies that prepared glass lantern slides in Toronto: the Rainbow Lantern Slide Co., and Charles Potter's company, both listed in *Might's*

City of Toronto Directory. The slides for the reunion dinner were prepared by A.J. Reading, University of Toronto. Reading was not the trip photographer: he is not listed on the *Megantic* manifest, and some of the slides are Gleason photos. Arthur John Reading (17 May 1856 – 1 December 1941) was an art teaching master for the Ontario Department of Education, 1888. In 1918 he was working for the Presbyterian Lantern Slide Department, *Star,* April 19, 1918. The University of Toronto Archives has glass slides prepared by Reading from the 1920s and 1930s for the Botany Department. A2003-0019/16. Department of Botany, 3rd, 47.60.03. A.J. Reading is identified as a photographer in a publication in 1912, E.M. Walker, University of Toronto Studies, Biological Series, 11. The North American Dragonflies of the genus Aeshna. University of Toronto. Plate 2, Fig.1, "From Photograph by A.J. Reading." I think that Reading began making glass lantern slides for the professors at the University after his time at the Presbyterian Lantern Department.

867 The *Globe and Mail*, January 7, 1939:4.
868 1910 Trip Reunion Menu, AQOR SC25, F24.
869 Toronto *Star*, January 7, 1939:7.
870 The *Globe and Mail* January 7, 1939:4.
871 Toronto *Star*, January 7,1939:7.
872 Toronto *Star*, January 7, 1939:7
873 Toronto *Star*, January 7, 1939:7.
874 The *Globe and Mail*, January 7, 1939:4.
875 Toronto *Star*, January 7,1939:13.
876 *Globe and Mail*, September 22, 1939:13.
877 Toronto *Star*, January 7, 1939: 7.
878 The *New York Times*, March 9, 1939:21.
879 The *Times*, March 10, 1939:18.
880 The *Star*, March 9, 1939;1,33.
881 The *Star*, March 9, 1939:1,33.
882 The *Globe and Mail*, March 13, 1939:10.
883 The *Star*, March 13, 1939:20. This would have been the 1906 trip.
884 The *Globe and Mail*, March 13, 1939:10.
885 The *Globe and Mail*, March 13, 1939:10.
886 The *Star,* March 13,1939:20.
887 Edward Enright, May 27, 2023.
888 The *Globe and Mail*, June 13, 1955: 13; *The Globe and Mail,* June 13, 1955:6.
889 The *Globe and Mail*, June 13, 1955:6.
890 The *Globe and Mail*, August 19, 1943.
891 *Might's City of Toronto Directory,* various years.
892 The *Globe and Mail*, May 27, 1944:9. I am the youngest child of that second marriage.
893 The *Globe and Mail*, March 11, 1964:51.
894 *London Free Press*, May 28, 1964:4.
895 The *London Free Press*, August 10, 1957:12, 14.
896 https://museumlondon.ca/exhibitions/thrill-arthur-a-gleasons-aerial-photography
897 The *Star*, July 28, 1967:26. *Might's City of Toronto Directories.*
898 *Might's City of Toronto Directory, 1955.* The *Globe and Mail*, August 7, 1959:18.
899 There are no donation details. Shaun Kelly, email June 22, 2023.
900 The *World*, October 4, 1910:7.

901 The Toronto *Star*, June 28, 1926:4.

902 The Toronto *Star*, January 7, 1939:7.

903 The *Globe and Mail*, March 9, 1939:4.

904 David Roberts, "PELLATT, Sir HENRY MILL," in ***Dictionary of Canadian Biography***, vol. 16, University of Toronto/Université Laval, 2003–, accessed July 5, 2023, http://www.biographi.ca/en/bio/pellatt_henry_mill_16E.html. Carlie Oreskovich, *Sir Henry Pellatt: The King of Casa Loma,* McGraw-Hill Ryerson Press, Toronto, 1982. Nicholas A.E. Mouriopoulos, "A Serious Piece of Business."https://qormuseum.org/2014/09/15/a-serious-piece-of-business-part-i/

905 The *Globe and Mail*, January 6, 1939:13..

LIST OF FIGURES

Figure 1. Jim Brown's worn photograph of five of the English Trip reporters: L to R, Jim Brown, Jim Scroggie, Jaffray Eaton, Jack MacLaren, and Ned Sheppard. Fred H. Foster, photographer. Brown Family collection.

Figure 2. Scroggie's artistically annotated photograph of five of the cubs identifying the reporters' newspapers using their logos. "Ned has a look of consternation ."(AQOR) Scroggie Scrapbook #02232 (S) :9. Fred H. Foster photographer.

Figure 3. Québec Tercentenary Fireworks and Electrical Display on the St. Lawrence, Québec, (P.Q.) 1908. July 27, 1908. LAC 1971-034 NPC, Box Number 60000.

Figure 4. Unveiling of the South African War Memorial, University Avenue and Queen Street West. City of Toronto Archives. Fonds 1568, Item 523. Image number 147629.

Figure 5. Henderson and the band at the far right in front of the pageant stage. E.F. Gunther Scrapbook, AQOR 00290:71.

Figure 6. The setting for Laura Secord's story in the pageant. E.F. Gunther Scrapbook, AQOR 00290:70.

Figure 7. Performers with Lady and Sir Henry Pellatt in front of Victoria Memorial with Canada Gate. AQOR 2018.07.056, no. 86.

Figure 8. Sir Henry Pellatt (left) and Lady Pellatt (back) receive guests at the garden party. Ceremonial beefeater is to the right holding the HR sign. In the background is the painted canvas backdrop showing the Canada Gate. City of Toronto Archives, Fonds 1244, item 4016.

Figure 9. Sir Henry Pellatt in Queen's Own Rifles uniform and Mohawk clothing, CNE Grandstand. City of Toronto Archives, Fonds 1244, item 4012.

Figure 10. The "Living" Union Jack made quite an impression. E.F. Gunther Scrapbook, AQOR 002990:70.

Figure 11. Jim Brown (R) and an unknown reporter. Two cub reporters at Toronto's first aviation meet. Brown Family collection.

Figure 12. The list of names and their numbers of the men in the press gang tent. AQOR.S:49

Figure 13. The ENGLISH TRIP list of personal supplies needed for each private. AQOR.S:47.

Figure 14. Gleason's photograph of the QOR Marching in Montreal. This was published in the *Canadian* Courier, Vol. VIII (No. 12):7. AQOR, 2018.07.056.no.7.

Figure 15. Ferry teminal, from Lévis to Québec City, 1908. LAC, PA-032679.

Figure 16. "The QOR's A-Company Getting Rifle Instruction from a Ross Rifle Expert." Rifle Instruction, Québec Camp. August 1910.This was published in the *Canadian Courier* Vol. VIII (No. 13):9. AQOR, 2018.07.056, no. 77.

Figure 17. The Disturbance Committee, Québec. (Sixth from left, Salvaneschi ? [holding a baton], Third from right Charlebois?) AQOR, 2018.07.056. no.66.

Figure 18. Wrestling match on the *Megantic.* AQOR 04845. No. 15.

Figure 29. This photograph was published in the Toronto *Star Weekly*, September 24, 1910:1, with the title, "The Star Weekly Arrives in Camp and They All Want Ito see It." And the caption "The *Star Weekly* is a prime favourite with the Queen's Own boys, and when the Canadian mail arrives there is always a rush for copies of the *Weekly* that have been sent to the members of the regiment." AQOR. 2018.07.056. no.39.

Figure 30. Foot care at Aldershot. AQOR, 2018.07.056. no.61.

Figure 31. The QOR at Aldershot. AQOR 2018.07.056, no.75.

Figure 32. Scroggie's London membership cards. AQOR.S:31.

Figure 33. Filling water bottles from the portable water cart. AQOR, 02069.14.

Figure 34. Review of the Queen's Own Rifles by the Duke of Connaught at Avington Park, September 7, 1910. AQOR, 00502.

Figure 35. On manoeuvres from Aldershot 1910. AQOR, 2018.07.056. no.18.

Figure 36. The QOR being presented to the King at Balmoral, September 12, 1910. AQOR 04873.

Figure 37, The QOR men arriving at the Chelsea school, September 13, 1910, AQOR 02069.16.

Figure 38. Three cheers for Lord Roberts, at the Duke of York School, Chelsea, September 16, 1910. AQOR. 2018.07.056, no.2.

Figure 39. The march to the Guildhall through the streets of London. *Canadian Courier*, October 1, 1910. This is a Gleason photograph from the *Canadian Courier* Vol. VIII (No. 18):7. Toronto Public Library,

Printed in the USA
CPSIA information can be obtained
at www.ICGtesting.com
LVHW011726101124
796066LV00014B/711